Wakefield Press

BREAKOUT!

Robert Cox's eight previous books include three volumes of short fiction and four of Tasmanian history. His most recent book, *Broken Spear: the untold story of Black Tom Birch, the man who sparked Australia's bloodiest war*, was longlisted for the 2024 Dick and Joan Green Family Award for Tasmanian History.

What readers said about Robert Cox's *Broken Spear*

This is the most honest, fair, comprehensive and complete story of this time in our Tasmanian early history I have ever seen. Absolutely enlightening!
Lyn Rainbird

An extraordinary book ...
Pete Hay

A compelling history, beautifully written.
Nancy Birch

A master writer ...
Ian Lipke

So very, very well written, this book is also an extremely useful and generous resource, with so many important details, incidents, dates, places and referencing all brought together with attention to and provision of details that are so rarely included in popular histories, and from a huge range of sources. This is scholarship.
Julie Gough

An excellent book ...
Alison Alexander

Broken Spear is a carefully balanced yet detailed work that creates a cohesive story from the chaos of Tasmania's invasion, building a scholarly biography from a galaxy of confusing fragments.
Ray Kerkhove

Broken Spear is a most rich, quite remarkable achievement. I was pleasantly aware throughout of being both instructed and entertained.
Michael Briggs

One of the most salient Tasmanian books of our generation … A masterful work of historical investigation.
Simon Bevilacqua

Will still be relevant fifty years hence.
Leigh Swinbourne

An amazing, disturbing and eye-opening account of our untold history.
Moya Sharpe

An imposing book … written with great skill. Mr Cox writes with flair and elegance and is a born storyteller.
Henry Reynolds

A very readable, informative and moving account.
Jacob Atkins

A riveting portrait … destined to become a classic of our time.
Lyndall Ryan

BREAKOUT!

The Tasmanians who terrorised Victoria

ROBERT COX
Foreword by Henry Reynolds

Wakefield Press

Wakefield Press
16 Rose Street
Mile End
South Australia 5031
www.wakefieldpress.com.au

First published 2024

Copyright © Robert Cox, 2024
Foreword Copyright © Henry Reynolds, 2024

All rights reserved. This book is copyright. Apart from
any fair dealing for the purposes of private study, research,
criticism or review, as permitted under the Copyright Act,
no part may be reproduced without written permission.
Enquiries should be addressed to the publisher.

Original maps of Tasmania and Victoria by NordNordWest/Wikipedia
https://commons.wikimedia.org/wiki/File:Australia_Tasmania_location_map_blank.svg
https://commons.wikimedia.org/wiki/File:Australia_Victoria_location_map_blank.svg

Edited by Maddy Sexton, Wakefield Press
Typeset by Jesse Pollard, Wakefield Press

ISBN 978 1 92304 272 8

 A catalogue record for this book is available from the National Library of Australia

 Wakefield Press thanks Coriole Vineyards for continued support

Dedicated to the memory
of three loved and loving women

Emma Parsons (1885–1965)
Phyllis May Cox (1922–1999)
Kirsten Helen Cox (1949–2021)

My brothers, in our own country a long time ago we were a great many men, a great number. Then white men killed us all; they shot a great many. We are now only a few people ...

Wurati, 1838

The genocide of the Tasmanian Aboriginals ... was part of an historic record which brought the benefits of civilisation to a quarter of the world.

William Rees-Mogg,
The Times, 20 April 1998

Ghosts of the night mist, set me free.
Forgive, until the past is called
Wisdom, and history can be
told in some last redeeming world.

Gwen Harwood, 'Evening: Oyster Cove'

Contents

Glossary of Palawa Names	x
Foreword by Henry Reynolds	xiii
Preface	xvii
Prologue	xxiv

Part One: Lutruwita
1. 'The African slave trade in miniature' — 1
2. 'The cry of welcome was evinced' — 9
3. 'Plenty much blood, plenty cry' — 14
4. 'Make haste, black fellow run away' — 37
5. 'Greatly at a loss how to proceed' — 45
6. 'We will kill them all by and by' — 53
7. 'They are not at liberty to do as they choose' — 70
8. 'The entire Aboriginal population are now removed' — 84

Part Two: Flinders Island
9. 'We don't want to live here' — 99
10. 'Too much dead man' — 107

Part Three: Port Phillip
11. 'Get plenty of guns ready' — 143
12. 'It was a big big country' — 158
13. 'Now was the time for revenge' — 174
14. 'They would fight to the last' — 188
15. 'By ¼ past 6 it was all over' — 196
16. 'Shooting at Watson would hang them' — 209
17. 'He hung beautiful' — 234

Epilogue	242
Acknowledgements	251
Bibliography	253
Notes	257
Index of Names	277

Glossary of Palawa Names

Name in original source	Person referred to
Ben Lomond	Rolepana
Black Tom	Kikatapula/Kickerterpoller
Bob	Timme
Cape Grim Jack	Pevay
Coates's Jack	Batman's Jack
Count Alpha	Wurati/Woorraddy
Cranky Dick	Teengerreenneener
David/Davy Bruny	Myyunngge
Dick	Teengerreenneener
Fanny	Planobeena
Friday	Nikaminik/Nicermenic
Isaac	Prupilathina
Jack, Jack Napoleon	Pevay
Jack Allen	Batman's Jack
Jemmy	Timme
Jenny	Numbloote
Jock (f.)	Planobeena
King George	Rolepa
Kit (f.)	Nollahalaker
Lacklay	Prupilathina
Lalla Rookh	Trukanini/Truganini
Little Jemmy	Prupilathina
Lydgugee	Trukanini/Truganini

Glossary of Palawa Names

Mannalargenner	Manalakina
Maria	Mathabelianna
Matilda	Mathabelianna
Matilda	Planobeena
Maulboyheenner	Timme
Mutteellee	Wurati/Woorraddy
Napoleon	Pevay
Peter Bruny	Droyyerloinne
Pompy	Teengerreenneener
Probelattener	Prupilathina
Richard	Teengerreenneener
Robert	Timme
Semiramis	Numbloote
Smallboy	Timme
Sydney (f.)	Numbloote
Timmy	Timme
Tom	Kikatapula/Kickerterpoller
Tunnerminnerwait	Pevay
VDL, VDL Jack	Pevay

Foreword

During much of the twentieth century Australia's First Nations were generally left out of the national story; some widely used historical works failed to mention them at all. It was an omission famously condemned by the leading anthropologist W.E.H. Stanner in his Boyer Lecture for the ABC in 1968 entitled 'After the Dreaming'. Stanner talked of the 'Great Australian silence' and of a 'cult of forgetfulness practised on a national scale'. At the time I was in two minds about the Stanner attack. It was clearly justified when national historiography was concerned but it did not really apply to Tasmanian history. The frontier wars of the 1820s had always featured in local histories. Their full brutality was revisited in 1948 by Clive Turnbull in his *Black War*. And then in 1966 the Tasmanian Historical Research Association published *Friendly Mission*, the voluminous papers of George Augustus Robinson. It is likely that Stanner was unaware of what was clearly one of the most important books in the field published anywhere in Australia at any time since 1788.

Relevant books continued to appear in the 1980s and 1990s. But suddenly in 2002 Tasmanian history became the focal point in what became known as the 'History Wars', perhaps the most intense public debate about historiography in living memory. The opening salvo was launched by conservative commentator Keith Windschuttle in his book *The Fabrication of Aboriginal History: Volume One, Van Diemen's Land, 1803–1847*. As the title declared, the revisionist history of frontier conflict had been made up, or, as he put it, 'fabricated'. The violence of the frontier had been grossly exaggerated and had been done so for overtly political reasons. The book whipped up a storm of controversy that was widely reported in the media and debated before overflowing public meetings. Windschuttle had a considerable public following, many people feeling that they had been relieved of the need for any feelings of doubt or regret about colonisation. They could return to those comforting historical narratives that had dealt with heroic pioneers and uniquely peaceful settlement. But opposition to Windschuttle was, in the long run, more consequential than the support of his camp followers. Established scholars returned to old research notes with renewed vigour. Many new, and often younger, writers opened a fresh chapter in Tasmanian history. Books, articles and theses were published, often locally. In the 20 years since the Windschuttle intervention the scholarship on the frontier wars and their aftermath has resulted in a harvest of historiographical richness, unrivalled anywhere else in Australia.

Robert Cox was one of the early responders who entered the history wars with his 2004 book *Steps to the Scaffold: The untold story of Tasmania's black bushrangers*. He continued to work with the remarkably rich documentary sources available for the period in question and in 2021 published *Broken Spear: the untold story of Black Tom Birch, the man who sparked Australia's bloodiest war*. His new book, *Breakout! The Tasmanians who terrorised Victoria*, follows as a natural sequel to the two earlier books. His two main characters, known at the time as Pevay and Timme, were young Tasmanians who had been taken to Victoria by George Augustus Robinson. With three Tasmanian women they did indeed break out and terrorise the fledgling Port Phillip colony during 1841, Cox explaining that 'embers of resentment and desire for freedom' finally flared 'into a brief and violent flame'. The five were eventually captured and tried, and Pevay and Timme were convicted and publicly hanged.

Breakout! displays all the characteristics of the two earlier books in the trilogy. Cox's mastery of the contemporary sources is again evident. Assertions and arguments are alike soundly based on the records, which are always appropriately cited. But the detail, while abundant, does not obstruct the easily flowing narrative. Cox is indeed an accomplished prose writer. His style combines clarity and precision – and is also a pleasure to read.

Foreword

In this book Cox follows his characters across Bass Strait to the new colony of what was soon to become goldrush Victoria. And that provides some interesting new themes. Port Phillip, as it was then called, and South Australia were in their founding years. Both were determined to distinguish themselves from New South Wales and Tasmania, which were indelibly marked with the 'hated stain' of convictism. The ubiquity of frontier violence was also well known. The leaders of both new colonies wanted to keep the ex-convicts – variously called 'the Van Diemonians' or 'the Othersiders' – away from their borders. Cox's two main characters Pevay and Timme were seen as embodiments of the all-too-apparent disorders of Van Diemen's Land. There was therefore an urgent need to run them down, prosecute and convict them, and then hang them as both a public spectacle and a political statement.

The terrible fate of the two young men points us in the direction of another wider theme that Cox has been thinking about since he wrote *Steps to the Scaffold* 20 years ago. It comes down to the question of how to interpret the violent 'breakout' of young Aboriginal men well after the frontier wars had, in one way or another, come to an end. This was a phenomenon apparent all over Australia and across the generations. The young men in question had grown up either within or at least on the fringes of settler society. They spoke English and had often worked for white men. They knew how to ride and were often handy with guns. But they also retained many traditional bush skills. This combination made them both invaluable servants and equally dangerous enemies. Were they therefore bushrangers rather than tribal warriors? Were they both? Jimmy Governor, who rampaged across rural New South Wales at the turn of the nineteenth century, declared that he was a bushranger. The society at large thought he was a throwback to the frontier wars and, as a result, much more challenging.

In the last 10 years there has been keen debate about the significance of Pevay and Timme's 'breakout'. It emerged into public consciousness when the Melbourne City Council decided in 2012 to erect a monument on, or close to, the site of their execution. It was officially unveiled in September 2016. It was quite emphatic about the significance of the young men's short, tragic lives. A plaque with copies of their portraits declared: 'Lest We Forget' The Freedom Fighters. Speaking at the event, Aboriginal elders declared that the memorial would 'forever stand as an unambiguous reminder of the brutal impacts of displacement, dispossession and despair that was inflicted upon our people and their homelands and all those who bore the brunt of that invasion and paid the ultimate price'.

Henry Reynolds

Preface

This is a story of a young man's struggle to find a place for himself in a world that denied him the freedom to choose his own. It is also a tale of his bond with another young man, like him a Palawa (Tasmanian Aborigine), and how they unintentionally made history. At first strangers to each other and to the three women who became their comrades-in-arms, they were thrown together by war and calamity, linking their lives on a path to involuntary exile in alien country, a rebellion, a dramatic climax, a violent end. Their names were Tanaminawayt (traditionally Tunnerminnerwait) and Malapuwinarana (Maulboyheenner), although they are better known to history as Pevay and Timme, which, for the sake of that familiarity, is how I refer to them in these pages, satisfied that both names were variations or derivatives of natal names. This is the first time their story has been fully told, from boyhood to grave. Like so much Australian history, past and evolving, it is a tragedy rooted in racism.

Breakout! might be seen as a sequel to my most recent book *Broken Spear: the untold story of Black Tom Birch, the man who sparked Australia's bloodiest war* (2021). Both volumes are a corrective to a fallacy suggested by the subtitle of my first book, *Steps to the Scaffold: The untold story of Tasmania's black bushrangers*, in which I used the term 'black bushrangers' to refer to some Palawa who violently resisted the British usurpation of their Country. In using the term I was parroting a coinage of Keith Windschuttle who, in *The Fabrication of Aboriginal History*, had wrongly derogated Palawa resistance fighters as 'bushrangers who happened to be black'.[1] In the closing pages of *Steps* I repudiated his claim by declaring that 'I could not disagree more', although for reasons that now elude me I left the subtitle unchanged.[2] It remains a regretted and irritating error and I have withdrawn the book from sale.

Most recently, in *Broken Spear* I refuted the very notion that Palawa resistance to colonisation was in any way criminal. Colonisation is low-intensity war driven by racism and sanctified by colonisers' racist belief that those being colonised are a lesser form of humanity whose subjection and consequent deaths are therefore irrelevant – an unfortunate concomitant of the forced imposition of an alien culture. Resistance to colonisation raises the level of that warfare and *Broken Spear* was a biography of Kikatapula or Black Tom, the warrior who first incited resistance to the British invasion of Tasmania and then led the fight against the invaders for four years before agreeing, under threat of execution, to change sides. For the rest of his life, while purporting to help the British he was instead subverting and sabotaging their efforts to capture and exile those of his race not yet incarcerated or annihilated. Kikatapula was one of the Palawa I had written about sketchily in *Steps*, but my subsequent research had established that he was indeed a patriot, a hero, and also by far the most important and influential Palawa in history, fully worthy of the decade of work that his story took me to tell. Aged about 30, he became ill and died in May 1832 while serving the British, at which point *Broken Spear* ended, as had, only a few months earlier, the eight-year Black War he incited.

The subjects of this book, Pevay and Timme, were younger than he and might be seen as his disciples. As very young men they travelled with him in George Augustus Robinson's Friendly Mission, where they heard campfire tales of his and other former guerrillas' martial deeds. And if by that time the fighting was over, the embers of resentment and the desire for freedom nevertheless glowed in their souls for another decade before finally flaring into a brief and violent flame.

§

Five Tasmanians terrorised Victoria in 1841 but *Breakout!* is the biography of only the men, for two of their three women companions appear to have been relatively inconsequential to the rebellion that gives this book its title. The third, Trukanini, has already been the subject of at least two biographies since 1981, so repeating her story is unnecessary. Historian Henry Reynolds has pointed out that she and other Palawa women were largely responsible, through their diplomatic efforts, for the success of Robinson's Friendly Mission as it extirpated Tasmania's Indigenous people, and her part in what happened in Port Phillip in 1841 was not minor.[3] She was among the first to shake off the restraints imposed on the transplanted Palawa who were languishing unhappy, homesick, and restless in that colony, and she would take a viciously active part in the killings that sent her two male companions to their deaths, although she managed to exculpate herself and survive into old age. She is usually viewed as a tragic heroine, but her part in the devastation of her race needs to be remembered. She was one of Robinson's longest-serving emissaries and perhaps the most faithful. Her saving his life in the wilderness of western Tasmania in 1832 was a pivotal point in Palawa history. Had she not done so, the story of Aboriginal Tasmania would likely have had a different and less tragic outcome and she might subsequently have disappeared into the wilderness and from history. Although in part my subjects' story necessarily follows the same route as hers, I have avoided stepping in her footprints, preferring to let the two men's lives and actions follow their own course. If Trukanini is sometimes present in the same place at the same time as Pevay and Timme, I have focused my lens on them. Their lives are my subject.

My research for this book revealed a difference in their characters that changed the tenor of the narrative as I wrote and further narrowed its focus. Pevay, who was a notably cheerful, happy-go-lucky, peaceable youth, became the stronger and angrier man over the years he spent in an unwanted colonial yoke. He was at first a follower but grew into a leader, while Timme, who as a teenager had twice escaped incarceration and participated in attacks on settlers, became placid and compliant, never more than Pevay's acolyte. It was Pevay who drove the Port Phillip breakout; Timme was merely his follower. A newspaper in 1842 summed up how Europeans viewed their difference. Timme was 'lively, pliable, and capable of affection; [Pevay] was sullen, but daring; the latter was the leader in all the depredations that closed in their ignominious death; the former revolted at the crimes committed but was compelled to submit'.[4]

Regrettably, their story cannot be told from their point of view. Palawa were a non-literate people, so their story survives only in the parts recorded by the invaders. Inevitably there are gaps, but, as Norman Mailer has written, 'If half the pieces in a jigsaw puzzle are missing, the likelihood is that something can still be put together. Despite its gaps, the picture may be more or less visible. Even if most of the pieces are gone, a loose mosaic can be arranged of isolated elements.'[5] For Pevay and Timme, many such elements exist. Much of their adult lives was spent within the orbit of George Augustus Robinson, an indefatigable and sometimes exhaustive chronicler. Whatever his faults as a man – and they were numerous – it is largely due to him that a Palawa mosaic can be constructed at all.

Some other minor difficulties need to be noted. Palawa often had more than one natal name; up to five have been recorded for one individual. In addition, those who coexisted with Britons were invariably saddled with unwanted new ones – English forenames or silly and demeaning nicknames – by which they often appear in the records. In these pages I have restored the dignity of their parentally bestowed names to my Palawa characters, using today's *palawa kani* preferred spellings where available. So the warrior that Britons feared as Tom Birch or Black Tom but sometimes referred to by his given name, which they usually spelt Kickerterpoller, is herein spelt Kikatapula. Guided by the same contemporary preference, I have written about the woman habitually and wrongly called Truganini (or some variation thereof) as Trukanini because that is how she pronounced her name. That fact was recorded from her own lips by a Hobart lawyer named John Woodcock Graves who befriended her in her final years. In a letter to a newspaper in 1876 Graves wrote that '[W]hen [she was] dining at my house only a few months before she died, I importuned her so much about the proper pronunciation of her name that she at last grew impatient . . . she had already replied half a dozen times, distinctly, "Trucanini".'[6] So that is incontrovertibly its correct pronunciation and Trukanini is its preferred *palawa kani* spelling.

George Augustus Robinson, whose journals were a major resource for this book, sometimes had the irritating and confusing habit of using two or more different names or nicknames for one person in a single passage – for instance, referring to Pevay by that name as well as calling him Tunnerminnerwait, or Jack, or Napoleon, or VDL in that one paragraph. Further confusion arises because of Robinson's (and his contemporaries') understandably inconsistent spelling of Palawa names. He sometimes spelt Nollahallaker as Nollewsalleke, at other times Nollerallic. Since the problem obviously occurs only in original sources such as Robinson's own writing, I have in some instances – when quoting from such a source and confusion seems likely – replaced nicknames or scrambled spellings with the person's natal name in brackets. In my own text I call them by their Palawa names. When necessary, the Glossary of Palawa Names at the beginning of this book will help to clarify the matter for readers.

In a similar vein, wherever possible I have provided surviving Palawa place names alongside today's European-bestowed toponymy. But if multiple Palawa names are known for a place or topographical feature, I have randomly chosen one rather than encumber the text with several. My intention is not to be encyclopedic but to remind us that those names existed, have very deep roots, and might have been in place for millennia. Names given by Europeans, on the other hand, are at most only two centuries old, often obsequious, and all too often unimaginative and shopworn, having been chosen for the very familiarity that would 'annihilate distance with sameness'.[7] As such, they are spiritually meaningless in the ancient Tasmanian landscape, whereas to acknowledge the original names is to commemorate those who conferred them and the descendants whose imperishable legacy they are.

Throughout this text I have referred to the native inhabitants of Tasmania as *Palawa* in preference to the European-bestowed *Aborigines*,

Tasmanians, or *Vandemonians*. Although not all Tasmanian Aborigines of the colonial era referred to themselves as Palawa – just as not all contemporary Aboriginal Tasmanians do – I have used the word because such a recognisable collective term aids comprehension, usefully differentiating the Indigenous people of Tasmania from the natives of mainland Australia, some of whom also appear in this story and whom I refer to as *Aborigines*. Such general use of the word Palawa will not be agreeable to all contemporary Aboriginal Tasmanians, but no disrespect is intended and none should be inferred. I have used it only as an aid to clarity.

The neo-traditional language that is presently being reconstituted by contemporary Aboriginal Tasmanians is called *palawa kani*. I have chosen to use *palawa kani* spellings, where available, for Palawa personal names and band names – again except in direct quotes – and I am grateful to the Tasmanian Aboriginal Centre for their cooperation in providing them. Individuals' alternative names are shown in parentheses. Not all my orthographical choices will be approved by every Aboriginal Tasmanian community – some indeed may be deemed culturally inappropriate – but I have used them only to aid comprehension, never because of insensitivity to or disrespect for Indigenous people or culture past or present.

Three published volumes of the collected journals of George Augustus Robinson were a major resource for this book. The volume mined for my Part One: Lutruwita, which covers the years 1830–1835, has twice been published as *Friendly Mission*, first edition 1966, second edition 2010. To simplify referencing I have cited the date of the relevant journal entry that was its source, rather than the relevant page number of *Friendly Mission*. But wherever I have quoted from notes or other incidental material in *Friendly Mission*, I have cited the relevant page and edition number, the pagination of the second edition being different from the first.

Part Two: Flinders Island draws on Robinson's journals for 1835–1839, published as *Weep in Silence: A History of the Flinders Island*

Preface

Aboriginal Settlement. Here I have applied the same protocol, again citing dates rather than page numbers when quoting specifically from the journals. When the quote is from material other than Robinson's journal entries, the page number is cited.

All references from Robinson's Port Phillip journal in the final part of the book, Part Three: Port Phillip, are dates.

Finally, three orthographical points. Where necessary I have converted imperial weights and measures to their metric equivalents, but because one yard is roughly equivalent to one metre I have not given yards-to-metres conversions. Further, in accordance with Australian nomenclature practice I have omitted the possessive 's' from English-language place names – for example, writing *Maloneys Sugarloaf* rather than *Maloney's Sugarloaf* – except in quoted text. And I have used the generally understood term Black War for the bloody conflict that engulfed Tasmania from 1824 to 1831, although it might more properly be called the War of Palawa Resistance.

Prologue

Even before seven o'clock that morning, 20 January 1842, the six-year-old settlement named Melbourne, then part of the colony of New South Wales, sparkled with a festive air. It was bright midsummer and a crowd of between 4000 and 5000 people had risen early, dressed in their Sunday best, and gathered, abuzz with expectation, on a small hill east of Swanston Street, opposite the new public library.

The size of the assembly was unprecedented in the infant settlement. A census nine months earlier had determined its population to be just 4479, so virtually every inhabitant, including women and children, had turned out that morning, some with picnic hampers, to enjoy the free entertainment provided by a novel public event, the first of its kind in the fledgling town.[1] 'It was the Christmas holiday tide', reported a newspaper, 'and there was consequently a sprinkling of gay young bucks of bushmen, well-mounted, and got up in the fashionable style of the period, in buff breeches and top boots, or strapped trousers and shining spurs, as excited and jovial as if mustering in a hunting field or on a racecourse'.[2]

Such a large assembly ensured competition was keen for the best vantage points. Some spectators, young and limber, sought to improve their perspective by clambering onto incomplete walls on an adjacent building site. Several Aboriginal people, also eager for an unimpeded view of this unique experience over the heads of the milling mass, scaled trees around the area to watch the proceedings from aloft. A military detachment marched in, summer-sweaty in full fig, adding a splash of pageantry to the scene. A further dash of colour and excitement was contributed by the appearance of 'The most prominent figure in the whole assemblage . . . a well-known publican, named Byng, – a tall, well-developed, Yankee blackfellow, who was dressed in the latest style prevailing in town, and astride a well-appointed, prancing white horse'.[3]

Prologue

Everything compounded to charge the atmosphere with excitement and expectation and commotion and colour. The many women in the crowd 'were as loquacious as chattering monkeys', said one attender.[4] 'From the laughing and merry faces which were assembled ... the scene resembled ... a race-course', said another, likening the huge crowd's eager anticipation to the excitement of spectators at a boxing match or a bull-baiting.[5] But it was not a horse race they had come to see, or a boxing match, or any other kind of sporting event. Nor was it an oration, a concert, or a play.

They had come to watch two men being put to death.

The festive occasion was Melbourne's first execution. The condemned men were two Palawa – Tasmanian Aborigines – who had been rounded up and removed from Country, exiled first to a Bass Strait island and later to the new southern colony not yet named Victoria, where they were dumped on an Aboriginal reserve and left to their own devices. Bored, dissatisfied, alienated, homesick, nursing many grievances, they and three Palawa women had rebelled and broken out, seizing the freedom to live as they chose. Falsely told that one of their friends had been murdered by a colonist, they rejected the restrictions white society imposed on them and set out to avenge his death. For weeks they were afoot in sparsely settled countryside, terrorising Dandenong and Mornington Peninsula and Western Port, raiding farmhouses at gunpoint, panicking settlers, stealing firearms and ammunition, and easily eluding a large posse of police, soldiers, and civilians sent to hunt them down. During their breakout they slew two Europeans, wrongly believing them to be their friend's killers, and wounded four others. They led pursuers on a frustrating six weeks of hide-and-seek before being cornered and captured in a blaze of gunfire. After a rigged farce of a trial they had been condemned to death.

Now Pevay and Timme were about to pay with their own lives, and the whole white population of Port Phillip was jostling for the best viewing places around the scaffold, cheery and impatient, loudly calling for the entertainment to begin.

Part One
Lutruwita

Ethnic cleansing is defined as a comprehensive,
systematic, predetermined program
to rid, to cleanse, an area of its residents.

Janine Di Giovanni
Madness Visible: A memoir of war

1

'The African slave trade in miniature'

What ended violently in a crowded Melbourne street had begun with peaceable intentions in remotest Tasmania 12 years earlier.

Mid-afternoon on 1 February 1830, in an isolated bay on the south-eastern tip of Lutruwita, as Indigenous Tasmanians called their homeland, two small craft were nosing toward shore. For millennia the bay had been known as Leillateah, but in 1792 French explorers had entered it on their charts as Recherche Bay. *Swallow*, the larger craft now coming to rest in its calm waters, was a former cutter extended at the stern to convert it to a schooner.[1] The other vessel, *Maria*, was a whaleboat, about nine metres in length, with a mast and six oars. Together they were carrying a remarkable expedition led by an ambitious English autodidact, missionary, and lay preacher named George Augustus Robinson who, as events would prove, was also self-servingly devious, mendacious, and hypocritical. His party comprised his pubescent son Charles, six convict servants thought trustworthy, 12 Palawa to act as guides and interpreters, and nine crewmen (three for the schooner and six for the whaleboat) – 29 people in all, plus four dogs and enough supplies for 10 weeks. However, it would be a full year before the expedition returned to Hobart, whence it had embarked a few days earlier.

Officially its task was diplomatic. Bound for Toogeelow (Port Davey) in Tasmania's unexplored far south-west, the mission was under government orders 'to effect an amicable understanding with the aborigines of that quarter, and through them, with the tribes in the interior'.² Because it was a peace mission, it is remembered in history by the name Robinson gave it: the Friendly Mission.

Sound reasons existed for this first official probe into the unmapped wilderness. In the colonised parts of the island – those in the east, north-east, Midlands, and north that the colonial government had decreed to be settled districts – a vicious racial war had been raging since 1824, when dispossessed and desperate Palawa had begun a belated resistance to the British usurpation of their Country, which had started in 1803. But by the time the first angry spears were flung, the Palawa population, which was only about 5000 when the first colonists arrived, had been devastated by murders and introduced diseases and a serious gender imbalance caused by colonists' abductions of Palawa women and girls. As a result of that, and of the chaos caused by settlers' incursions into and usurpation of Palawa Country and resources, 'Within a single generation of British occupation of Tasmania, approximately 90 per cent of the Aboriginal people alive at the time of British arrival were dead'.³ So when Palawa finally began the hit-and-run raids that were their only means of resistance, there were fewer than 1000 of them – men, women, and children – left to do the fighting.

Despite that, the Black War, as it became known, proved to be 'per capita . . . one of the most destructive wars in recorded history'.⁴ Many colonists had died, many more had been wounded, buildings and crops had been burnt, livestock slaughtered, farms and flocks abandoned. At the end of 1828, provoked by mounting casualty numbers and settlers' clamorous demands for decisive action, colonial authorities had dispatched armed roving parties into the settled districts with orders to eject all Palawa from them and to kill those who resisted – a desperate strategy whose efficacy proved to be chiefly psychological. A year later, as a precautionary measure, the government sent Robinson and his mission to contact and befriend the Palawa of the South East and South West nations, who were believed to be peaceable, to assure them that British intentions toward them were benign and amicable.

'The African slave trade in miniature'

Such assurances, it was hoped, would forestall any intention they had of entering the war.

But in July 1829, six months before Robinson led his mission into the wilderness, a Palawa woman on Lunawanna-alonnah (Bruny Island) gave him startling contrary information. She told him that far from being peaceful, the South West nation's Ninene band – the Port Davey people – were in fact those responsible for several recent raids on settlers. 'It now appears beyond the shadow of a doubt', Robinson wrote, 'that the Port Davey tribe are in league with others who have conjointly carried on their bloody massacre'. He believed what the woman told him, noting that 'this very tribe has been above all others most active in the perpetration of those atrocities which have filled our newspaper columns and caused such a general consternation throughout the settled districts of this colony'.[5] Such information would have been vital to the colonial government at that stage of the conflict, yet Robinson chose not to pass it on. Lieutenant Governor George Arthur had sanctioned the Friendly Mission less than three weeks earlier and it was still months away from starting out. Only by keeping this radical intelligence to himself could Robinson ensure his expedition would be allowed to go ahead, which, for personal reasons, he desperately needed it to. Although he was sincerely committed to and active in several humanitarian and benevolent causes, he intended this, as he did all his endeavours, to improve his own social and financial standing.

At that time his ascension badly needed a fillip, his most recent enterprise having been disastrous. On 7 March 1829, months before he offered to lead the Friendly Mission, he had been appointed to oversee the Palawa ration station on Bruny Island, in the D'Entrecasteaux Channel south of Hobart. A lowly builder by trade, he expected the post to provide him with a measure of personal recognition and improved status by his taming and civilising the island's Palawa population, educating them, and transforming them into model Christian farmers. But he had arrived on Bruny Island to find that only 19 of them were left alive, where a few years earlier there had been 160, and despite his best efforts they continued to sicken and die. Six months after his arrival only nine were living. He realised that they and therefore his enterprise were doomed. After contemplating other possibilities for self-advancement he had proposed to the government that he lead a mission to the Port Davey people, and he had subsequently been appointed by the lieutenant governor to do so. Had Arthur known what Robinson knew about Ninene attacks on colonists, a punitive party would have been despatched instead of a peace mission, which would have been counter to both Robinson's humanitarianism and his ambition. It would also have left him in hapless charge of Bruny Island's moribund Palawa population and overseer of its imminent extinction. No kudos was to be had from that.

Although self-interest was a major motive for his suggesting the mission, his altruism and his concern for Palawa were genuine; as he told his wife, 'to benefit the heathen is dear to my heart'.[6] Both factors had been bolstered by his interview with two Palawa women in Hobart jail on 10 October 1829. They were *tyrelore*, women who had been abducted as children to be the sex slaves of Bass Strait sealers and whalers. One, identified only as Mary, told Robinson that the sealers 'carry on a complete system of slavery', that *tyrelore* were bartered among them for flour and potatoes, and that 'white men beat black women with a rope'.[7] The other woman confirmed Mary's testimony. Her name was Planobeena (aka Fanny or Jock) and in 1841 she would participate in the breakout that terrorised the embryonic colony of Port Phillip. But even as early as 1829 she seethed with resentment, as Robinson noted.

> The aboriginal female Fanny, who speaks English well and knows not a word of the aboriginal tongue, said there were fifty women at the straits and plenty of children . . . [and] that this slave trade is very common at the straits, and that the women so bartered or sold are subject to every hardship which their merciless tyrants can think of

and that from the time their slavery commences they are habituated to all the fatiguing drudgery which their profitable trade imposes.[8]

Robinson was appalled. 'Surely this is the African slave trade in miniature', he wrote, 'and the voice of reason and of humanity loudly calls for its abolition'.[9] Now he had a sound motive beside self-interest for undertaking the mission – and a further justification for keeping secret his new knowledge about Ninene raids. He placed Planobeena in his Hobart home and took Mary with him to Bruny Island (where she died the following month), after which preparations for the Friendly Mission continued. It would proceed as planned, setting him on a path to a controversial place in history and two young men on track to a violent death at the end of a rope.

§

While Robinson's sweating convict servants were carrying supplies ashore at Recherche Bay that February afternoon, his Palawa contingent pursued more congenial pastimes. Some cooled off in the bay, others gathered a favourite food plant called pigface, another caught a platypus in the creek, and some went into the bush to hunt. This late in the devastation of the Palawa population they comprised a motley dozen – females as well as males, children as well as adults, former guerrillas side by side with those who had never shaken a spear at the invaders. They were also heterogeneous; some, indeed, eyed one another warily because their natal clans had been antagonists. But by now old enmities had had to be suspended; merely to be Palawa was bond enough. Consequently they had this in common: all had adapted to the invasion, with its shattering of their culture and destruction of their people, by putting aside ancient animosities and learning to coexist in heterogeneity with one another and to survive in uneasy comity with the invaders, whose regime they complied with or pretended to.

Paramount among them in Robinson's eyes was Kikatapula

(historically spelt Kickerterpoller), a man known to and much feared by Britons as Black Tom Birch, who had incited and led Palawa resistance to British settlers for the first four years of the Black War. His former traditional enemy Umarrah, a minor guerrilla leader from the Tayarinutipana band of the North Midlands nation, was another of Robinson's guides, as was Umarrah's follower Parewareatar, a Tayarinutipana man lame since boyhood, whom Kikatapula had once tried to kill.[10] Two other men's natal origins are unrecorded: Robert, a very young man who had been raised from infancy by settlers and spoke only English, and Trepanner, who had joined Robinson from hospital in Hobart on 15 December 1829 but whose prior history is unrecorded.[11] Three other males were surviving Bruny Islanders from the Nununi band: Wurati (historically Wooraddy or similar) and his sons Myyungge (aka David Bruny) and Droyyerloinne (aka Peter Bruny), both young boys. Other guides were a young woman named Draymuric (aka Dray), who was a Ninene from Port Davey, and two Nununi women from Bruny Island: Pagerly and a pretty teenager who had recently married the much older widower Wurati. Her name was Trukanini and she was on her way to a unique and tragic place in history.

Born *circa* 1812, she grew to be a petite woman under 150 centimetres tall who was notably attractive to – and attracted by – men. From childhood her life had been devastated by violent events at the hands of colonists, some of which she related many years later.

> We was camped close to Partridge Island when I was a little girl when a vessel came to anchor without our knowing of it. A boat came on shore, and some of the men attacked our camp. We all ran away, but one of them caught my mother and stabbed her with a knife and killed her. My father grieved much about her death and used to make a fire at night by himself when my mother would come to him. I had a sister named Moorina. She was taken away [abducted] by a sealing boat. I used to go to Birch's Bay. There was a party of men cutting timber

for the Government there . . . While I was there two young men of my tribe came for me; one of them was to have been my husband; his name was Paraweena. Well, two of the sawyers said they would take us in a boat to Bruni Island, which we agreed to. When we got about halfway across the channel they murdered the two natives and threw them overboard. I tried to jump overboard, but one of them held me. Their names were Watkin Lowe and Paddy Newel.[12]

She (or the friend who retold her story) failed to mention that both men had subsequently raped her. Paddy Newel was probably the Paddy she told Robinson had once flogged her while four men held her down, another incident she apparently neglected to mention to her friend. Her litany of brutal experiences also omitted mention of the fate of her uncle, known as Boomer Jack, who was shot dead by soldiers intent on raping his wife.[13] Whatever scarring she bore from such horrors, Trukanini survived to be the longest lived and best known of the five Tasmanians who would terrorise Victoria – indeed, to be the best known of all her people.

Another member of that inceptive quintet, a stranger then to Trukanini (although in time they would become lovers and partners in homicide), was the twelfth of Robinson's dozen Palawa companions: Malapuwinarana. Although only in his middle teens, he was a former resistance fighter who had been captured with Umarrah and Parewareatar. In early encounters with whites he had acquired the nickname Jemmy, but he would later become infamous as Timme – sometimes spelt Timmy – which was said to be a native name.[14] His life, like Trukanini's, would be historic and tragic.

Unlike hers, it would also be brief and brutally ended.

§

Robinson decided to trek overland from Recherche Bay to Port Davey, supported from the sea by the schooner and the whaleboat. In a straight line the two places are about 80 kilometres apart, but there are no straight lines in the wild and forbidding landscape that separates them, only 'mountains and hills . . . deeply intersected with very steep gullies and gorges running in all directions and mostly clothed with very thick scrub or forest'.[15] Estimating that the trek would take three days, Robinson led his party away from Recherche Bay into the wilderness on 3 February, but only after 11 torturous and sometimes dangerous days did they reach Port Davey, having had to struggle through some of the most difficult terrain in Tasmania – 'mountain tiers as far as the eye could see', Robinson wrote – whose frigidly malign climate and foul weather made progress as arduous as it was hazardous. They had to wade through waist-deep flooded marshes, force their way (sometimes on hands and knees) through near-impenetrable bush, cross rivers, traverse lofty tiers, and negotiate perilous escarpments, even though some expeditioners were weak and ill and all were short of food. The settler-raised youth Robert endured the hardship for only a fortnight. On 18 February he absconded, a loss Robinson shrugged off because he expected the young man's ignorance of bushcraft to ensure his early demise in that extreme country. (Robert survived, however, later rejoining the mission in unrecorded circumstances.)

Despite the difficult terrain, Robinson boasted that 'we travelled as fast as some people travel on the road', and the mission's four remaining youngsters found the trek particularly debilitating.[16] On 1 April he took pity on them. He sent his son Charles, Wurati's two little boys, and the youth Timme back to Hobart aboard the *Swallow* while the mission pushed on overland. During his two gruelling months with Robinson Timme had not drawn attention to himself in any way, garnering only an innocuous single mention (on 27 February) in Robinson's copious journal entries. That would change. History would have reason to remember him.

2

'The cry of welcome was evinced'

As Robinson's party, now without its juvenile members, continued to push farther northward along the west coast, the three exhausted Palawa boys were disembarking from the *Swallow* in Hobart. At first they were housed in Robinson's Aboriginal annexe while they recovered from their travail, but on 13 May 1830 it was reported that 'the two elder boys Jemmy [Timme] and Davy [Myyungge] are in good health and fit to be admitted into the male orphan school', so both entered the institution that day.[1] Despite his youth, Timme had already been in jail twice, but he plausibly found the King's Orphan School worse. Even by the standards of the time it was brutal, and he was black. Like the convict system whose offshoot it was, the school functioned by regimentation, discipline, and punishment. The boys were housed in a converted distillery on New Town Rivulet that was unheated and overcrowded. They were undernourished. Severe beatings, neglect, and systemic abuse were recorded. (The year after Timme's admission, the headmaster beat a 14-year-old inmate to death.[2]) What a black youth with limited English might have suffered under such a regime is best left unimagined, but Timme chose not to endure it. He absconded within days of admission, reportedly because he wanted to see his mother, and was soon back on Country in the far north-east.[3] It was there, six months later, that Robinson next had news of him. By that time the Friendly Mission, after following the coastline clockwise halfway around Tasmania from their south-eastern Recherche Bay start, had reached Swan Island, off the north-eastern tip. From the island they saw that Palawa on mainland Lutruwita were signalling with smoke, and Robinson's guides, reading the smokes, informed him that Timme was there.[4] That greatly surprised Robinson. As far as he knew, Timme was still at the Orphan School in Hobart, about 240 kilometres south.

Timme's escape from the school was not his first flight from British custody. Born about 1815 into the Pyemairenerpairener band of the North East nation, he was the son of a leader named Rolepa and his wife Luggenemeener.[5] He is believed to have had brothers or half-brothers named Rolepana (aka Ben Lomond), Tillarbunner (aka Batman's Jack), and Walter George Arthur (natal name unrecorded), although the matter is confused and the relationship unverifiable.[6] When still a boy of about 11 Timme witnessed the wreck of the schooner *Sally* in Ringarooma Bay, so he was on Country in June 1826 when that occurred.[7] By the spring of 1828, now about 13, he was part of a small remnant mob led by the Tayarinutipana man Umarrah, whose 'determined purpose [was] . . . to make repeated incursions, and to destroy all the whites he possibly can, which he considers a patriotic duty' and who was said to be responsible for several raids on settlers in the Campbell Town region.[8] Umarrah, his wife, and three of his band were captured on 14 November 1828 when a roving party led by Gilbert Robertson, the chief district constable of Richmond, raided their camp at Mellareremertitter (probably Black Johnnys Marsh near Little Swanport).[9] Guided there by Kikatapula, who was a traditional enemy of Umarrah, Robertson's men attacked at dawn while Umarrah's people were asleep. Although several of them managed to flee in the ensuing chaos, Robertson seized a boy who was trying to escape through the back of a bark hut. Once the boy and the other captives were secured, Kikatapula interrogated them and was able to identify each by name, telling Robertson that the boy was called Jemmy.[10] The prisoners were marched first to Richmond and then, on 18 November, into Hobart, where Lieutenant Governor Arthur intended to put them on trial for their lives. But Robertson argued that they should be as prisoners of war, not criminals. Arthur conceded, incarceration without trial was decreed, and the five were escorted back to Richmond and confined in the jail.

It was Jemmy's first experience of prison and it was not to be his last, but he did not suffer durance long. After three months' incarceration he contrived an escape. As well as an English nickname, he probably had some knowledge of English because he fooled Chief District Constable Robertson into believing he was willing to become a guide for the black rangers, as Robertson's roving party was called. Robertson then arranged for him to be escorted to Peter Dudgeon's stock hut for attachment to a small military contingent based there, but Jemmy had other ideas. A newspaper reported the success of his ruse.

> Gibbs parish, Salt pan plains, 2d March [1829]. Last Monday [23 February], Jemmy, one of the black natives so long confined at Richmond, made his escape from Prior, a field police Constable in this parish. Jemmy had volunteered to guide Mr. Gilbert Robertson's party, in pursuit of his sable brethren, and was on his way from the Coal river [Richmond], to join Mr. Robertson at Malony's sugar loaf, when he adroitly gave Prior the slip.[11]

Free again, Jemmy found his way back to Country. He was probably part of a band of about 60 to 70 Palawa, which included his mother Luggenemeener, who were camped east of Ben Lomond when attacked by the settler John Batman and his men on 1 September 1829. Most escaped but 15 were thought to have been fatally wounded and Luggenemeener and her infant son Rolepana were captured. Eight days later Batman set out on another sortie, this time along St Pauls River toward Oyster Bay. After a week's searching he encountered some farmworkers who said they had been attacked by Palawa and knew where they were camped. Early in the afternoon of 18 September Batman found them.

Breakout!

> [As I saw] a number of Natives approaching towards us I ordered the men to lay down and not to fire upon them – but when I should whistle to rush forward and seize them . . . when they approached us within 40 yards I gave the signal . . . we all ran forward and secured three women, two young children, three Boys, and two young men . . .[12]

Jemmy was among those captured; six others escaped. The captives were escorted first to Campbell Town and then to Oatlands before finally being herded south for incarceration in Richmond jail.

> RICHMOND, Sep. 29, 1829.–Eleven of the Aborigines captured lately by Mr. Batman, were this day brought here under an escort of a party of the 63d regiment and constables from Oatlands. Two of them are very young men . . . They halted at the court house. A native man and woman taken by a party of the 40th regiment with Mr. Robertson's party in the month of November last* . . . were sent for from the gaol [to greet them], immediately on their coming in sight of the newly arrived party, the cry of welcome was evinced . . .[13]

The 'native man and woman' were Parewareatar and Umarrah's wife Laoininneloonner, two of Gilbert Robertson's captives from the raid at Mellareremertitter, and they clearly knew some of the newcomers.[14] One of them was the Jemmy who had escaped from Constable Prior, and he was now forced to endure a second three months' incarceration in the cramped and crowded prison. It was not a pleasant experience. Despite his lameness, Parewareatar was for some reason singled out for harsh treatment and kept handcuffed in a cell, and all of them were undernourished and badly fed. Their rations included only salt meat, which they detested, instead of fresh. When Kikatapula, still guiding for Robertson, learnt of their mistreatment he complained to him on their behalf. The chief district constable interceded and in due course the lieutenant governor ordered better treatment for them.[15]

★   Umarrah's band.

That the incarcerated Jemmy was in fact Timme is verifiable because it was from Richmond jail on 4 January 1830 that Robinson freed the youth he later called Timmy.[16] After liberating him and other Palawa prisoners – 'three women, two infants, one man and two boys' – he took them to Hobart and interned them in the colonial hospital where they could be securely confined with the lunatics. Jemmy languished there until 15 January when Robinson transferred 'two native lads, one from Jorgen Jorgenson's party and the other from Mr Gilbert Robertson's' to the building adjacent to his Elizabeth Street home, which was newly appointed an Aboriginal annexe.[17] On the seventeenth, a Sunday, he took all those housed there to St David's church in Macquarie Street where 'Their conduct was . . . very decorous and satisfactory', he noted. 'The grandeur of the edifice, the crowded and highly respectable audience, together with the sacred music . . . was too much for their untutored imaginations. Their attention was deeply riveted on this imposing spectacle . . .' They were less impressed, however, by a Wesleyan service he took them to next day.[18]

Later that month Luggenemeener was allowed to return to Country. Timme and Parewareatar were dragooned into the incipient Friendly Mission and sailed with it on 27 January toward its starting place in Recherche Bay.[19] Timme's service with the mission was brief and inconspicuous before he was sent back to Hobart and the Orphan School, but he and Robinson would soon meet again, and this time the union would endure until severed by death.

3

'Plenty much blood, plenty cry'

Before that, back in May 1830, as Timme was suffering his brief spell in the Orphan School, Robinson's mission had continued to labour northward on the west coast. At Trial Harbour on 12 May, six weeks after the four youngsters were shipped back to Hobart, Robinson lost three more of his Palawa companions when Umarrah, Parewareatar, and Trepanner absconded, leaving him with only four or five guides: Trukanini and her husband Wurati, Kikatapula and his new wife Pagerly, and possibly the shadowy and inconstant Robert. They shouldered the extra loads and pressed on. Despite having replenished their supplies the previous month during a week's respite at the Macquarie Harbour penal settlement, they were almost out of provisions. But the weather was good and so was the hunting; on 18 May they caught seven kangaroos. Two days later they rendezvoused with the *Maria*, which brought them further supplies: 'one gallon of wine, half a gallon of lime juice, preserved soups and meats; some writing paper, three pencils and sealing wax'.

As they pushed northward they had occasional encounters with Toogee, the Palawa they were seeking to conciliate, although the guides easily subverted Robinson's efforts to contact them. Sometimes, when they found tracks or other signs indicating Toogee were nearby, Robinson's Palawa companions made undue noise to warn of their approach. It exasperated him. 'Had the greatest difficulty keeping my natives quiet', he complained; 'frequently put my hand over their mouths to stop the sound of their voice'.[1]

'Plenty much blood, plenty cry'

At midday on 13 June he climbed to the summit of Wobberricker (Mt Cameron West) and surveyed the landscape ahead.

> From the top was seen broad extensive plains covered with grass and small grassy hills, and small belts of open forest interspersed throughout . . . Had a view of the Straits north of Robbins Island, the Pelican Island,* the Doughboys, the Black Rock, the Petrel Islands, the East and West Hunter Islands, Cape Grim &c.

At the extreme north-western tip of Tasmania, Laggenner (Cape Grim) is about 30 kilometres north of where Robinson was standing. The extensive plains he saw included part of a vast holding of more than 1000 square kilometres of usurped Palawa land that in 1826 had been granted to the Van Diemen's Land (VDL) Company to establish a wool-growing enterprise. As the first British outpost the mission had encountered since leaving Macquarie Harbour, now at least 180 arduous kilometres behind them, it was a welcome sight. After 19 weeks' trekking from Recherche Bay through the most testing terrain in Tasmania, they were physically spent and short of rations. Encouraged that Cape Grim was in sight, they pressed on, eager for whatever respite and comforts might be offered at Woolnorth, as the grant was named.

By 15 June Robinson was ensconced in the cottage of Joseph Fossey, a VDL Company surveyor, where initially he rested and wrote in his journal. Soon, however, he took to his boat and began investigating the nearby Bass Strait islands where he expected to find sealers and their *tyrelore*, whom Lieutenant Governor Arthur had authorised him to free from their captors. On 19 May he landed on Padereker (Robbins Island), at 99 square kilometres the seventh-largest of the 334 islands that comprise today's state of Tasmania. From ancient times Padereker had been the country of the Parperloinnher band of the North West nation, and as Robinson began to explore it on foot he saw in several places evidence of their recent occupation. Wildlife was

---

*   Probably Penguin Island.

abundant, which made him think the Parperloinnher must have been well provided for before the sealers came and 'were very numerous but have been destroyed by the sealers and by the tribes with whom they are at war, and are now but few in number'.[2]

The weather was fair, so he camped on the island overnight. Late next day he caught up with the *Maria*, which he had sent ahead. The crew had already spoken with some of the sealers living on the island. They had six *tyrelore*, including a sister of the absconded guide Parewareatar, as well as 'one male aborigine who had come to them about seven days before and was a native of the part'.[3] His name, the young man told Robinson, was Tanaminawayt, also known as Pevay, and he would promptly attach himself to the Friendly Mission. More than a decade later, he would lead the Tasmanians who forced Port Phillip settlers to flee their homes in terror.[4]

§

Pevay was born *circa* 1812 into the Parperloinnher band. His father was Keeghernewboyheenner and his siblings included brothers Pintawtawa (historically Pendowtewer), Wymurrick, and Penderoin; a sister, Pordeboic, who was about his own age; and possibly one other sister whose name is not recorded.

A few events are known of his life before he joined Robinson, two of them youthful experiences with ruthless foreigners. The first was in 1820 when he was aged about eight. He told Robinson he was in a food-gathering band of men, women, and children at Cape Grim when nine sealers rushed from concealment and attacked them. They abducted several women and murdered two Palawa men who tried to stop them. Robinson noted that Pevay's story 'agrees with the account the sealers give'.[5] Some years later Penderoin told Robinson that he too had been in the Cape Grim party when it was attacked, verification of his brother Pevay's presence.[6]

Despite such early experience, Pevay was inquisitive about the alien race that was beginning to proliferate in the north-west. In 1826 the Van Diemen's Land Company had established its headquarters, Highfield House, close to present-day Stanley and had planted a store and the germ of a settlement at Konenerrinehe (Emu Bay), also on the Bass Strait coast but about 80 kilometres to the south-east. Palawa mainly kept aloof but observed and studied the newcomers. Occasionally they made peaceful contact. 'In some cases the old men seemed to have welcomed the chance to send the young away to work for Europeans for the difficult and often prolonged period between puberty and marriage . . . to relieve some of the pent up pressures of traditional society intensified by rapid change.'[7] One who made contact during 1828 was a Palawa youth believed to be Pevay. At first this young man concealed himself in the bush near Emu Bay's Blackman Point, where the VDL Co. had established its store, from where he watched an employee's small children at play. In August the following year he felt secure enough to approach some of the company's employees at Maluta (Circular Head). He did so in a friendly and no doubt inquiring manner, but they made him a prisoner and took him to the company's manager Edward Curr, although he twice tried to escape on the way. Curr, who was under pressure to improve relations with local Palawa, chose to comply by incarcerating the inquisitive young man and keeping him confined for months, as he reported to his London head office.

> A youth, about 16 years of age, came voluntarily to some of our people who were in a boat near the isthmus*. They brought him to me not without his making one or two attempts to escape and I have put him on board the *Friendship* for security where I intend him to remain until he knows at least enough of our language to be made to understand that we mean no hostility to his tribe and then probably after a few months he may be allowed to rejoin his people if he wishes to do so . . .[8]

Curr named the young man 'Thursday' and kept him a virtual prisoner

---

*   The Neck at Circular Head.

aboard the *Friendship* until the following year. During that time the vessel plied between Circular Head and Emu Bay, and it seems that although Thursday was taken ashore from time to time, he made no attempt to escape.

On 16 November 1829 Curr sent his directors a report of his progress with the captive.

> Thursday the native youth who gave himself up to our people ... is still on board the *Friendship* and behaves very well except that he is incorrigibly idle. He is extremely intelligent and tractable and is a great favourite with everyone. Mr Hellyer* writes me that when he went on shore with him at Emu Bay 'he told Mrs Heaton he had often been in the bush there close to the little children and described their having little Baskets which they filled with stones, and Mrs Heaton said that must have been twelve months ago; but it shews Thursday had no wish to hurt them'.⁹

Mrs Heaton, mother of several small daughters, was the wife of John Heaton, a VDL Company employee at Emu Bay. Helyer's note indicates that in 1828, the year before Thursday revealed himself to Curr's men at Circular Head, he had several times visited the little settlement, observing from concealment its people and activities – the action of an adventurous and inquisitive youth. Given the 80-kilometre walk from Emu Bay to Robbins Island, he was not deterred by indolence in his quest to learn about the newcomers. He was clearly free of hostility toward them, wanting only to observe and learn.

After keeping Thursday captive for five months Curr realised his efforts to tame the youth were not progressing, so in January 1830 he liberated him, but not before first attempting to convince him that he was being released so he could become an intermediary between the company and the Parperloinnher. In reporting Thursday's liberation to London, Curr provided a brief pen portrait of his prisoner, whom he described as having 'a cocky air'.

---

*   A Van Diemen's Land Company surveyor.

My object in keeping him for some time being answered, namely by treating him with kindness to make him understand that we were good white men and that we had no wish to injure his Countrymen. I asked him when I was last at Woolnorth in the Friendship [29 November–4 December 1829] whether he would like to go back to his Countrymen. I told him that he must make ready to go to them and bring them all with him to my house at Circular Head, where they should all get Bread Blankets and Tobacco for he had become very fond of the latter Article. In a few minutes he presented himself again, his jacket lined with slices of damper and cold pudding as provisions for his journey, highly delighted apparently with the prospect of seeing the people of his tribe. He took a fire stick in his hand and set forward to Robins [sic] Island where he said they would be, and where I have no doubt he found them as I saw their fires soon after he left me. Thursday was a great favourite with every one, a good-natured intelligent fellow who would laugh, talk, eat and drink the day through, but do no work. He has not since made his appearance according to promise, and I now think he will spend his summer in the bush whilst Kangaroos, birds, eggs and Shellfish are plentiful, and that he will come to us again for shelter and food in the Winter. He has met with nothing but good treatment here and I think cannot have any other than friendly feelings towards us.[10]

Having headed after his release straight to Robbins Island to rejoin his people, Thursday was clearly a Parperloinnher, and it was on Robbins Island five months later that the Parperloinnher youth Pevay was first recorded. Moreover, as Robinson was soon to note, Pevay 'spoke the English language tolerable well', which is a skill likely learnt during his months as Curr's captive pupil.[11] Little doubt remains that Thursday was Pevay.[12]

Curr's last comments about Thursday were to the colonial secretary.

I learnt from him some curious facts regarding his countrymen, particularly that they burn their dead, who are then supposed to go to some very distant place over the sea to the North West, which they call moo.ai. He has be[en] as far as the Surrey Hills but knows nothing of Launceston [more than 100 kilometres farther south-east], and his language was entirely different from that of the Eastern tribes.[13]

This 1830 word-portrait of a man who was certainly a Parperloinnher and undoubtedly Pevay is invaluable. It paints a man in his late teens who was inquisitive, intelligent, not belligerent or aggressive, tractable, popular, good-humoured, and fond of conversation and laughter. In the following dozen years, all of them spent with colonising white men, his character would undergo a complete and drastic change.

With his experience of the Cape Grim attack and his involuntary confinement by Curr, Pevay might by now have learnt that white men were best avoided. Yet in June 1830, only five months after Curr freed Thursday, Pevay attached himself to sealers living on Robbins Island. Any wariness about whites he might have had quickly proved to be justified. Within a week he began to suspect they meant to kill him.

§

The Robbins Island sealers were resentful and uncooperative when Robinson told them he intended freeing all their Palawa women; they said he could have Pevay instead. But Robinson was firm. 'I would not have him on those terms . . . I should take him and the women if I thought proper', he responded. Eventually the sealers relented and let the women go.[14] Pevay, fearing for his life if he stayed, was happy to leave with Robinson and the six liberated *tyrelore* on 21 June. While they waited at Leendimrooer (Welcome River) for the boat to come for them, Robinson talked with Pevay and recorded Parperloinnher vocabulary for inclusion in the lexicon he was compiling. Pevay also provided him with information about Walyer, the so-called Aboriginal Amazon who was then leading a small mob in attacking Palawa and white colonists alike in the north-west. Although what he told Robinson was detailed enough to imply some first-hand knowledge, his declaration that she was 'no good' suggests his information came from unpleasant personal experience.[15] It was not to be his last.

When the boat arrived, Robinson and his seven new recruits sailed to Cape Grim and stayed for a few days at Woolnorth. Pevay and the six women now joined Kikatapula, Pagerly, Wurati, and Trukanini in Robinson's mission – Robert, the other remaining original guide, had absconded again – which resumed travelling on 25 June. Strangers at this time to one another, three of the five Palawa who would stage a violent breakout at Port Phillip were now together in Robinson's mission.

After a few days camped by Welcome River they returned to Robbins Island to search for more Parperloinnher and soon encountered some.

> 4 pm on ascending a small a small range of hills the PAIR.RE.HE.HOIN.NE aborigine [Pevay] descried the natives. I desired him to take off his clothing and go after them. They fled, when TUN.NER.MIN.NER.WAIT [Pevay] hullooing for them to stop, he presently got to them. One of the natives (who proved to be his brother) came to him, when they conferred together. I desired the people to remain and to make a fire and I would go to the natives. Having walked about a mile I perceived TUN.NER.MIN.NER.WAIT, accompanied by one of the aborigines. We shortly met and TUN.NER.MIN.NER.WAIT introduced him to me as PENDOWTEWER [Pintawtawa], his brother. He shook hands and we conversed together from a vocabulary which I had formed of their language. He laughed heartily and seemed pleased with his new acquaintance; I was equally so with mine. I desired TUNNERMINNERWAIT to go back to the rest and bring them. Myself and PENDOWTEWER remained. We sat down on the ridge of hills; enjoyed each other's company much. PENDOWTEWER is a fine young man, appears to be about 18 years of age. He is very cheerful and has a pleasing aspect on his countenance . . . Requested PENDOWTEWER to accompany (me) to the rest of his countrymen. He acquiesced

> but very reluctantly. Having come within a hundred paces of them TUNNERMINNERWAIT came to me accompanied by a female whom he also introduced as NARRUCKER. Poor creature, she seemed filled with apprehension. I endeavoured to cheer her. She was reserved and a sullen gloom pervaded her countenance . . . (These people have accompanied me to Emu Bay; they are three in number.)[16]

Pevay's new-boy eagerness to please was limited by youthful caution, however, as Robinson discovered on Robbins Island soon afterward.

> Having taken breakfast, took TUN.NER.MIN.WAIT and went on a hill to reconnoitre. My native companion quickly descried one man at a distance, standing upon a hill. Proceeded and crossed the plains and went towards him. Upon arriving near to the place my companion stopped: said I might go but he would stay. Asked him if he was LAB.BE.RID.DE.KER, frightened; said, yes.[17]

On 6 July, with the mission back on Robbins Island, the six *tyrelore* absconded. Robinson chose not to pursue them, instead rationalising that 'although it would be the greatest act of humanity to take them out of the hands of their enemies, time is an essential consideration in this undertaking'. Events soon changed his mind. Eight days later, at Circular Head, he learnt of a potentially lucrative government proclamation made six months earlier. Dated 25 February 1830, it offered a cash bounty for every Palawa captured: £5 for each adult and £2 for each child. Robinson's altruism immediately metamorphosed. Conciliator became capitalist.

> Having been informed of the proclamation offering reward for the apprehension of the aborigines, I this day despatched my boat to Robbins Island in quest of the aborigines there.[18]

It has been observed that 'Robinson's action in sending his boat to Robbins Island to try to capture the natives there, marks the beginning of his commercialisation in relation to his work among the aborigines'.[19] Recapturing the six *tyrelore* would have enriched him by £30 — a year's wages for many working men — but despite its alacrity, his response was futile. The boat returned two days later without captives.

At midday on 24 July the mission departed from Circular Head, where Robinson had been sojourning for several days as Edward Curr's guest, and set out for Pinmatik (Rocky Cape). 'The country is very rugged', Robinson noted two gruelling days later, 'the mountains covered with scrub and terminating in steep rocky cliffs'.[20] Although he saw such evidence of Palawa presence as a newly made hut, he saw no Palawa.

On 27 July his boat brought him two new captives. One was a club-footed young man named Nikaminik (historically Nicermenic) whom Pevay was overjoyed to see, for Nikaminik was an old friend. He had once been employed by the VDL Company (and acquired there the nickname 'Friday') but had left them after promising to return with his family. 'He not only failed in this but subsequently became most notorious for his repeated outrages upon the Company's people' after he joined the hostile mob led by the Amazonian Walyer. Consequently, the company declared it would kill him on sight.[21] The other new captive, Linermerrinnecer, had been lured into the boat by the coxswain. Robinson gave each a pair of canvas trousers and then, bounties in mind, dispatched Linermerrinnecer, Pintawtawa, and Narrucker in the boat to Emu Bay, whence they would be forwarded by sea to Launceston and on to Hobart, thereby boosting by £15 the Robinson coffers.

Pleased with this lucrative transaction, he sent Nikaminik and Pevay into the bush in quest of more Palawa. The two friends disappeared for a few days — Kikatapula and Wurati, sent to find them, returned and claimed they could not — but they eventually rejoined Robinson and accompanied him to Emu Bay. From there on 4 August Robinson sent Nikaminik aboard the *Friendship* to be shipped with Pintawtawa, Linermerrinnecer, and Narrucker to Launceston for forwarding to

Breakout!

Hobart, a £5 boost to his bounties and a total of £20 worth of human cargo. But easy money for Robinson was a source of grief for Pevay. Robinson was surprised at the depth of the Parperloinnher's distress at this peremptory parting from his friend and his brother.

> The affection of these people is very striking – the vessel on weighing her anchor caught a breeze and was soon distant, TUN.NER.MIN.NER.WAIT keeping a longing and wishful eye upon her and bursting into tears. With them had fled his hopes. His brother and his companion had all gone. NIC.ER.ME.NIC had been his former intimate acquaintance and friend . . .[22]

It was now plain to Pevay that his life and those of his friends and family were no longer their own, that they could be denied their freedom and willingly or unwillingly removed from Country. His own incarceration by Curr and now the involuntary exiling of Nikaminik, Pintawtawa, and Linermerrinnecer must have driven home to him that freedom could no longer be taken for granted. Palawa lives could be and were being constrained or even ended by the inexplicable whims of white men who wanted them gone. He contemplated escape.

From Emu Bay the mission moved on again, headlong into harsh midwinter, and was soon slowed by bitter weather and relentless rain. With their laboured breaths steaming icy air they toiled through deep snow in Hampshire Hills. Trees all around them were spangled with icicles 30 centimetres long. Progress became painful.

> At 9 am proceeded on my route accompanied by McKay, WOORRADY, TRUGERNANNA and TUN.NER.MIN.NER.WAIT. Thick hazy weather with rain. Travelled a north course for several hours in order to obtain a pass to the mountains, the plains very bad to travel from the large tussocks of grass, water &c . . . In the direction we were travelling it was several miles across, the whole laid with snow up to the knees and sometimes up to the middle and with a sharp bleak wind, thick cloud and frozen rain. The rain had rendered the snow compact and

each one of the party trod in the footsteps of the other. It became exceedingly laborious to have to pull the foot out of one of these snowboots, some of which reached up to the thighs ... One of my feet was so benumbed with cold that I was obliged to plunge it into snow water to obtain animation.[23]

Some became sick in the brutal conditions. On 23 August Pagerly and Robert were so ill that Robinson sent them back to Emu Bay and soon had to join them there himself, having developed an abscess on his kneecap that made walking unbearable. While he was recovering he discovered to his great displeasure that three of the four Palawa captives he had shipped to Hobart in the *Friendship* had been allowed to return to Circular Head, from which they had vanished into the bush. Because Nikaminik had been the only one delivered to Hobart, Robinson's expected £20 bounty was winnowed to £5, to his strongly expressed annoyance. When Pevay learnt his brother was back on Country, the desire to abscond and join him there became irresistible.

The mission left Emu Bay for Launceston via Port Sorell as soon as Robinson's knee had sufficiently improved. It was spring and the weather was better and the travelling easier, but they encountered little sign of Palawa – until, near Rubicon River on 20 September, voices in adjacent bushland brought them to a halt. 'These sounds were welcome sounds to me ... and I lost no time in going in quest of them', Robinson wrote. He grabbed a handful of trinkets and ordered Pevay, Wurati, and Trukanini to strip off their clothing so they could go forward with him as emissaries. After a short sortie into the bush they found two huts where Palawa had recently been making spears – their fires were still burning – and they soon spotted the spearmakers' trail.

> Followed their tracks for about three miles [five kilometres], when on descending the declivity of a hill [we] saw the natives walking along in single file, quite naked, blacked over with charred wood and carrying spears. They were all big men, eight in number ...

> They were not more than fifty paces of me and PEE.VAY recognised them as [Walyer] the Amazon's party . . . Followed after them and on winding round the aclivity of a hill heard a faint sound of human voices, which seemed to proceed from the top of this hill. Concluded immediately that these were the women and children. Was now between the two parties. Saw plainly that the eight men was on a murderous expedition . . . [O]n perceiving them to cross the western river [Rubicon River] and take a direction to where I had encamped the day before, I plainly saw that they were going to attack me and my little party . . .
>
> Upon crossing the river I sent the three natives forward to try to get an interview with them, fearful lest my approach should affright them, and remained a short distance behind . . . The band of warriors proceeded by a circuitous route to my former encampment and having discovered that the object they were searching for had fled, immediately returned, tracking my footsteps, when they unexpectedly met with MUTTEELLEE [Wurati], PEE.VAY, and TRUGERNANNA. The warriors pointed their spears, calling to each other MANG.HER.NER DRACK.ER (throw spears), and my natives, on seeing the danger to which they were exposed, fled and returned to where I was . . .²⁴

It was a dangerous situation; Robinson and his three guides were unarmed. They hurriedly backtracked to the hill where they had heard women's and children's voices. Although no one was there, they found tracks that led them to a small valley where voices were again audible.

> I approached them unobserved to within ten yards. The men had returned and were relating their exploits. I had stood a few moments listening to their conversation and observing their actions, when they observed our approach and immediately made off . . . I run towards them, calling upon them to stop . . . Some of the natives got into a thick scrub and I desired PEE.VAY, who spoke their language, to tell them I would not hurt them. After a short parley I desired the people [his three guides] to come away . . .²⁵

Either ignorant of or foolhardy about the great danger he had been in (and still festering about his deprival of three bounties), Robinson chose to consider his escape from the hostile band as just another lost commercial opportunity. 'Had I power to act as my judgment would direct I should have deemed it advisable to capture the whole of this tribe, but the ill-advised measure of sending back those aborigines that I had desired to be sent to Hobart Town, induced me to act agreeable to the letter of instructions of conciliation', he rationalised.[26] He was not specific about how, outnumbered and armed only with trinkets, he might have captured eight armed and belligerent warriors and their women and children.

Although the encounter left the mission unscathed, they were fortunate to have escaped. Pevay, who knew and feared the murderous Amazon and her band, was rattled. It was too close a call for his liking and he was unnerved by Robinson's imprudence. It was time to seize his freedom, time to go home.

Next day two Palawa youths from Circular Head were delivered by boat to the mission. One of the new captives, Merappe, was about 17; the other, Lettelowhe, was thought to be two years younger. Both were orphans and both knew Pevay and spoke his language, Robinson commented, noting too that they had been with white people and could swear. Without effort he was able to reconcile bounties with benevolence. 'It is not only unwise but inhuman to turn these poor creatures in the bush', he reasoned. 'Surrounded on all sides by their white foes they would have been shot, or having no tribes to go to they would have been enticed to join an hostile tribe.'[27]

Pevay had differing ideas. When he told the two newcomers of his intention to return to Country and family, they were happy to follow his lead. Next day, in pre-dawn darkness, the three slipped away. Although angry, Robinson was able to shrug off another monetary loss.

Although the [white] men were sleeping in the same tent with them, they allowed them to go away – the men are of little use in this work! The two lads [Merappe and Lettelowhe] was set at liberty by the government and I therefore could not think of detaining them. Making captives was not my duty. They were at liberty to go where they were inclined. They had moreover three companions behind them, PEN.DOW.TE.WER, NARRUKER and LINE.NER.RIN.KNE.ER having returned to their country, and it was natural to expect that they would feel desirous to join them. The circumstances of PEE.VAY going will do good, as he knows me and the nature of my business and my friendly pursuits towards the natives. He had been a long time with me* and spoke the English language tolerable well. But I was entering a country of people which he knew nothing of, and he could therefore render me little service. He was an exceeding willing and industrious young man, about nineteen years of age, stout and well made, of good temper, and performed his work equal to any white man.[28]

Robinson and Pevay were not to be parted for long, however. Their paths would soon converge again, and after that would intermesh until 1842 and the infant colony of Port Phillip.

§

Free now, the three young Palawa moved quickly through the early morning back toward Country, intending to join Pevay's newly emancipated brother Pintawtawa. But they were not long at liberty. Soon after absconding they were attacked by Walyer's mob, from whom they escaped only by plunging into Mersey River and swimming to the opposite bank. There they sought sanctuary with Captain Malcolm Laing Smith, a magistrate, but he notified the authorities of their presence. Four days after they fled Robinson's camp a military party marched them into Launceston, where they were confined in the jail in Paterson Street.[29] Although their incarceration

---

*   Three months.

was brief, prison conditions were harsh and the spring of 1830 was a particularly bad time for a black to be in white detention in Lutruwita. The Black War was raging fiercer than ever in the settled districts. Hostility to Palawa was universal. Three sealers who had just come from Launceston met Robinson and told him that 'nothing was heard or thought of than shooting the natives'.[30] The deteriorating situation had forced the government on 1 October to declare martial law, a dramatic move followed by something even more drastic – launching the largest military operation ever undertaken in Australia against Indigenous people, a campaign that became known as the Black Line. Beginning on 7 October, a vast human chain of more than 2000 well-armed police, military, and civilians would sweep in a long tight line south-easterly across the settled districts, driving all remaining Palawa before them with a gradually closing dragnet. As the net tightened it would force the entire hostile native population across narrow Teralina (Eaglehawk Neck) onto Turrakana (Tasman Peninsula), where they would be corralled in perpetuity. But the campaign proved a costly failure. Only two Palawa were captured and two shot dead; all the others easily broke through and escaped, killing two colonists and wounding nine more as they fled westward to safety.[31]

Even Launceston jail was suffused with the prevailing antagonism to Palawa, and the three black youths were badly treated. Pevay suffered much. '[T]he gaol was no good and the white men was bad white men' was his angry comment.[32] He had time to brood. White men were not to be trusted. Freedom was no longer a birthright. It was necessary now to seize it and be prepared to defend it. Yet he was so alarmed by the prevalent hostility that he refused when Lettelowhe and Merappe urged him to escape. In the present climate he was safer in prison, he believed, although again being under Robinson's protection now seemed the safest option. So he resisted the pressure to escape. Robinson would come again and take them out, he said.[33]

Robinson did. After reaching Launceston on 2 October he 'Went to the gaol to see the natives . . . Found them with all the prisoners.

They were pleased to see me, wanted to come out. PEE.VAY fretted very much. I endeavoured to quiet his mind, poor fellow. Cruel treatment!'³⁴ He arranged for Pevay's release, although not before using his imprisonment to scare the other mission Palawa into greater dependence on him.

> Told my natives how PEE.VAY was in gaol. They cried then and said the commandant was no good, and seemed much alarmed when I told them the commandant was going to put them in gaol. I told them not to fear, they were safe with me.³⁵

When the mission left Launceston for the north-east on 9 October, Pevay left with them. He was glad to be away from the jail, the prisoners, the town, the aggressive and abusive population – 'extirpationist to a man' – and grateful for whatever certainty travelling with Robinson provided.³⁶ In warming spring weather he joined the other guides in hunting and enjoying a semblance of traditional life as they journeyed. At night they danced and sang and told stories around their campfires, and Pevay heard more about the exploits of Kikatapula and Wurati. He listened, and perhaps the deeds of Kikatapula, the spearhead of Palawa resistance during the Black War, became seeded in him.

§

Sobered by his prison experience, Pevay remained tractable. The infrequent notes of him in Robinson's journal during his first post-prison weeks were merely brief logs of menial events: accompanying a convict servant to get supplies, being issued with a pair of shoes, discovering the tracks of a Palawa man and a dog (which Robinson thought not worth following), going with Wurati to fetch water. For the moment he felt safe, glad to be under Robinson's protection and enjoying freedom of a sort.

The mission travelled north along Tamar Valley to George Town and then, on 15 October, turned north-easterly to follow the coastline as far as Noyhepunnetter (Waterhouse Point), the north-eastern tip of Tasmania. It was rich country. Robinson commented appreciatively on the abundance of Palawa food sources: oysters, mussels, crayfish, abalone, ducks, pelicans, swans, and other birds. Kangaroos and wallabies were plentiful. An emu was killed and eaten. Sometimes they came across immense shellfish middens where many generations of Palawa had feasted, but they saw no native people in that formerly populated region. Writing in his journal near St Helens Point on 30 October, Robinson observed that 'Some years since [ago] they must have been numerous, but from George Town on the north to Georges River on the east there is no indications except at Cape Portland of natives having been, not the least track, no bush burnt'.

Two days later, however, near the valley of Anson River, the mission encountered four men and a woman.[37] They were reluctant to join the mission so Robinson chose to scare them with an exaggerated description of the Black Line and its dangers. 'I . . . told them . . . a story of soldiers killing the blacks' and 'the sooner we got away the better as the soldiers was coming', he said.[38] The five quickly decided to go with him. Fearing they would abscond while he went to search nearby islands for sealers and *tyrelore*, he isolated the five with his guides on Warenekomekar (Swan Island), an unappealing 239-hectare speck eight kilometres offshore. When he returned to the island on 25 November he was given news of two Palawa he knew, a former guide and a former captive. 'Informed that the aborigine Robert was taken and put in the penitentiary, and that NIC.ER.ME.NIC was apprehended in company with two females, who are also in gaol at Launceston.' Next day he had more news, this time of a former companion he had not seen for seven months. 'The natives said they saw PANNER, i.e. native smoke [from mainland Tasmania], and that Timmy who was at my house [in Hobart] was with them.' That was a shock. Having sent Timme back to Hobart in April for admission to the Orphan School, Robinson had no reason to believe he was not still an inmate there. It was to be his last news of the youth for several months.

On his return to Swan Island Robinson found that Pevay was physically ailing, and during the next few days he noted several times that the young man was very unwell. Concerned about their sickly companion, other Palawa fastened a curative amulet around his body, and by 12 December the patient was recovering.

A day earlier Robinson's coxswain James Parish had returned from Truwana (Cape Barren Island) with six *tyrelore* liberated from sealers there. The newcomers 'soon recognised their relations and kindred and friends among those natives brought from the main[land]', Robinson wrote. 'Their joy was unbounded and it was truly affecting to witness the kind of feeling exhibited . . .' After much delighted chatter among themselves, the Palawa danced and 'This hilarity was kept up for several days'.[39] Their elation is understandable. 'There was not a woman kept in captivity but what earnestly desired and longed for their liberty', Robinson observed two days later, 'and many attempts had been made by them to get away and several of them had lost their lives in the attempt – many have been flogged by the sealers for attempting the same'.[40] One *tyrelore* told Robinson that 'the white men tie the black women to trees and stretch out their arms . . . and then they flog them very much, plenty much blood, plenty cry – this they do if they take biscuit or sugar'.[41] Some had suffered even worse barbarities. A sealer named Munro told Robinson 'that the sealers tied up a black woman to a tree and then cut the flesh off her thigh and cut off her ears and made her eat it' as punishment for having run away.[42] Another claimed that 'the sealers have been known to burn their women alive', a horror confirmed by testimony that 'As an incentive to exertion, if the females showed any tendency to relax their efforts, it was not uncommon for those white devils to fasten their women to the ground face downwards and put coals of fire and hot ashes upon their naked backs'.[43]

One of the new liberated women was Planobeena, the *tyrelore* known as Fanny whom Robinson had interviewed in Hobart jail in 1829. A native of Mueterminner (Pipers River), Planobeena, born about 1805, had a sister called Woretermoteteyer (aka Pung) and another named

Pierrapplener (aka Diana), as well as a brother, Woreternattelargener.[44] It has been suggested that Planobeena was Fanny Hardwicke, a young Palawa girl who had once worked as a maid for a settler at Longford and was possibly abducted from there by sealers.[45] But information given to Robinson by a woman named Meterlatteyar (Sally), who had been abducted with Planobeena, refuted both claims by providing a credible account of Planobeena's early life. Meterlatteyar told Robinson that 'My country is Big Forester River twenty day island;* I was taken from my country by [sealer Michael] McKenzie when a little girl; Fanny alias Jock [Planobeena] and Juliet [Warrameenaloo] was taken at the same time; when McKenzie was drowned [sealer James] Thomson took the three women and kept them as his own property'.[46] Acquiring the nickname Jock along the way, Planobeena had also cohabited with a sealer named John 'Black' Baker, the man with whom she had voluntarily left Robinson's home and returned to Launceston after being freed from jail in 1829.[47] She spoke only English and was noted as strong, intelligent, and able to navigate a schooner.[48] Having earnt a reputation for defiance, she was known to nurture simmering resentment against whites. A sealer named Turnbull told Robinson that Planobeena had 'so mastered the sealers that she would do very little for them'. He warned Robinson about her, saying she 'was a woman that would do a deal of mischief if put on the main[land], and that she has frequently said that if she was on the main she would teach the black fellows to kill plenty of white men'.[49]

§

Pevay remained on Swan Island while Robinson set out on 4 January 1831 to walk to Hobart with Kikatapula, Pagerly, Wurati, Trukanini, and a Little Swanport woman named Tikati (historically Tekartee), one of the *tyrelore* Parish had brought in. They were gone for two months. Two days after their return, Robinson transferred all the Palawa – he now had 60 of them in his care – to Preservation Island, and from

---

* Ninth Island.

there to tiny Gun Carriage (now Vansittart) Island. Their housing on the 800-hectare Gun Carriage Island was inadequate, their water supply was brackish, and game was scarce. Two Palawa died and 15 more sickened, including Pevay. On 16 April Robinson took the ailing young man in the cutter *Charlotte* to Launceston, docking in the town the following day.[50] There to buy supplies, Robinson also sent for two Palawa who were employed by settlers at Norfolk Plains. They were 'a lad' named Tillenner (aka James) and Teengerreenneener (aka Richard, Dick, Cranky Dick). The latter arrived 'in a shamefully ragged state, not having sufficient to conceal his nakedness', so Robinson ordered a suit of clothes and a blanket for him and the same for Pevay, who had remained aboard the cutter, too ill to go ashore. On 23 April Robinson noted that 'TUNNERMINNERWAIT was very unwell; had been badly attended to by the people in the cutter', but on 27 April he recorded that 'Pevay convalescent'.

It was two days later, while he was still recuperating aboard the *Charlotte* at George Town, that Pevay probably first came face to face with Timme, the young man who was to be his lifelong friend and comrade. The meeting was not chronicled and Timme was not mentioned by name, but his presence and the circumstances can plausibly be deduced.[51] After he escaped the Orphan School in April 1830 he went back to Country in the north-east, as indicated by the smoke signals Robinson noted in November that year during the dying days of the Black Line. After that there is no record of him for six months, until 4 May 1831 when Robinson, shortly after returning from Launceston, noted in his journal that Timme was present on Gun Carriage Island. It seems that he had collected Timme during his stay in the town in circumstances that can convincingly be extrapolated.[52]

On 23 April Robinson had gone downriver from Launceston in a borrowed whaleboat to rejoin the *Charlotte*, which was in George Town loading timber, and he took Tillenner and Teengerreenneener with him to join Pevay, who had remained in the cutter. Six days later, still at George Town, Robinson's servants took aboard the *Charlotte* 'one native from Dr. Smith's'.⁵³ (Dr John Smith kept a George Town inn.) Thus when it sailed that day, 29 April, there were four Palawa in the *Charlotte*. When Robinson went ashore on Gun Carriage Island the following day he took 'with me four natives' – obviously the four from the cutter: Pevay, Tillenner, Teengerreenneener, and the unnamed Palawa from Dr Smith's. That Timme was the newcomer is evinced by an entry in Robinson's journal four days after landing on the island. It named Timme as one of several Palawa there who were about to be shipped elsewhere.

> Embarked on board of the cutter fourteen natives for Swan Island, viz. WOORRADDY and wife, TRUGGERNANNA, Black Tom and wife PAGERLY, Dick [Teengerreenneener] alias Pompy, Jock [Planobeena], PUNG [Woretermoteteyer], LOETHERBRAH, TUNNERMINNERWAIT [Pevay], Davy and Dick (two children), Jumbo [Pulara], TIM.ME and Tibb [Tanganuturra].⁵⁴

No record has been found of Timme's presence on Gun Carriage Island before that date, so he was evidently the unnamed Palawa taken there from Dr Smith's. It is not known why he was at Smith's – captive? refugee? employee? – or whether he left there and joined Robinson voluntarily.⁵⁵ Nor is it known where he was and what he was doing between escaping the Orphan School and boarding the *Charlotte*. He was certainly on Country during that 12-month period and was credibly one of the Palawa who were, in the first four months of 1831 especially, raiding settlers in the neighbourhood of Ben Lomond.

§

Together now aboard the *Charlotte* sailing toward Preservation Island en route to Swan Island were four of the five Palawa who a decade later were to terrorise Port Phillip. Strangers at first, they were shards of the shattered peoples of Lutruwita: Pevay from the Parperloinnher band of the North West people, Timme from the Pyemairenerpairener band of the North East nation, Trukanini of the Nununi band of the South

East people, and Planobeena, who was believed to be from the Coastal Plains people's Poorrermairrener band. Firm new partnerships would form: Pevay would wed Planobeena, Timme would marry Trukanini. A strong bond would be forged between the two young men. They would become great friends and comrades-in-arms, and although circumstances would separate them from time to time, henceforth their lives would be in tandem.

Likewise their deaths.

'Make haste, black fellow run away'

On 8 May the 14 Palawa from Gun Carriage Island were landed on the bleak and windswept Swan Island, where a depot had been established. 'Snakes are numerous on the island', Robinson wrote, 'and what with the screeching of the penguins at night and the howling of the tempest, the whole combined has a tendency to engender painful and gloomy forebodings . . .'[1] Not many days passed before he recorded that several Palawa were unwell; then he too fell ill. The dour climate was depressing as well as unsalutary. On 2 June, weary of the 'exceeding bleak' and boisterous conditions, he decided to move his encampment and all the Palawa to Little Musselroe Bay on the north-eastern tip of Tasmania opposite the island. He put his servants to work there building huts for the Palawa while he began preparations for his next mission. The relocation was welcome. 'Natives much pleased with the change of situation and in being on the main where they can get plenty of kangaroo', he wrote next day.

Two days later he sent Planobeena and Woretermoteteyer, whom he described as 'the two most efficient aboriginal females of all the natives', to Tamar Valley to assist a colonist named Clucas. He gave each woman a ration of tobacco and they went off in care of Tyrell, a servant of Robinson's. But Clucas had gone, so Tyrell and the two women set out after a few days to return to Little Mussel Roe. In the meantime the Palawa men in the new location were noted only as 'generally employed in hunting kangaroo, which are tolerably abundant in this part'.[2] At night, when they danced and sang, Robinson joined in 'to gratify their wish'.

Breakout!

Constant adverse weather delayed his departure, but by 20 June he felt he could wait no longer. He led the mission back into the wintry north-east that day, destination Ringarooma River. He proposed taking Kikatapula and Pagerly, Wurati and Trukanini, Tanganuturra, Robert, and Teengerreenneener, plus eight whites, two horses, and a dog, but later noted taking nine Palawa.[3] One of the additional two was Timme; his participation was recorded on 7 July. Pevay was left behind at Little Mussel Roe with the other Palawa before being transferred on an unrecorded date to Gun Carriage Island, where he remained until 5 August.

Robinson's mission was to locate and then conciliate his former guide Umarrah, who had absconded again and was waging war on settlers in the north. Trekking through bitter weather – Lalewongener (Mt Cameron East) was shawled with snow – the mission saw no recent signs of Palawa. The dearth surprised Robinson. On 6 July, somewhere north-east of white-wimpled Turapina (Ben Lomond), he concluded that although they were traversing country 'formerly occupied by the PY.EM.MAIR.RE.NER.PAIR.RE.NER[*] [sic], who were a fierce people . . . They are now extinct.' The Pyemairenerpairnener were Timme's natal band.

Next day the mission found a *markenner*, a Palawa road leading toward Tamar Valley where Umarrah had lately been raiding. Close inspection suggested it had recently been used, sending Robinson's hopes soaring. But Kikatapula seized the moment to subvert. He shouted at the dogs to hunt and they responded with noisy enthusiasm, dashing into the bush and raucously advertising the mission's presence. Robinson was incensed and was not mollified even when Kikatapula and Timme came back from the chase with two kangaroos to alleviate the mission's food shortage.[4] The following day he was even angrier when they discovered a new hut nearby, proof that Palawa had indeed been close until the dogs' tumultuous fanfare.

They slogged on. Through short frigid days of limpid winter

★   A band of the North East people.

sunlight and others of cold teeming rain they walked with ease over good country and laboured cursing through bad. Near Great Forester River on 12 July they found evidence of recent spear-making, and sometimes they passed through country that had been burnt, but they saw no Palawa. 'It is evident that only a small remnant of this once formidable race of aborigines remains', Robinson mused.[5] On 26 July, five footsore and frustrating weeks after setting out, he gave up and they trudged back to their base camp on the coast.

Robinson's next move was to send to Gun Carriage Island for Manalakina (historically Mannalargenna), a respected leader and wise man of the North East people; his Country, Kallerenenannener, was between Mt Pearson and Ringarooma.[6] Robinson hoped Manalakina's knowledge of the north-east would provide a crucial advantage in a renewed search for Umarrah. On 5 August Manalakina arrived, bringing with him Pevay and little Jemmy, an adolescent male whose natal name was Prupilathina (historically Probelattener).[7] Several years hence, Prupilathina would be the unwitting catalyst for the killing of two men and the consequent death on the scaffold of two others.

With Manalakina now leading the way, the mission resumed on 10 August. Robinson had with him his son, another Briton, and 11 Palawa. From the coast they headed south-westerly, the guides hunting as they travelled. 'The aborigines are passionately fond of hunting', Robinson observed on the 15 August. He occasionally liked to participate too, and three days later he described a kill he and Pevay made.

> I proceeded on a hunting excursion, accompanied by my old acquaintance TUNNERMINNERWAIT and the dog Rodney. Having crossed a large heathy plain, came to the verge of an open forest. Several kangaroos was seen bounding away at a considerable distance from us. The dog appeared unwilling to hunt and kept behind, being tired. On reaching the forest referred to, my sable friend descried on the ground the impression of a boomer kangaroo. He took the dog

to the spot, when, having got the scent, it followed after the animal. Myself and TUNNERMINNERWAIT kept after him. Having got sight of the game the chase began: the animal, which was exceedingly large, took to flight, followed by the dog and us. The dog biting him on the hind leg, the animal would then stop and fight the dog, and the dog, fearful of close attack, would bark at him. This gave us time to come up, but on perceiving us he fled, followed again by the dog, which kept close after him. He would again stop and face the dog, and then run and stop &c, until much tired he allowed myself and TUNNERMINNERWAIT to come up to him and he faced us both. Seeing the dog was quite unable to master him, and he having clawed the dog, I told TUNNERMINNERWAIT to throw a waddy at him, but he was afraid and said by and by. Anxious to put him out of his misery, I went to him and threw a stick at his head and hit him, when he made a jump at me. The native called out 'He will catch you'; and which would have been the case had not the chief's [Manalakina's] dog, attracted by the barking of Rodney, came to us and fastened on to the animal, when Rodney caught him by the throat and got his head down. Wearied, the animal laid down panting for breath and the dog beside him; and at this juncture the native beat on his head and killed him.[8]

The two of them (with Rodney) repeated their success next day while out scouring the landscape for sign of Palawa. Game they found aplenty, but Umarrah and his band were nowhere seen.

Ten days after starting out, a disheartened Robinson admitted that 'No indications presented themselves to guide us to the long neglected and wandering aborigines'.[9] But as they were making camp that evening Pevay, who had gone up a nearby hill to reconnoitre, signalled that he could see smoke. Kikatapula and Manalakina joined him and confirmed the sighting, then persuaded Robinson that the smoke was too distant to investigate so close to nightfall. Best wait until daylight. Next morning Kikatapula and Manalakina, with Robinson's son and two unnamed Palawa, left camp in heavy rain to investigate the smoke. When they returned that afternoon they brought with them Planobeena, Woretermoteteyer, and the servant Tyrell, returning from their failed attempt to find Clucas. 'They had been seven days on their journey from George Town and had seen no signs of natives', Robinson noted.

But later that afternoon, as the guides left camp to hunt, they found fresh footprints and the remains of a fire only 100 metres away. Palawa had not merely been close, they had been spying on the mission, but the spies vanished at the guides' approach. While Kikatapula and the others set off after them, Pevay sprinted back to camp and gasped out the news to Robinson. 'The black fellow run away, the black fellow run away! Make haste, gone this way!' Robinson was briefly befuddled. Do you mean Manalakina? Yes, said Pevay, misunderstanding him. Still incredulous, Robinson repeated the question, and this time Pevay grasped his meaning. 'No no – *paner* [black man]!' he replied. Now Robinson understood. They ran back to the spot, where Pevay pointed out the tracks and the embers of the fire. Setting out to follow the trail, Robinson was surprised to meet Kikatapula coming back, fearful of being speared by those he was tracking, but Robinson ordered him to rejoin Manalakina and keep searching. Planobeena hurried after Kikatapula, saying 'I'll follow them up'. Robinson returned to camp. As a precaution he took Pevay, 'against whose tribe these people were at enmity and would doubtless slay him if unacquainted with the circumstances in which he is connected with me', he wrote.[10]

The guides' search proved fruitless. Not until eight wearisome days later did Manalakina, who claimed to be guided by spirits, lead them to a place on the coast near Noland Bay, an area of heath-covered plains interspersed with lagoons and open forest. 'I was at a loss to conjecture why [Manalakina] took this route', Robinson mused, sceptical about spirit guides, 'as I did not myself expect to meet with natives in this situation'.[11] But they did. As Robinson sat writing in his journal on 29 August, two guides who had been out hunting hurried into camp with the news that 'the natives was coming, that there was plenty of smoke coming this way that the natives were making as a signal of their approach'. Manalakina, Kikatapula, and Planobeena had located Umarrah, a woman, and five other men and were leading them back to the mission. The men included Woreternattelargener (Planobeena's brother), Memerlannerlargener (brother of the absconded guide Parewareatar), Ningernooputener, and probably Kulipana (historically Kolebunner), who was Umarrah's brother.[12] Robinson was elated. 'This tribe is called by the white people the Stoney Creek tribe, and are supposed to have perpetrated some of the most daring outrages that could be conceived', he wrote. 'They are the people that murdered the people on the banks of the Tamar and have committed the outrages upon the inland settlement [Campbell Town].'[13] Timme confirmed the identification, informing him that 'those natives had murdered plenty of people, that they had speared some men when they sawed wood on the banks of the Big River, i.e. Tamar, and had taken away plenty of flour, tea, sugar, knives &c'.[14] That night, joined by a jovial Robinson, the newcomers and the Palawa guides sang and danced together.

But lingering late-night harmony was shattered next morning when a gang of armed sealers barged into the camp and demanded that Robinson give up Planobeena. A sealer named Everitt, whom Robinson referred to as a murderer, was abusive and threatening. Fearing bloodshed, the Palawa became edgy and prepared to flee; Robinson was able to stay them only with difficulty. Although in time the intruders left without Planobeena, the incident unsettled all the Palawa, and their disquiet persisted. Uncertainty and old antagonisms surfaced to blight the bonhomie of the previous night. Manalakina was an enemy of Umarrah, who had once speared him, and he also nursed an old grievance against Umarrah and another man because they had killed his son Plairnrooner. Soon he was conniving with Kikatapula to foment discord among the newcomers. Squabbles broke out over women. But despite all the fret and fuss, a former *tyrelore* was finding romance. 'One of the women told me she was going to get married to one of the fresh natives', Robinson wrote on

2 September, four days after the two parties had merged. Two days later the woman, Planobeena, told him that Memerlannerlargener was now her husband.[15] The union shone rare sunlight into her life. After years of slavery she was finally free and on Country – she was from Pipers River – with some of her own people, and now, for the first time, she had a husband instead of a master. Memerlannerlargener had demonstrated a bold and perhaps alluring machismo by grabbing a venomous snake and putting his finger in its mouth, after which he 'played with it for some time; laid hold of the sting and pulled it out; skinned it and took out the fat and greased himself with it'.[16]

Despite nuptials and sporadic outbursts of conviviality, however, the strife continued. On 10 September four of Umarrah's mob – three men and the woman – absconded. One of the absconders was Memerlannerlargener, Planobeena's new spouse, and although she pursued the fleers she failed to overtake them. Her distress elicited only indifference from Robinson. He warned her she must not think of following Memerlannerlargener's example.[17] '[He] had not evinced much love towards his new consort by going away and leaving her', Robinson sneered. 'He also took away her clothing and knives.'[18] Worried that she and her brother might try to flee despite his warning, he marooned them with Umarrah and most of the Palawa guides two kilometres offshore on Wayterkobuner (Waterhouse Island) while he sailed with Pevay, Prupilathina, and Robert to George Town to liberate Palawa from the jail there, thence to Launceston for the same purpose. On 21 September he sent for all the Waterhouse Island Palawa, who joined him and the others in Launceston on 1 October.

§

With Umarrah pacified once more, the Black War was all but over. Only the united Oyster Bay and Big River peoples were still warring on colonists, and Lieutenant Governor Arthur wanted Robinson to find them and bring them in. The Executive Council had already decided what was to be done with them and every Palawa already in captivity. All were to be exiled from Lutruwita and incarcerated on a remote Bass Strait island where they could never again interfere with the theft and redistribution of their Country or be a danger to the advance of colonisation.[19] Only one dissenting voice was raised, that of the colony's chief justice John Lewes Pedder. His objection was compassionate and tragically prophetic.

> Notwithstanding Mr. Robinson's opinion to the contrary, however carefully these people might be supplied with food, they would soon begin to pine away when they found their situation one of hopeless imprisonment.[20]

The Executive Council, however, was desperate to end the war and willing to countenance genocide if needed.

> Even if the Aborigines pine away in the manner the Chief Justice apprehends, it is better that they should meet with their death in that way, whilst every kindness is manifested towards them, than that should fall a sacrifice to the inevitable consequences of their continued acts of outrage upon the white inhabitants.[21]

Decision made, Arthur and Robinson conferred in Launceston and agreed that only by putting 50 kilometres of Bass Strait's toss and tempest between the island prison and Lutruwita could they ensure that the internees never again set foot in their homeland or stood in the way of the usurpation of their Country. A Launceston newspaper summarised their decision.

> The natives, when caught, are to be placed upon an island in the immediate vicinity of the one at present occupied as a depot for Aborigines, known as Great Island [now Flinders Island] . . .[22]

So was sealed the fate of a free people.

5

'Greatly at a loss how to proceed'

Before they could be exiled, however, the few who were still attacking colonists had to be located, pacified, and brought in to be shipped out to their permanent island prison. Although Robinson believed that the remaining hostile Palawa – the combined Oyster Bay and Big River peoples, the two largest nations – were 'the most sanguinary in the island', he was undeterred. Fired by his usual optimism and the potential for boosting his financial and social standing, on 8 October 1831 he led the mission out of Launceston toward Campbell Town, 70 kilometres south. His departure was reported by a newspaper.

> Mr. Robinson left this morning in prosecution of his mission of conciliation to the aborigines. His expectation of success with the Oyster Bay and Big River tribes, which are said to have united, are most sanguine.[1]

On 15 October, after a week's provisioning and preparation in Campbell Town, the mission, which included three whites, shouldered their loads and departed, accompanied by one riding horse, one pack horse, and several dogs. Although Robinson said he had 'thirteen natives of VDL' with him, there were actually 15: Pevay, Timme, Planobeena and her brother Koleteherlargenner, Trukanini and her husband Wurati, Kikatapula and his wife Pagerly, Prupilathina, Robert, Tanganuturra, Umarrah and his wife Wulaytupinya, and Manalakina and his wife Tanalipunya.[2] For a day they headed east, then turned southward into Oyster Bay country. West of Tooms Lake on 21 October they had news of Planobeena's absconded husband when Manalakina identified embers they found at a campsite as 'ME.MER.LAN.NE.LAR.GEN.ER's fire ... he and KOLEBUNNER had gone to the westward to meet the natives at Quamby's Bluff'. The mission moved on, crossed the Eastern Tiers and then the Eastern Marshes. As usual the guides hunted as they travelled 'and when they had obtained a kangaroo would cut off the tail and hind legs, leaving the thighs and the carcase behind'.[3] Their habitual hunting also served a second purpose, which Robinson was not yet aware of: subversion. Not suspecting anything untoward, he frequently reported having to reprehend them 'for hunting and making a noise instead of looking out for the natives'. They feigned but did not demonstrate penitence. Life was good when they could hunt every day and by doing so also avoid betraying their people.

It was spring and nights were cold. In camp Pevay and Timme ate with young men's healthy appetites and then piled their fires high and sat close and attentive while the older men diverted them with elaborate tales of their exploits, martial and otherwise.

> UMARRAH entertains the other natives by telling them stories every night, many of them so long as to take upwards of an hour in reciting, keeping them awake until twelve or one o'clock listening to his relation. The manner of relating these stories is by singing them, each verse ending in a chorus, and consist of long journeys or travels with their various adventures, of amorous adventures, exploits in war &c.[4]

For three weeks the mission scoured the heart of the Oyster Bay nation's sprawling Country almost as far as the coast, but they saw no Palawa and the guides said they saw no Palawa sign.

> This morning sent the white man Stansfield with three natives to look out for smokes, and MANNALARGENNA, UMARRAH, Tom, WOORRADY and Timmy went in another direction ... Pm, the natives returned. They had been on the Swanport Tier but had seen no sign of natives.[5]

'Greatly at a loss how to proceed'

In early November, sensing that the guides were deliberately wasting his time, Robinson abandoned the Midlands and turned the mission westward, passing south of Sorell Springs and then south of Oatlands, where earlier that month marauding Palawa had inaugurated a savage new phase in their resistance by attacking women and children – the first recorded assaults on British children and only the second on a British woman. (The first had been more than four years previously.[6]) On 4 November the mission crossed the Hobart–Launceston road before deviating north-westerly toward the Central Highlands – Big River country. Aware that it was likely where the hostile Palawa were havened, the guides baulked, contriving specious reasons for their reluctance. Big River country was very cold, they said, so they would surely die there. Robinson retorted that it was spring; warmer weather was nigh. Kikatapula, who was very familiar with the highlands, countered that Wulaytupinya, a Big River woman, had told him 'there was plenty of devils in that country and that they would kill strange black people, especially if they saw them carrying knapsacks'. Robinson scoffed and turned the mission toward distant Lowlunyer (Lake Echo).

Umarrah and Manalakina had professed that it would give them great pleasure to lead Robinson to their traditional enemies the Oyster Bay and Big River people, but the guides' efforts remained less than wholehearted. They had become distrustful of his promise to let them stay on Country after all other Palawa had been incarcerated on Flinders Island, so they stalled and stymied. Umarrah dallied. Kikatapula lit warning fires in the grass and guided the mission awry. Others skived off into games or hunting while purporting to scout for Palawa sign. The women made smoke by burning dead bark. By mid-November even the teenage Timme was aligning himself with the saboteurs. Robinson noted the youth's first subversive action.

> On crossing this stream* [I] observed a large smoke in the direction from whence we had come [south from Lake Echo]. Supposing it

---

*   Probably Kenmere Rivulet.

had originated in my fire [I] ordered one of the natives to accompany me back. On our arriving there [I] found the grass and bush on fire and the strong wind wafting it, so that the fire burnt rapidly and in a few hours the atmosphere was covered by dense smoke. Myself and sable companion exerted ourselves to extinguish it, but without much effect. Directed all the people to assist and in a short time succeeded in extinguishing it. On enquiry I found that this fire had been kindled by Timmy, an aboriginal adolescent, whether by accident or intention I could not learn.[7]

What he subsequently did learn proved the fire was no accident. On the day he lit it Timme had found evidence of Palawa that he did not tell Robinson about. Only on the following day was Robinson 'Informed that the lad Timmy had discovered the previous afternoon the impression of a dog's feet and which they said was natives' dogs'. If he suspected a link between Timme's discovery and his setting the scrub ablaze, he did not mention it.[8]

Factions as well as friendships having formed among the guides, Timme was demonstrating in other ways that he had allied himself with some of those undermining the mission. He had joined Kikatapula and Manalakina in threatening to kill Umarrah and Woreternattelargener, putting Umarrah and his wife in fear of their lives.[9] Pevay, however, remained unaligned. Planobeena had been single again for two months and he may already have been contemplating a match with her, making it politic for him not to align himself with Kikatapula and Manalakina because of their threat to kill her brother Woreternattelargener. His neutrality was rewarded. He and Planobeena would soon become man and wife, beginning a long-lasting union that would be sundered only by his death a decade later.

§

During November the mission looped around Lake Echo and then followed a meandering course southward to a point south-west of

Bothwell before turning northward, back toward Lake Echo. Although farms and huts were burgeoning across the region, Robinson was wary of the tendency of trigger-happy Britons to shoot Palawa on sight. He steered the mission clear of settlements unless they needed flour, sugar, tobacco, or tea, any shortage of which brought complaints from the guides. They rarely lacked meat. They hunted kangaroos, wallabies, possums, platypuses, wombats, a quoll, thylacine cubs, and a variety of birds. Timme was one who demonstrated his hunting prowess as they travelled, Robinson several times noting his ability. 'Timmy . . . knocked down a crane with a waddy'.[10] Later, 'Timmy speared a fish resembling an eel . . .'[11] The youth also proved to be an excellent shot with a musket, but Robinson, admiring his marksmanship, had no reason then to see it as ominous.

By 27 November they were again in sight of Lake Echo. During their trek northward they had found several recently built Palawa huts and had sometimes seen the smoke of distant Palawa fires, but their quarry remained elusive. Robinson was forced to to lead them farther north 'to the unexplored and unsettled parts of the territory' as far as Skittleball Plains, before deviating east to Yingina (Great Lake). Mere days short of summer, the erratic weather and mercurial climate of the region often slowed progress and undermined morale. '[Y]esterday it was exceeding hot; today it is very cold with snow, rain, wind and sleet', Robinson griped on 28 November. Three days later he noted 'A continuation of rain, snow, sleet and boisterous winds, accompanied by thunder and lightning . . . and frost and snow are here frequently met with in the midst of summer'. The terrain, rarely less than testing, impeded their progress with natural obstacles: dense scrub, near-impenetrable forest, tarns, marshes, and fallen timber. Even the extensive open tracts were often minefields of foot-befuddling rubble. Fatigue and irritation aggravated the guides' boredom. They had been afield for two months; the country was harsh; they were suffering capricious extremes of weather. Indifference mutated into obstinacy and then mutiny. On 7 December, after a rest break, they refused to go any farther. Robinson lost his temper and berated them 'in severe terms'. They took up their packs and sullenly moved on.

From Arthurs Lakes they searched in a meandering circuit of Western Tiers, which returned them to Arthurs Lakes on 14 December. After trudging south to Lagoon of Islands they circled eastward around Lake Sorell and Lake Crescent and back to Lagoon of Islands. Despite seeing old huts and other Palawa signs, they encountered no Palawa. 'The LAIRMAIRRENER [Big River people] was seen to go away in a contrary direction to that we were travelling', Timme told Robinson.[12] The comment further wilted his spirits and deepened his desperation, for he was unwell. Even as he berated his guides for their apathy and lack of cooperation, a dispatch from the lieutenant governor berated him for his lack of progress. Two days after Christmas he admitted that he was 'Greatly at a loss how to proceed'.[13]

But he pushed on, and four days later, a few kilometres west of Lake Echo, his doggedness was rewarded. Distant smoke led the mission to the camp of the last Oyster Bay and Big River people, whom they succeeded in approaching peacefully. Although not intimidated, the remnant band needed little inducement to agree to a ceasefire. A generation earlier their combined population had been perhaps 1000 people, but now only 25 adults and one infant remained, all of them battle-scarred and war-weary. '[T]here was scarcely one among them – man, woman, or child – but had been wounded by the whites', Robinson recalled years later.[14] On New Year's Day 1832 hunters and hunted forsook the highlands for the long march to Hobart, which they reached on 7 January, three months after the mission's departure from Launceston, and this time Robinson was hailed a hero.

§

Ten days later, all the Palawa, captives and guides, were shipped from Hobart in the *Charlotte*, bound for Preservation Island. It was probably during this brief stay in Hobart that some guides, including Pevay and Timme, had their portraits made in pencil and watercolour by Thomas Bock.[15]

Although 40 Palawa embarked for Preservation Island, only 39 arrived, the *tyrelore* Tikati having died during the voyage. Nine of the guides were subsequently carried on to Launceston, where they disembarked on 4 February to await Robinson's arrival. He remained in Hobart for nearly six weeks, basking in the lieutenant governor's public approbation of his success with the Oyster Bay and Big River people, although it was not enough to loosen the purse strings of the Aborigines Committee, the body responsible for determining his reward. He was not impressed with their parsimony. When they offered him only £100 for yet another dangerous mission, this one to capture all the remaining Palawa in Tasmania – the reportedly 200 on the north-western and western frontier – he refused, insulted. Committee and conciliator negotiated further and eventually the committee relented. They offered him an extraordinary £1000 – four times his already substantial annual salary – to undertake the task. As a bonus they promised to appoint him superintendent of the Flinders Island establishment and all its Palawa prisoners. Both blandishments were to his liking. Emoluments settled, his own future secured, he travelled overland to Launceston to begin his new mission: to denude Tasmania of the last remaining Palawa – every man, woman, and child in the west. It was an extreme, heartless, and unnecessary measure. The western bands were not at war with whites and posed no threat. Neither the government nor any settler wanted their land. What the colonists wanted was complete peace of mind, assurance that their usurpation of Lutruwita could never again be challenged or threatened. The Palawa had to go. Only complete removal from their homeland and permanent incarceration in a place they could never escape from would suffice.

Waiting in Launceston for Robinson were nine guides, of whom Pevay was the only single man. The others were couples: Kikatapula and Pagerly, Wurati and Trukanini, Umarrah and Wulaytupinya, and

Breakout!

Manalakina and Tanalipunya. No mention was made of Planobeena or Timme; apparently they had remained on the island after the others sailed to Launceston. When Robinson reached the town on 16 February he took the nine guides aboard the *Charlotte* and sailed back to Flinders Island with them, arriving six days later. Sickness had become prevalent there. An internee died soon after Robinson arrived, and 17 days later, when he returned to Launceston ready to begin his new mission, some of the Palawa he took with him were also ailing. Two of the invalids soon succumbed, Robert on 23 March, Umarrah the following morning. They were buried in Launceston with the surviving guides as mourners. Others sickened too, delaying the mission's departure. When Robinson finally set out on 4 April he was on horseback and had a horse-drawn cart to carry supplies. His companions included his son, four other white men, and the surviving guides, 'three of whom were invalids and two dangerously ill' – mortally ill, as it ensued.[16] Robinson himself would have a close brush with death not long afterward in remote Takayna – not from disease but from Palawa spears and waddies.

6

'We will kill them all by and by'

After the mission had been travelling for a few days, Robinson could see the ailing guides were not improving. He ordered the cart to be unloaded to carry them but the gesture made little difference, and when the mission arrived at Hampshire Hills on 19 April the sick were no better. Travelling through bitter autumn weather had not been salubrious. Torrential rain fell. Biting westerlies battered the mission and sliced through wet clothing. By 26 April most guides were afflicted with dysentery. Kikatapula, Pagerly, Teengerreenneener, Wulaytupinya, and a woman named Karnebutcher were so weak they could no longer walk. Robinson ordered them taken on horseback to Emu Bay ahead of the mission. When he and the others joined them there on 6 May after being stalled for days by the incessant deluge, they found two of the women unimproved and Kikatapula sinking. The mission moved on, their immediate destination being Peewungar (Cam River), leaving the sufferers behind to be given whatever medical care Emu Bay offered. Mid-May Kikatapula died, and a few days later so did Wulaytupinya. But Karnebutcher, Teengerreenneener, and the newly widowed Pagerly improved enough to rejoin Robinson at Circular Head on 28 May. The other guides gave 'a shout of joy at their arrival', but when they learnt of the two deaths 'all was mournful silence'.[1] The relentless rain continued.

§

It was still wet and windy when the mission arrived at Woolnorth on 4 June. The company's superintendent greeted them cordially, telling Robinson that local Palawa had not been troublesome and were expected to continue peaceful. Robinson preened, claiming in his journal that his 1830 trek through the west and north-west had been responsible for their being peaceful, although he was honest about the wrongs that had caused the Black War.

> The excitements to which they have been exposed are many indeed. Their country has been torn from them, their wives and daughters violated and carried into captivity, the men have been murdered for sport and cruelties at which the mind revolts have been practised upon them, but though slow to enrage they never forget an injury.[2]

On 14 June 1832 the mission rounded the north-western tip of Tasmania and proceeded southward along the west coast. Pevay, now on Country, soon demonstrated his local knowledge. Near Nongor (West Point) he and a former *tyrelore* named Nollahallaker (aka Kit) showed Robinson a herb used for seasoning muttonbirds. Nollahallaker too was on Country. She told Robinson that sealers had abducted her from Robbins Island when she was only a girl, so she, like Pevay, was a Parperloinnher, one of the eight bands that comprised the North West people whose Country the mission was now traversing.[3]

Pevay was torn. Being on Country strained and tested his loyalties and raised new doubts about his participation. Travelling through distant territory with Robinson, helping to round up and exile Palawa from other nations, had been one thing – they were strangers, possibly even enemies – but it was quite another to betray your own people, your family and friends, knowing they would be removed from Country for ever. They had played no part in the war that had so inflamed other parts of Lutruwita and made whites desperate to expunge them from it. His people were peaceful. Some, like him, had attempted friendly association with the interlopers. Should they not be allowed to remain unmolested?

As the mission pushed farther into Pevay's Country, Robinson sensed the guide's growing uncertainty. It began gnawing at his own confidence. Although rarely impeded by self-doubt, he soon succumbed to fear that he might fail this time. Contributing to his unease were the magnitude of his undertaking and his reliance on the guides, especially those who were on Country. In icy midwinter he was venturing back into what he knew to be a vast and unforgiving wilderness in the remotest part of Tasmania, far from his own kind and the possibility of help. When he had first traversed this region in 1830 his assignment had been only to contact and befriend the Palawa he encountered. This time his task was to persuade all of them to abandon their Country without any good reason and go away with him, a stranger, a white man, to an alien place, never to return. It was an outrageous ask. 'The aborigines of VDL are patriots', he had once observed, 'lovers of their country'.[4] It made him nervous and uncertain. More than ever before, he would need the full cooperation of his guides, especially such local people as Pevay and Nollahallaker, whom he had no choice but to rely on. Yet he could feel their unease. He feared it might tempt them to abscond, to reunite with family and friends and disappear into the wilderness. Even the briefest separation from them now made him anxious. 'I frequently was desponding lest I should not succeed . . . My only hope was in PEEVAY and Kit, and if they abandoned me my hope was lost', he admitted. 'At one time yesterday Kit was absent for two hours, having walked by herself, and I began to fear lest she had absconded . . .'[5]

> Today I altered my order of travelling. Having disencumbered PEVAY and Kit of their packs, I requested them to precede the rest of the people; and on our arrival at MOON.DER.ER.COW.DIM.MER [Bluff Hill Point], PEVAY, who was some distance in advance, made signs that the natives was near and beckoned me to advance quick. On coming to him he said the natives was near, that he heard them hunting. I ordered the people to conceal themselves and sent PEEVAY and Kit off again to reconnoitre. At this time it was raining fast. They came back and told me they had seen the natives and that they had made a little fire. I

now desired the two ambassadors to divest themselves of raiment and the woman attired herself in her native costume, a kangaroo mantle which WOORRADY had lent her. They then proceeded. We were all suspense and earnestly hoping they would get to them . . .[6]

For two anxious and uncomfortable hours when 'it rained and blew and was exceeding cold', Robinson waited on tenterhooks, uncertain whether the two guides would even come back. In the afternoon Nollahallaker returned alone; Pevay had remained with the newly located Palawa. There were seven of them, she told Robinson, but when Pevay approached them 'they became alarmed and looked about and asked if there was any NUM, i.e. white men, about'. If there were, they said, they would flee, and they advised Pevay to do the same. Mindful of the Black Line and its associated hostility, Pevay responded that the white men would shoot him if he did. Six of the strangers – three men and three women – promptly disappeared into the bush, leaving him with the seventh, a man named Pannabuke. Robinson found the two of them waiting for him in a hut.[7] Pannabuke, who was estimated to be about 20, agreed to join the mission as a guide but was shy at first, reluctant to sample bread or tea, foodstuffs the other guides relished. But after two days he was consuming both and seemed content in his new role.

Adding Pannabuke to the mission did nothing to lessen Robinson's pessimism and added to his doubt about Pevay's loyalty; after all, he had just let six Palawa escape into the bush. In Robinson's mind it confirmed the guide's lack of accord with the mission's objective; it might even portend his and others' imminent abscondence. '[T]he natives that I depended on to effect a communication, i.e. PEVAY and Kit and the stranger [Pannabuke], might abscond, in which case my object would at once be obviated', he fretted. Further underscoring his uncertainties was a prophecy Manalakina had made: that Robinson would be killed during this expedition. He knew from experience that the old warrior's auguries were sometimes unnervingly accurate.[8] The gloomy prediction preyed on his mind.

'We will kill them all by and by'

Next day Pevay and Pannabuke returned to Robinson after a short reconnaissance and reported that Palawa were camped only 300 metres away. Robinson joined them as they hurried back. Pevay led the way, keen this time because in the camp were members of his family whom he had not seen for a long time. Such was his eagerness that he ignored Robinson's instructions.

> My aborigines, contrary to my wishes, continued to approach the native encampment with their raiment on and knapsacks. On arriving within ten yards of the natives I prevailed upon [the guides] to divest themselves of their clothes and knapsacks, and sent PEEVAY, Kit and the stranger [Pannabuke] to the natives, followed by MANNALARGENNER and WOORRADY. The other natives remained with me until a communication had been effected. In a few minutes we heard a shout, by which we knew the aboriginal delegates had succeeded. This was a shout of joy and surprise, a mode of welcome usual with savages: it was a welcome shout to me . . . [Then] a whoop was given for us to advance. I proceeded to the encampment.[9]

Some fled at Robinson's approach and hid in the surrounding tea-tree scrub. One who stayed was Pevay's brother Wymurrick, the band's leader, a towering man Robinson estimated to be at least two metres tall (although the short and stocky Robinson often overestimated the height of taller men). Gradually, cautiously, others emerged from hiding: a teenage boy, a pubescent girl, and then another of Pevay's brothers, a young man named Penderoin. Eventually seven of the band, including an old man, gathered to listen to Robinson's spiel as he tried to persuade them to go with him. But the situation deteriorated when the skittish Manalakina began gathering the strangers' spears and Wymurrick tried to wrest them from him.

> Another man got up and also laid hold to assist WY.MUR.RICK. I was now apprehensive that the natives would either resent the insult thus offered to them or else abscond. I ordered MANNALARGENNA to let

go the spears and let the people have them. Jack [Pevay] and Kit sat as though they were panicstruck and did not speak. I desired Pevay to tell his brother not to be alarmed. Pevay now got up and laid hold of the spears and each party still kept hold . . . I stepped forward and insisted upon MANNALARGENNA giving up the spears. I gave them to the chief and he was highly pleased at my interference . . .[10]

Although tensions were eased, Robinson ordered his guides to take their packs and go away. Pevay and Nollahallaker stayed with him, making presents of their blankets and necklaces to Wymurrick's people. Harmony restored, it was agreed that five of the seven would go with Robinson while Wymurrick and the old man searched the bush for the rest of the band. After that they would join Robinson at West Point, they said. Robinson then herded his latest captures back to Cape Grim, where three of them became ill. More sickened in following days, forcing Robinson to postpone his departure for West Point and the rendezvous with Wymurrick. Only on 13 July was he able to resume his mission.

In the interim Pevay and Nollahallaker had had further misgivings about betraying their own people. Their reluctance to cooperate became even more pronounced, and the constant rain and frigid conditions further dampened Robinson's expectations. 'I could not help but looking at the dark side', he admitted the day after starting out, 'and thought it by no means improbable that not only the strange natives but Kit and Jack also might abscond. Should such an event take place I knew that all further attempts to remove these people would be fruitless.'[11]

In late afternoon on 15 July they noticed smoke smearing wet sky between Tyberlucker (Green Point) and Mt Cameron West – the direction Wymurrick had taken after their parting three weeks earlier. Robinson urged the mission forward, but Pevay and Nollahallaker baulked. 'Kit did all she could to dissuade me from going in quest of those natives . . . [and] Jack was the same way of thinking', Robinson grumbled.¹² As they approached the smoke, he warned them to be as quiet as possible but they defied him, talking and laughing louder. After going ahead to reconnoitre, Nollahallaker came back to report that they were too late. No one was there. Wymurrick must have gone to Robbins Island, the guides opined, declining any further action to locate him. It was dark and cold and the torrential rain had not let up. Robinson's fears intensified. What to do now? 'If Jack and Kit and the other natives left me – and it was hard to depend upon them – I knew not how or whether I should succeed at all', he fretted. 'My mind was excited above measure.'¹³ He ordered a rough camp to be prepared for the night and discussed the situation with the guides, who said it was Pevay's and Nollahallaker's fault that Wymurrick and his band had escaped. They should have made surrender more attractive, they told Robinson. They should have highlighted how much tea, sugar, and flour Wymurrick's people would be given if they submitted. Pevay derided the notion, scoffing that 'they would not eat it'. Anyway, he said, 'they like the bush', meaning Wymurrick and his people intended to stay where they were.¹⁴ Wet, frozen, and uncomfortable, a desperate Robinson resorted to bluff. He declared that Wymurrick would be found. He boasted of his own invincibility and the inevitability of his success. '[I]t was folly for them to think they could escape me', he crowed, 'that I who had sought out and subdued all the natives could find them out'. In his journal, however, he admitted that his bragging was only 'a *ruse de guerre*' and that the Palawa could easily elude him if they chose.¹⁵

Next morning he tried a gentler approach, but Pevay and the others were now openly rebellious. They ignored him.

> I again counselled my aboriginal friends to use their utmost endeavours to effect a communication with their sable brethren, and pointed out how desirable it was to get to them, that our work in a great measure would be accomplished; that those blacks could then go back with us to Cape Grim where they could hunt and have plenty of bread, tea, blankets &c; and that when warm weather came we could

go in quest of the TARKINE PANEER, i.e. the other natives at Sandy Cape. To all my arguments Jack [Pevay] and Kit and the other natives paid but little attention.[16]

Nevertheless, they found and followed tracks and soon spotted smoke from Wymurrick's fire. As emissaries Robinson sent forward Pevay, Nollahallaker, and four other guides, and although the usual shout of welcome soon rose from Wymurrick's camp, it was not enough to diminish Robinson's gloom. He believed the guides' rebellious attitude had now metamorphosed into outright hostility and that, reinforced by Wymurrick's band, they might violently turn on him. Full of apprehension, he awaited their return.

> I knew not what the result of this conference would be, or whether I should be successful in removing these people from the main territory or not; or whether the four strangers as also PEVAY and NOLLEWSALLEKE (Kit) would not join them . . . or whether they might not spear us . . . At length I heard them shouting and advancing towards where I was standing . . . PEEVAY on seeing me called out in English, 'here he is, here he is, here's Mr Robinson'.[17]

Robinson tensed, but Pevay had brought with him Wymurrick and 21 men, women, and children, including his sister Pordeboic, her husband Paddedevenehenoke, and their child Noringbake. Another member of the band was Narrucker, whom Robinson had shipped to Launceston in July 1830 for the bounty. Now she told Pevay how she had been ill-treated at that time. She had been abused by white men before and after her release, she said, and she told him his brother Pintawtawa had also been captured and had then suffered cruelly at the hands of a ticket-of-leave man named Alexander McKay, formerly Robinson's coxswain and now a VDL Company employee, before being removed to Flinders Island. It did not improve Pevay's affection for whites in general or his sense of shame at having betrayed his people. The cleft in his loyalties widened.

Wymurrick's band went with Robinson to his camp at Green Point before moving on to Mt Cameron West. Friends and family reunited, they travelled joyously, but Nollahallaker warned Robinson that they might flee. 'She whispered that I must keep the people before me, as though my individual exertion would prevent their absconding', he wrote.[18] The rain had ceased but it was still damp and windy as the party – including 'twenty-three strange natives, *viz* ten men, five women, two male and two female adolescents, and four children' – proceeded toward Cape Grim. When they arrived on 17 July Robinson faced the problem of how to prevent the captives from dispersing once he left them and resumed his mission down the west coast. His solution was to maroon them on Warehebenuke (Hunter Island), about 20 kilometres offshore, although how he would feed so many of them while they were there was another problem. That there was no obvious solution did not matter. 'I explained to them that they would have to live upon the islands and eat mutton birds, but how to get them away at the present time I knew not. There is no inducement: the birds are not in.'[19] Despite knowing it was not muttonbird season, he did not let it concern him. The important thing was to incarcerate them securely until a vessel arrived to ship them to Flinders Island. All he had to do for the moment was persuade them to go to Hunter Island.

> Being informed that both the sealer's boats was at the jetty, I thought I would try the experiment of getting the natives removed to the islands . . . I proposed to Jack [Pevay] to go with me and look at the boats, to which he very readily assented. On arriving at the boats I began to praise them, and said what an excellent opportunity it would be to go to the islands. Jack readily assented and wanted to go alone, but this was not what I wanted . . .

Pevay's offer was perhaps a ruse to separate Robinson from Wymurrick's people, which would have allowed them the opportunity to disappear into the bush, or even a tactic for Pevay himself to escape alone and return to Robbins Island. But Robinson was not fooled.

> I said that we would all go . . . I now went back to the encampment with PEEVAY, and with an air of indifference proposed to the natives to make an excursion to the islands. Jack capered about quite delighted at the idea, but the strangers stared and gaped, appearing quite indifferent . . . I appeared careless and said I should go without them; they might come if they chose. They soon followed after me . . .[20]

On Hunter Island they were to remain until they could be shipped to Flinders Island. Sickness and death blemished their wait.

§

On 4 August Robinson learnt that the government had rescinded its offer of cash bounties for captured Palawa. Although annoyed, he was able to rationalise the loss to appease his ego. 'I did well to engage with the government for the capture of all the natives, for if I had been restricted to their first offer I should not have seen any natives and they would have been dissatisfied and would have held from me their reward', he wrote. 'By taking the whole I gain not only the reward but celebrity.'[21] All he had to do was locate every remaining Palawa in the west and north-west, survive potentially hostile encounters with them, persuade them all to capitulate, and then ship them, with all those now interned on Hunter Island, to Flinders Island, nearly 300 kilometres away across the chop and churn of wild Bass Strait waves.

§

When Robinson resumed his round-up mission down the west coast on 29 August 1832, his companions, who were 'in ecstasies of joy' at leaving Hunter Island, he said, included four of the future Port Phillip rebels. His party included 12 veteran guides, all but one of whom he named in his journal over the next few months. The 11 identified were Pevay, Timme, Wurati, Trukanini, Teengerreenneener, Karnebutcher, Pagerly, Nollahallaker, Manalakina, Prupilathina, and Numbloote, a woman from Panatana (Port Sorell). The unnamed twelfth guide was

Manalakina's wife Tanalipunya. Some of Wymurrick's band also went: Wymurrick himself with his wife Larratong; Pevay's sister Pordeboic with her husband Paddedevenehenoke; Pevay's brother Penderoin; Pannabuke; and a stout man named Heedeek.[22]

From the outset all were uncooperative, their fortnight's incarceration on Hunter Island having given them enough experience of exile to harden their opposition to Robinson and his mission. A day after starting out he sent them up a hill to search for smoke from Palawa campfires. They 'descried a smoke in a southerly direction, in the woods near where I had before seen and obtained the natives', but they did not tell him and he was angry when he found out. 'My old aboriginal companions wanted to conceal [that] fact from me', he fumed. Later that day, when they found tracks at West Point, Robinson decided to camp there near a small stream. The guides ignored the many footprints visible around the campsite and Robinson continued to gripe about it. 'My people are very remiss in their endeavours to look for the natives', he wrote that night.[23] Their overt rebelliousness continued. On 1 September, after sending Timme and Trukanini with some others on an advance scout, Robinson had cause to complain again about their attitude: 'My old natives continued to give me much trouble'.[24]

With a few guides he crossed Maydim (Arthur River) on a makeshift raft the following day, 3 September, and then dispatched two of the women to hunt while he made a fire. One soon returned with the news that 'plenty of blackfellows was coming'. Led into Robinson's camp by an old man named Wyne, the new arrivals were from the Sandy Cape, Port Davey, and Pieman River bands. As Robinson distributed gifts among them, he grew uneasy, observing that all were well armed with spears and there were no women. Something was suspicious about them, he thought. 'They were shy and sullen, yet bold and full of bravado . . .' It made him wary, although his guides were relaxed and 'never informed me that these natives premeditated an attack upon me'. After a while he too relaxed a little, noting that

'They all appeared in exceeding good spirits and were very friendly'. Wyne in particular was amiable, although Robinson thought him 'very covetous . . . wanted his and other people's things'.

Late that afternoon, after Wyne's men returned from hunting, they sat at their fires and began to sharpen their spears, which Robinson thought indicated a change in their plans. 'This had a suspicious appearance', he wrote, 'since, I thought, if they meant to go with me they did not require spears'. He believed it signified their intention to abscond that night.

As darkness approached, he was proved perilously wrong. Paddedevenehenoke warned Pevay, his brother-in-law, that Wyne's men were not planning to escape but to kill Robinson and any guides who resisted. Pevay alerted Robinson, telling him that Paddedevenehenoke had cautioned him to stay awake all night because Wyne's men intended to kill him and the guides. 'This was immediately communicated to me', Robinson wrote, 'and there was much whispering; which I wished to prevent, for although I felt assured that the taking of mine and my people's lives was premeditated, still I wished to avoid everything that might lead them to suppose that I suspected them'. The reason for their spear-sharpening was now terrifyingly clear. He was unarmed. His situation was dire. Manalakina's grim prophecy suddenly had alarming luminosity.

The newcomers' deadly intent was confirmed when they began dancing. 'The strange natives corroboreed first, and corroboreed that they would kill all of us . . . and said make haste and dance for we will kill them all by and by.' More than a little agitated, Robinson observed that 'Of the strange natives only a part danced, a sullen reserve being depicted in the countenance of most of them, and a foreboding that something fatal was intended seized my breast'. Foreboding became outright fear when a relation of Trukanini's warned him the strangers 'would spear us at daylight next morning'. The guides shared his trepidation. Wurati urged Trukanini to flee but she refused, saying she would not leave Robinson to be killed.[25]

Writing about it after the event, Robinson claimed an improbable *sang-froid* as he contemplated the gravity of his situation that night.

> I spread my blanket and took off my clothes and retired to rest, and whilst the natives were dancing I slept for a short time. My people blamed me for sleeping and said I ought not, but should take care and watch. However I considered this the only opportunity and was therefore better prepared to watch the remainder of the night. I affected not to entertain the least suspicion that the strangers meant to harm us . . . One of my natives told me the strangers meant to spear us: I smiled and said it was all nonsense, to which he replied 'you see by and by' . . . The chief of the Pieman River aborigines [Wyne] sat at the foot of my bed . . . preparing his spears with which he purposed destroying me, and . . . at the same time would leer at me with a savage grin thinking that I was asleep, but I was watching his actions and only pretending to sleep.[26]

During the night Penderoin warned the guides that the strangers were again sharpening their spears and told them to beware. When Robinson asked which Palawa were friendly, Pevay pointed out a group on the right. Only they were friendly, he said; those on the left were hostile. Robinson reported remaining calm, although he admitted 'It was a night of great anxiety'.[27]

At daybreak the hostile group on Robinson's left made a fire and resumed sharpening their spears, of which they had many. The friendly Palawa began to do the same, although each man had only a single spear, and Wurati was alarmed to discover that his had been stolen during the night. Pevay and Penderoin now started to argue with Wyne's men, telling them they should not kill Robinson, which suggests Pevay was ambivalent. Despite his misgivings and his recent rebelliousness, he owed some loyalty to Robinson, who had protected him at the time of the Black Line and liberated him from jail. Probably with mixed feelings, he advocated for Robinson's life. 'They argued the subject with great vehemence', the fearful Robinson observed.

Breakout!

Expecting to be attacked at any moment, he dressed, packed his knapsack, and went to speak with Pevay, who seemed dejected and said they had better go. Robinson tried to defuse the situation by responding that Wyne and his men did not have to go with him; they were free to leave. But his attempted mollification failed dramatically.

> I had scarcely spoke ere the wild natives jumped up with a shout and surrounded me. Their spears were all poised in the air. My natives gave a cry of alarm and fled ... I escaped between some trees and pursued my way through some scrub in a NE direction to an angle of the river.[28]

He could not swim, yet he knew his one hope was to reach the safety of the opposite side of the fast-flowing Arthur River. Trukanini, a strong swimmer, could save him, so he raced after her.

> I was sensible that I ran a great risk in following her as she was the woman they were anxious to get ... I was not long ere I gained the river. TRUGERNANNA was in the greatest possible alarm, and in much agitation called to me to hide myself in the bush, for the blackfellows were following after our tracks, and in a faltering tone said they had already killed Jack [Pevay], WOORRADY and the other natives. I looked up ... and saw one of the wild natives with his spear and waddies.[29]

Somehow the man, Loathdiddebope, did not see him, although Robinson was in full view on the riverbank. Needing fast and decisive action to survive, he manhandled a five-metre spar into the river and tried to launch himself onto it, but it foundered, forcing him to struggle back to the bank. Frantically stripping off his wet clothes, expecting at any moment to be speared, he cast about left and right until he found another manageable limb and shoved it into the water, hurriedly lashing the two pieces together with his garters. But they snapped under the strain. He ripped off his cravat and repeated the operation and this time the binding held. Clinging to the crude raft in the icy water, he called to Trukanini to 'shove me over'.

The current was rapid and it was with difficulty that I kept my equilibrium. The woman was calling out with fear that I should be drowned; said the natives was coming. I looked back and saw the natives. I desired the woman not to be alarmed about the blacks, for I well knew they would not cross the river. I found the woman wanted encouraging and I was not the least alarmed, although I had no thought of escaping. How I ventured to cross the river on those sticks can be attributed only to the choice of two deaths, drowning or being speared. I preferred the former . . . On arriving at the shore [I] climbed the rocks, and on looking across the river saw three of my aborigines walking upon a hill. Pursued our way to the encampment about a mile and a half [2.5 kilometres] distant, without shoes and having on only my shirt, and the woman naked.[30]

Most of the mission Palawa had scattered as soon as the attack began. In the general confusion Wyne's warriors did not immediately realise that Robinson had fled. When they found he was not there and learnt he could not swim, they searched around the camp for him, believing a non-swimmer would not have run down to the river. Later the guides tried to assure Robinson that Wyne's only intention was to acquire the mission's women and dogs, but there can be little doubt they intended to kill him and any guide who tried to defend him, as three of his attackers later confirmed.[31] Pevay, however, seemed not to believe himself in any danger despite Paddedevenehenoke's warning. He did not flee with the others and was able to stop Wyne from rifling through Robinson's knapsack, later restoring it intact to its owner. That made Robinson mistrustful. '[I]f he had influence sufficient to prevent them from taking those things', he brooded, 'he must necessarily have had influence to prevent the attack'.[32] And if he had neither tried to prevent it nor felt the need to flee from it, that implied his complicity with the hostile Palawa – either tacit approval of or indifference to Robinson's being slain. Both options amounted to treachery – immutably so, in Robinson's mind.

Breakout!

§

Fearing Wyne and Heedeek would try again to kill him, Robinson led the mission away from Arthur River, back to Cape Grim and then Hunter Island. When they landed on the island on 10 September he was surprised to find all his captives still there; no ship had come to transfer them to Flinders Island. Now he had about 50 Palawa to feed from supplies that were already dwindling, the VDL Co. having failed to maintain regular shipments. People were hungry, people were sick, people died, including Pintawtawa's wife Lawerick and a girl named Koinerbareake or Ryenbareoke. Tempers frayed. Wurati threatened to spear Trukanini, perhaps for some unrecorded infidelity. To force him to desist, Robinson had to intimidate him with a borrowed musket. On 2 October he sent Timme and Prupilathina to the mainland to hunt kangaroos, even as a shipment of 940 famine-relieving muttonbirds arrived from Bird Island. Nevertheless, by 7 October the island's supplies were again exhausted. In desperation Robinson took Wurati, Trukanini, and Nollahallaker to Albatross Island to buy birds and eggs from a sealer there, but it was no more than a stopgap measure. A hungry *tyrelore* absconded and took up residence at a sealers' camp on the southern part of the island. Other women followed. Fearing a total collapse of his enterprise, Robinson decided on an urgent return to Hobart to arrange for a ship to take all the captives to Flinders Island, after which he could resume his mission. But from now on he would use Macquarie Harbour penal settlement as his base.

Before leaving Hunter Island he arranged for the guides to stay there with his son and Anthony Cottrell, a former special constable, who with three Sydney Aborigines had joined the mission early that year. Then, on 28 October, he crossed to the mainland. But two days later, while he was waiting at Circular Head for a vessel to take him to Launceston, the *Charlotte* hove into view, bound for Hunter Island with supplies. Once unloaded, it would embark all the captives for transfer to Flinders Island; two armed soldiers were aboard to enforce their unresisting removal. Robinson declined to go in the cutter when it sailed the following day, preferring to wait for it at Circular Head 'to avoid unpleasant feeling at removing the aborigines'.[33] The *Charlotte* returned to Circular Head late on 3 November en route to Flinders Island with all the captives aboard. Next day Robinson joined the vessel for the voyage but sent the guides ashore. While he travelled on to Hobart, they and Cottrell would resume the round-up without him, trekking south toward Macquarie Harbour. Robinson told Cottrell he would meet him there after he had finished in Hobart.

For the moment he had a little more glory to bask in. He had removed 27 Palawa from the north-west to permanent Flinders Island exile. Moreover, and very much to his liking, the *Charlotte* had brought him letters of approval from Lieutenant Governor Arthur. To finish the job, he now needed to undertake the last leg of his mission and remove every remaining Palawa from the west, thereby voiding Lutruwita of the entire race whose home it had been for 40,000 years. Recent experience suggested it would be neither an easy task nor one without risk.

7

'They are not at liberty to do as they choose'

Robinson arrived in Hobart late on 13 November, having ridden overland from Launceston on a hired horse, and remained in town until April 1833. In the meantime, Anthony Cottrell, accompanied by Robinson's son, the three mainland Aborigines, and the guides, including Pevay, Timme, Planobeena (who was now Pevay's wife), and Trukanini, left Hunter Island on 21 November and headed down the coast toward Macquarie Harbour.[1]

Their first contact was the wily headman Wyne. The mission encountered him and about 30 of his Sandy Cape people on 26 November at Arthur River; they were on the opposite side. After the guides had parleyed with them next morning, their spokesman Heedeek – the portly warrior who had featured prominently in the attempt to kill Robinson – demanded to speak with the mission's leader.[2] Taking Robinson's son with him, Cottrell went to the riverbank and tried to persuade the Sandy Cape people to come across and join the mission. They refused, insisting that Robinson was there and that he intended to take revenge on them for their September attack. No, Cottrell said, Robinson was in Hobart and had already forgiven them. But Wyne kept insisting that the mission had firearms and intended to massacre his people. Two of his men were now making rafts. If Cottrell would allow them to cross over and inspect the mission's camp and they were satisfied there was no danger, he said, the rest of his people would also come over. Cottrell agreed. The rafts were completed and the two men crossed the river, inspected the mission's knapsacks, and reported to Wyne that there were no firearms. Wyne then insisted that a large raft be built to carry his women and children across. Cottrell had one constructed and sent Pevay and Wurati over on it, but the current quickly carried them away. They were forced to swim to shore, where they joined the Sandy Cape people and set about making another raft. Three Sandy Cape men, a woman, and a girl then crossed the river to the mission with them, but the others refused.

That evening Cottrell had the mainland Aborigines build a canoe. He sent one of them, Steward, across the river in it to bring the remaining Sandy Cape people over to the mission. Steward paddled across, but as soon as the canoe touched the opposite shore Heedeek and his men attacked him. Only a desperate leap into the river enabled Steward to escape the shower of spears and waddies hurled at him.

Sunrise next day revealed Heedeek's side of the river to be devoid of Sandy Cape people; they had told Pevay they were going to Surrey Hills. The mission had no choice but to return to Cape Grim with the seven of Wyne's band who had crossed over to them, whence they would be shipped for security to George Town. Wyne's continuing hostility had convinced Cottrell that peaceful conciliation was now unlikely. The mission would have to be armed. At Circular Head he procured all available firearms while assuring Robinson by letter that 'of course they shall not be made use of except to frighten them'.[3]

Thus armed, Cottrell led the mission back into the dense rainforests of Takayna where, on 9 January 1833, two of the mission's convict servants, William Stansfield and John Sharpe, drowned in Royenrim (Pieman River). Their makeshift raft, propelled by Planobeena, Trukanini, and Pagerly, had foundered, and although the three women stayed with the struggling non-swimmers and 'begged of them in the most earnest manner to get on their backs and they would take them to shore safe', it was unavailing.[4]

The mission moved on. One day after the drownings, still about 50 kilometres from Macquarie Harbour, Cottrell again encountered

Wyne and Heedeek and their band. It comprised 22 people – all the Palawa now remaining between Macquarie Harbour and Cape Grim, Cottrell believed – and this time they did not appear hostile. The two parties camped together overnight and in the morning the Sandy Cape people agreed to go with the mission to Macquarie Harbour. But after they had travelled about six kilometres together, Wyne's people suddenly melted into the bush. The sympathetic guides 'gave them every opportunity of getting away', Cottrell reported.[5] Robinson rebuked him by letter for allowing them to escape and for the two drownings.

On 5 February Cottrell met another Palawa band and induced two men, five women, and a boy to accompany the mission, although the rest of the band 'evinced a hostile feeling[,] shaking their spears at our people when they advanced towards them', Cottrell reported.[6] For security he marooned the new captives on Macquarie Harbour's tiny Grummet Island, whence they could be shipped to Hobart. The boy died while they were waiting.[7]

Cottrell had been expecting Robinson to meet him at Macquarie Harbour as arranged, but Robinson was not there when the mission arrived and had sent Cottrell no instructions. Irritated, Cottrell waited until Robinson appeared on 28 April, handed over to him six carbines and some other supplies, and quit the mission. He warned Robinson that the remaining Palawa would be taken only by force.

§

While the mission was at Macquarie Harbour a convict artist named William Buelow Gould painted some of the Palawa.[8] The group portrait survives but is historically and artistically worthless. None of the six blanket-wrapped subjects is identified and there is no indication whether they were captives or guides. In a reflection of contemporary British attitudes, Gould rendered them as simian caricatures.

On 10 May Robinson led his sons Charles and George, four convicts, and the guides on another sortie. For reasons unknown, perhaps just from general war-weariness, even the guides who had been least cooperative and most recalcitrant seemed resigned to the task. Or perhaps the firearms the whites carried engendered their newfound compliance. Subversion and sabotage were abeyant for the present as they headed south in pleasant autumn weather, the guides hunting as they travelled. Kangaroos were lacking in one tract they traversed but wombats abounded and they caught 10 in one day.[9] Two days later the women made fishing lines and landed many trout, which the Palawa would not eat, although the three Robinsons did. When the weather turned hazy and subsequently showery they huddled close to their campfires as nighttime temperatures plummeted. Having passed through much of this country in 1830, Robinson was familiar with it and enjoyed pointing out places of interest: here was where Parewareatar had absconded, there was the site of Robinson's camp with Umarrah, over there was where Dray had left him to go with the Port Davey people.

Of their quarry there was at first no trace. Only after a week's trudging through mostly wet weather did they find Palawa tracks. As they were heading for the south side of Rocky Point on a rainy 18 May, they saw 'numerous native footmarks . . . [including] numerous traces of children's feet'. More footprints were found along a stretch of beach. Near Elliott Bay the following day, after the male guides had been out to hunt and the women to gather crayfish and abalone, a guide told Robinson she had seen smoke on the other side of the bay. It was the news he wanted. To galvanise the guides he told them that 'as there were now only three remnant tribes, Port Davey, Macquarie Harbour and Pieman River, the sooner we got them the sooner we should be done and get back to Hobart Town. My friendly aborigines were quite elated at the idea of going to Hobart Town and promised to use all diligence to effect this desired purpose.' Whatever brought the mission to an end was conceivably desirable, and those who had been to Hobart had perhaps painted enticing verbal pictures of its wonders.

Near nightfall next day Robinson, his son Charles, a female guide, and Teengerreenneener, whom Robinson described as rather half-witted, were scouting for smoke along the coast near Drake Creek when they had an unexpected encounter. Coming toward them was Wurati. He was carrying a child across his shoulders and brought good news: plenty of natives were coming. Soon 12 Port Davey people appeared: three men, five women, and four children. Two others had run away and four more, including Dray, were elsewhere. Not altogether willingly, the 12 went with Robinson to his camp. When Manalakina began to sharpen his spears to intimidate them, the Port Davey people became agitated. One man, Towterer, shouted to his wife to flee. Pevay grabbed one of his arms and Manalakina the other but Towterer, a powerful man, shook them off and escaped with his wife. The rest sat sullenly. Robinson was forced to stand guard all night to ensure no others absconded.

Next morning he told his captives he wanted them to go with him to Macquarie Harbour. 'At this information they appeared quite astonished and said they wished to return to the remainder of their people, when they could all go together', he wrote, adding, 'This was only a ruse on their part'.[10] He advanced several arguments for their compliance but they countered with arguments of their own. They were adamant. They would not go with him to Macquarie Harbour. Force then replaced free will.

> My aborigines . . . said that I must make them go and that if I only shewed them the firearms they would be sure to go with me, for that they were much frightened of muskets . . . I resolved to adopt such measures to induce them as circumstances may warrant . . . I told the natives we must proceed. The strangers looked dejected and was preparing to run away. One man was sharpening his spear. I now ordered the two white men and my sons to uncover their fusees, and to file off on each side.* The friendly natives did the same with their

---

* Firearms. Samuel Johnson's *Dictionary* (4th ed., 1773) defined fusée as 'a firelock, a small neat musquet', synonymous with carbine.

spears, so that the strangers was in our centre. The wild aborigines now gave up all further thoughts of going away.[11]

Encircled by armed men, the Port Davey people had no choice. They were escorted under tight security to Macquarie Harbour, which they reached on 25 May. After initial incarceration on Grummet Island they were embarked on 5 June on the *Shamrock*, bound for Flinders Island. Neither voyage nor destination was a matter of personal choice. Conciliation had given way to coercion. The Friendly Mission was now nothing of the kind.

§

On 11 June the mission went out again, Robinson now carrying a pistol in his pocket 'to intimidate the natives'.[12] Three days later, near Pinderrenne (Low Rocky Point), Wurati found tracks that he said were made by Towterer, the escaped Port Davey man. That night the guides located his camp.

> They advanced with caution to the native encampment and was only guided by the smell of the smoke of the native fire. They went up in single file with the greatest caution. WOORRADY was the one in advance and when he looked in at the door of the hut the natives appeared panicstricken and turned their backs towards him, but made no noise. The children were frightened and cried out . . . They however became more reconciled and my aborigines crowded into the hut and remained with them the whole night . . . The next day my natives were anxious to get them along and the wild natives were as reluctant to go. They enquired of TRUGERNANNA where the country was of all the blacks and seemed frightened, and TOWTERER told his wife to run away. At this juncture MANNALARGENNA began to warm and sharpen his spears, as did Timmy. When TOWTERER was going to run away MANNALARGENNA laid hold of his arm and Jack [Pevay] hold of another, when he forced himself away and run off . . .[13]

After three days of searching, the guides located the fugitive Towterer and his wife, with five more Port Davey people: three men and two women including Dray, a guide on the first leg of Robinson's first mission. As Robinson herded his latest captives toward Macquarie Harbour, Deewooradedy, Dray's husband, gradually separated from the others, ostensibly to hunt. Robinson 'deemed it prudent to send after him as an example to the rest to let them know they were not at liberty to do as they chose'. He dispatched Manalakina and a convict servant to bring the recalcitrant back but Deewooradedy resisted, so Robinson ordered that he be threatened with a musket 'for I could not be trifled'. Deewooradedy sullenly complied.[14]

Travelling in freezing midwinter through torrential rain and razor wind, they reached Macquarie Harbour on 20 June. On arrival, Robinson wrote, 'I was so benumbed and chilly that I could scarcely speak and shivered as if I had the ague'.[15] When the captive Palawa were shipped to Flinders Island exile three days later in the *Tamar*, he provided a freshly slaughtered pig and some potatoes for their comfort and sustenance.

§

It was during the mission's subsequent recuperation at Macquarie Harbour that Pevay and Planobeena were first noted as man and wife. On 10 July, three weeks after arriving, they left with the other guides and Robinson on a quest 'to confer with the aborigines in the vicinity of Point Hibbs and Birches Rocks'. The following day he sent the guides off to search for them, people Dray assured him would go willingly with him, but by nightfall none of the guides had returned. More than a little peeved, Robinson was forced to go out himself the following day to search for them. He soon encountered Teengerreenneener, who told him the wild natives were coming. Plenty of them, he said.

They shortly after arrived, when I advanced and met them, and after shaking each one by the hand distributed some bread among them. They appeared shy. This reserve is peculiar to the aborigines of VDL ... We hastened forward to my encampment. I then took an opportunity as they passed to count them: they were sixteen in number, the entire tribe.[16]

The newcomers had fled at first sight of the guides, who ran toward them, calling on them to stop. When they failed to comply, the guides surrounded them. After explaining their purpose, they had, in Robinson's words, made friends with the band. Despite the newcomers' apparent submissiveness, when mission and strangers camped together at nightfall Robinson built up his campfires and stood guard all night.

Next morning the two parties began the 35-kilometre hike to Macquarie Harbour, but Robinson soon sensed his captives' restlessness. He feared it meant they intended to abscond, and before long Dray's one-eyed husband Deewooradedy vanished into the bush. Robinson blamed Pevay for the escape. Unburdened by a knapsack, Pevay had 'wandered away to hunt instead of looking after the natives'. Robinson sent Manalakina after the fugitive but he came back alone, and when Pevay returned from hunting he too claimed to have seen no sign of Deewooradedy. Robinson tightened security. He ordered the convict servants to brandish their firearms and the guides to stay close to the captives. As they travelled toward captivity, Dray kept looking back in forlorn search for her missing husband.

When the mission reached the settlement on 13 July, Robinson preened with pleasure because 'the astonishment of the people was great when they found I had brought in a tribe of natives. Some said I had a charm, some said I was an astonishing man. Indeed, the people were all in amaze [sic]. The officers said they was sure the Governor would be in raptures ...'[17] His captives, dumped for safekeeping on Grummet Island, a rocky outcrop usually reserved for the worst convicts, were less than rapturous.

Breakout!

§

With the end in sight, a new urgency propelled Robinson forward and the relentless round-up continued apace. After reprovisioning, the mission struck out northward from Macquarie Harbour on 19 July. Robinson took with him his two sons, seven other whites, and 14 guides. Backed up by the carbines they carried, intimidation was now the norm. The sheer size of the mission was additionally daunting: big enough to outnumber any remnant band likely to be left in the wilderness.

It took only two days for them to find fresh footprints near Pieman River. Although it was nearly dark, Robinson sent the guides to search for those who had made the tracks. Planobeena came back almost immediately. They had located their quarry, she told Robinson before returning to join the other guides. Robinson and his sons made a rough camp and waited. Knowing that these Palawa were 'led by the most sanguinary chieftain WYNE', he thought there might be trouble.[18] There was.

Wyne's little band comprised three other men, four women, two girls, and a boy, but two men were absent. The approaching guides had split into two parties, and although the nine fled at sight of the first, their flight was halted by the second group coming from another direction. Despite being outnumbered, Wyne refused to yield. He tried to spear Timme but Manalakina snatched the weapon from him. Wyne then grabbed Manalakina's spear and attempted to smash it across the old warrior's head but Tanilipunya wrestled it away from him. Still resisting furiously, Wyne broke his spears and one of Timme's to wield the points like knives. But superior numbers inevitably prevailed; Wyne and his band had to submit to the confiscation of their spears. During the night they attempted several times to escape but each attempt was thwarted.

Next morning, as the mission shepherded their surly captives back toward Macquarie Harbour, Pevay and Manalakina went off to hunt. Before long Wyne's two missing men joined the party, giving Robinson a total of 11 captives. They were, he gloated, 'the most ferocious of all the aborigines along the coast'. He led them toward Macquarie Harbour, but Little Henty River, in full spate after days of persistent rain, proved a serious obstacle. Although the guides built a rough driftwood raft, it was not buoyant enough to keep Robinson wholly out of the icy water when he tested it. Nevertheless, Trukanini, Planobeena, and Pagerly towed him across the river on the flimsy craft. One person at a time, mission and captives were all eventually transported to the other side. That night Trukanini suffered what Robinson described as 'a severe fit', perhaps an after-effect of prolonged immersion in the frigid river.[19]

Pushing on through foul and freezing weather, they reached the penal settlement on 24 July. Robinson was saddened to learn that one of the women captured earlier had died and that two male captives were dangerously ill. His conscience was untroubled, however. He reasoned that their accommodation 'was both warm and comfortable and secure and afforded abundant room, and had a large yard attached and secured by a high fence'. Nevertheless, he found the captives in a very sickly state. To add to their distress, petty racism had reared its mindless head. 'The natives said that the prisoners [on the floor above] did all they could to annoy them by pouring water through the boards, urinating upon them and hammering the floor.'[20]

Next day another captive died. Two days later a man and a woman perished. The guides, fearing for their own lives, isolated themselves on Swan Island,* on the north side of the harbour, while Robinson transferred the captives from the penitentiary to the hospital, away from the convicts. Noting the captives' distress at the deaths, he asked, in a display of staggering insensitivity, why they cried. 'Why black man's wife not to cry as well as white man's?' Dray retorted.

Aware of whom to blame for their situation, they made their

---

* Swan Island in Macquarie Harbour, not the island of the same name mentioned in Chapters 2, 3, and 4, which is off the north-east tip of Tasmania.

feelings plain when Robinson visited them in the hospital on 30 July. 'So soon as the natives saw me', he wrote, 'they took up their clothes and walked out and said they were frightened of the NUM [white man]; even the sick would not stop but walked out'. Next day Wyne died, then another man. Seven others were seriously ill. Robinson blamed the medical officer, calling him 'worse than useless'. On 2 August, when another captive died, his widow 'gave way to the bitterest grief'. Late that night another man died, although from injuries suffered in a fall. The others begged to be freed but Robinson refused. By the time he had responded by moving the survivors to the pilot station at the heads on 6 August, a dozen of the 27 Pieman River and Sandy Cape captives were dead.[21] Despite the pilot-station quarantining, the roster of dead and dying continued to grow. Robinson later described their illness to the lieutenant governor.

> This dire malady had every appearance of an epidemic. The patient seldom survived longer than 48 hours after being attacked[;] all ages and sexes fell victim to its ravages and generally expired in a state of delirium. They were all in apparent health when first brought to the settlement.[22]

§

During a month's respite in the crude comforts of wintertime Macquarie Harbour, Pevay and Planobeena found their marriage under siege. Robinson noted in his journal that the couple had been quarreling with Manalakina because the lusty old warrior hankered after Planobeena and said he would have her and all the women.[23] Others enjoyed less vexing diversions while they waited for the next sortie. Trusted guides and captives were given considerable freedom to hunt, sometimes with guns, sometimes while carrying out other tasks. Once, as Pevay and Timme and four other Palawa were setting out to hunt, Robinson loaded each of them with 11 kilograms of flour to be lugged to a Henty River supply dump for future use. Both were among those permitted to use firearms and both were expert marksmen, as Robinson observed one day after watching them shoot. 'These people are fond of shooting', he wrote, 'and would make excellent shots'.[24] His perception would be made lethally manifest eight years later at Port Phillip.

As preparations were being made for the next capture party, word reached Macquarie Harbour that 13 detainees on Flinders Island had died, some of whom were recent west coast captures. The news shrouded the guides in gloom as they readied themselves for departure. When they set out two days later, on 29 August, their reluctance was obvious. Unwilling to corral more friends and family for likely death in exile, they were uninclined to cooperate with Robinson, who was annoyed by their sullen defiance. 'My aboriginal attendants are dilatory in their endeavours to search after the natives . . . Their passion for the chase swallows up every other consideration.'[25] He had assumed they would be eager to complete the mission so they could go to Hobart, which he had led them to believe would be their reward at mission's end. They alone would escape incarceration, they thought, and he did not disabuse them.

Much rain fell and chill wind blew and rivers flooded as they travelled, making crossings as dangerous as they were difficult. Day and night they suffered the cold and the wet and the whipping wind. The guides did not bother to conceal their indifference or Pevay his animus. 'The natives very stubborn', Robinson noted one day, the next observing that Pevay was 'sullen and keeping considerably in the rear'.[26] But they trekked on and their obduracy had its desired effect. No Palawa were found, no captives taken.

As they were heading back to Macquarie Harbour, Pevay's brother Penderoin reassured Robinson that he would be successful.

> [T]he TARKINE and TOMMEGINNY natives would be sure to come to me, that they did not like another man. Said that Jack [Pevay] told him that all the blackfellows said that Mr Cottrell should not take them,

that they would look out for me*, that Mr C did not belong to the blackfellows, that me *one*'.²⁷

The statement has been described as 'the explanation of Robinson's successful relationships with the natives'. He travelled with them, spoke their language, ate the same food, endured the same dangers and hardships as they. It set him apart from other *num*, and as the Palawa world was engulfed they trusted him above any other. They had no option. He seemed their only hope of personal salvation, and Pevay, despite the widening gap in his relationship with Robinson, accepted that.

One way or another, Robinson had had enough. As soon as the mission reached Macquarie Harbour on 10 September, he began packing for return to Hobart. Twelve days later he embarked on the *Tamar* with all the captives and guides, who had to be housed in the ship's cells during the voyage. Robinson had trousers made for the men and caps for all and a pig slaughtered to feed them. After many delays because of bad weather, they sailed, disembarking on 9 October at the Port Arthur prison settlement on the eastern side of Lutruwita. Robinson left the guides to be accommodated at the prison while he travelled to Hobart. His arrival in the town was noted by the *Hobart Town Courier*.

> Mr. G.A. Robinson arrived in the Isabella on Saturday, bringing with him all the aborigines that remain of the three principal tribes formerly inhabiting the west coast of the island, amounting in all to the number of 30 ... There are now only 18 blacks at large in the island of Van Diemen's Land, all of whom are known to Mr. Robinson, and will be very easily obtained when that gentleman makes his next and final expedition to the west.²⁸

When the Palawa were delivered to Hobart in the *Tamar* a week later, he met the vessel at the wharf and took them to his home, erecting what he called 'an encampment' there for them. A week after that he accompanied them to Government House to meet Lieutenant

---

* That is, they would rather surrender to Robinson than to Cottrell.

'They are not at liberty to do as they choose'

Governor Arthur. 'The Governor gave them presents amounting to £5 which I purchased by his orders. The natives was highly pleased. The newspapers extol my exertions.' One journal referred to his 'very great and important service'.²⁹

He too extolled his exertions, notably in a written report to the lieutenant governor that in passing rationalised any personal guilt or remorse he might have felt at the result of his efforts, also ignoring that some of his captures had been made at gunpoint.

> [I]t cannot hereafter be said that these people were harshly treated[,] that they were torn from their kindred and friends[,] that they were forced from their country. No! their removal has been for their benefit, and in almost every instance with their own free will and consent. They have been removed from danger and placed in safety at a suitable asylum provided for their reception and where they are brought under moral and religious inculcation.³⁰

Some of the Palawa were soon 'daily more dissatisfied at being detained so long in Hobart Town', Robinson admitted.³¹ Wurati, Trukanini, Manalakina, and Tanalipunya, however, were diverted by posing for a recently arrived English artist, Benjamin Duterrau, who exhibited their three-quarter length portraits in his Campbell Street studio just before Christmas that year.³² Timme too posed during this seven-week Hobart stay; Duterrau's bland image of him, *Timmy, a wild native, address'd in a friendly manner by Mr. G. A. Robinson*, is dated 1834. Duterrau was an indifferent draughtsman, at least in his Palawa portrayals, and the image gives little indication of Timme's real appearance. His aboriginality is suggested mainly by an animal pelt wrapped decorously but inauthentically around his otherwise naked torso.

For those not entertained by posing for Duterrau, their dissatisfaction was only brief. After a month all the captives were shipped to Flinders Island, leaving the guides in Hobart with Robinson, who had more work for them. A handful of Palawa had evaded the round-up and were annoyingly still at large. Another mission was needed.

8

'The entire Aboriginal population are now removed'

Although Robinson left for his final mission on 7 December 1833, he did not reach the west until the following February, for he and his retinue had detoured to undertake an intervening assignment at the behest of the viceroy.

> [T]he Lieutenant-Governor is now desirous to follow up some measures with the aid of such of the aborigines as you can quite depend upon for the capture of the wild dogs, and His Excellency will be glad to receive your suggestions upon this important subject.[1]

Feral domestic dogs' predacity was said to be a serious problem in parts of the colony at the time. No dogs are endemic to Lutruwita but Palawa had quickly realised the value for hunting and security of those introduced by settlers. They traded for or stole them and adapted them into their culture. Some bands owned large packs of the animals, which bred unchecked, and as the Palawa themselves disappeared from the countryside their dogs remained, reproduced, and became feral and pestilent. 'It was the wish of the Governor that I should in my way [to the west] station the people in the neighbourhood of Campbell Town for a week or a fortnight as an experimental measure to see if they could be of service in tracing out the wild dogs', Robinson wrote, 'and then to proceed on the expedition'.[2]

The mission left Hobart a day before Robinson; he, on horseback, caught up with them at Constitution Hill. 'The expedition consisted of myself and two sons and seven white men, four horses and a cart, and fourteen blacks', he wrote. Although he did not name his guides, they included Pevay, Planobeena, Timme, and Trukanini – four of the five who would one day terrorise Port Phillip.[3]

After travelling through the Midlands in unusually hot weather, they reached Campbell Town on 11 December. Robinson was informed that the dog problem was most serious along the nearby Eastern Tiers. Next day he divided the mission into two parties, one black, the other white, and sent both to the tier to search in opposite directions while he collected his daughter Maria from a nearby boarding school and returned with her to Hobart. Late on Christmas Eve, his face badly sunburned, he rejoined the mission near Lake Leake. 'The natives were all away hunting', he wrote on his arrival. 'They soon returned. Had only seen one wild dog . . .'

One guide, however, did not return with the hunters. Pevay was missing. He had absconded, had 'gone away' two days before Robinson arrived (although without taking Planobeena, suggesting an impulsive rather a planned flight), but Robinson made no record of the cause or circumstances.[4] Nevertheless, he specifically noted that 'Black Jack had absconded'.[5] Abscondence was confirmed on 29 December when two of Robinson's servants returning from Mackerler (Ross) with supplies told him 'they had informed the constable relative to Black Jack'. A casual or temporary absence – a hunting trip prolonged, for instance – would not have needed reporting, and Pevay had been missing for a week by then.[6] Yet a fortnight later, as the mission finally headed westward from Launceston, Robinson recorded that it included 14 blacks – the original complement, indicating that between 29 December and 14 January Pevay had rejoined them or been recaptured, although in circumstances as long forgotten as those of his escape.[7] Robinson's journal recorded him back with the mission on 18 February 1834, but because the same entry suggested he was still contemplating escape (and encouraging others to do the same), his continuing rebelliousness is implied. That suggests he had been recaptured rather than returning voluntarily. His desire to be free would never diminish.

§

But that was in the new year. On Campbell Town Tier late in 1833, while Pevay was still missing, the wild-dog hunt was proving a wild-goose chase, not least because of the indifference to the task of Robinson's white assistants and his Palawa guides alike. The former searched for seven days but saw no dogs. The guides said the same, although, as Robinson grumbled, 'The natives were more intent on hunting kangaroo than dogs'.[8] Within a week he concluded that the dog problem had been exaggerated.

> My natives and white people have been out daily. They have seen a few straggling dogs, single ones, and on one occasion the white men saw two together . . . The story of their [sic] being dogs seen in droves is a mere groundless rumour invented by the stockmen and shepherds to create alarm . . .[9]

He dismissed the problem and resumed the mission. On a searing New Year's Day 1834 he rode with his party through drouthy countryside to a farm owned by Lieutenant Hill, where 'The natives were . . . astonished to see so many dogs' skins that lined the fences. They were wild dogs that had been shot and brought in for the reward.'[10] When they camped at Captain Robson's on 12 January he learnt that Robson's stockkeepers were killing 10 dogs a week. He moved the mission on without comment.

§

By the time this final Friendly Mission started west from Launceston on 14 January 1834, with Pevay present once again, they resembled a small army. The party comprised Robinson, his two sons, 'fourteen blacks, two whites (messengers), one cook, one clerk, one carter; cart and two horses and two saddle horses and dogs'. The mission's support boat, which had a crew of five, sailed the same day for Emu Bay.

Their travel was uneventful. But the guides, hunting as always, observed day after day what they had been seeing for many months wherever they went: the vast depeopled voids, a vacuum both incomprehensible and unignorable. Everything – family, friends, Country – was being taken, they saw, and sometimes their silent anger surfaced. When a settler refused an unnamed guide's request that he give her a dog, she snapped 'What you take my country for?'[11] That sounds like Trukanini or Planobeena, but it might have been Pagerly or Karnebutcher, both of whom absconded the following day at Middlesex Plains.* Their escape caused unrest among the other guides, although Robinson calmed his own concerns by commenting that 'the other natives deprecated their conduct and assured me of their fidelity and that they would not leave me'. They clung to the belief that staying in Robinson's or another white man's service would protect them from life imprisonment on Flinders Island. 'The natives have frequently mooted the question that by and by when I was done that I should give them to another gentleman', he wrote.[12]

They arrived at Circular Head on 1 February and left 12 days later, Robinson with a warning from settlers there that the western Palawa were extremely hostile. At Cape Grim he was given further local intelligence: 50 Palawa, including 16 children, remained at large – worryingly, many more than he had thought. But then the informant admitted he had not actually seen them, only heard their voices.[13]

As he had 20 months earlier when entering the North West nation's Country, Robinson began this crucial part of his mission concerned about the loyalty of some of his guides, not all of them locals. Pevay, who was now on Country, and Pagerly and Karnebutcher, who were not, had all absconded in recent weeks and were still restless and unhappy. Further, he wrote in his journal, he was concerned that Penderoin and Nollahallaker, who were also on Country, seemed to be preparing to flee. 'If I see them speaking in a low or undertone I am suspicious', he fretted. 'If they are absent I am fearful. I have today encouraged them and urged upon them the endeavour to

---

* They were later recaptured in unrecorded circumstances.

accomplish the work ere the winter commences, and I have received encouragement from their answers.' But he feared failure. 'I must confess I have for some considerable time felt great apprehension lest I might not succeed, for notwithstanding their paucity of numbers I may for aught I know experience greater difficulties than ever.'[14] Knowing that Pevay, Penderoin, and Nollahallaker were on Country especially troubled him. He also suspected they were trying to persuade others to abscond with them.

> Much of my hopes ... depended on PEVAY and NOLLEHOLLEKER. If these left me and joined the wild aborigines my hopes were gone, and I had painful forebodings that such would be the case ... Here was their brothers and sisters and friends. It was therefore natural I should feel apprehension. Hence, I became suspicious if they were away behind the rest, if I saw them whisper ... My expectations centred in those individuals ... I am fearful lest I may not succeed, and should Jack [Pevay], PENDEROIN and Kit leave it will be doubtful whether [the western Palawa] can be removed.[15]

Late in February Robinson sent the guides into the bush to search for the remaining free Palawa. Teengerreenneener soon returned with welcome news: they had found a band; the other guides were staying with them. That night Robinson had 16 kilograms of flour made into damper ready for their arrival next day. But as the sun rose so did his fears, which rarely left him now. 'Felt some apprehension about my aboriginal attendants. Was fearful lest they should not be able to succeed.'[16] Edgy, he set out with Teengerreenneener, who constantly led him astray, 'not however designedly but from a deficiency of intellect'. After searching without success they returned to camp to spend a restless night. But the following day the guides appeared, bringing with them a band of eight North West people – two men, two women, and four children – led by Nollahallaker's brother Rynuwidicer. They came uncoerced but unhappy. When Pevay first entered their camp, Robinson learnt, Rynuwidicer's immediate impulse was to spear this betrayer of his own people, but he desisted when the other guides appeared.[17]

Robinson transferred the little band to Hunter Island before leading the mission back into the wild, believing two families were still at large. Manalakina and Tanalipunya tried to convince him he was wrong, that 'there was no more natives, all the rest had gone a long way into the bush', and they tried to persuade the other guides to say the same.[18] He ignored their attempted subversion. But on 8 March, camped at Arthur River, Robinson agonised anew. Being fully rewarded depended on his rounding up every last Palawa, but he was unwell and his guides were bored and uncooperative and had lost interest in the mission's success. Hope was fading.

Late next day, however, they found fresh tracks, some of which Pevay identified as his sister Pordeboic's. But several subsequent days' searching for the Palawa who had made the tracks were unproductive, which further depressed and angered Robinson. 'I had been careful not to cherish too sanguine an expectation', he wrote, 'nor could I do so knowing as I did the uncertainties of the undertaking. Moreover, my aboriginal attendants was careless and indifferent . . . I had censured them for their careless conduct – for few people would believe the vexation and trouble I have with them . . .'[19] He sent the male guides back into the bush by themselves.

The following day Robinson and the women connected with Pordeboic, her husband Paddehevevehenoke, and their infant. Captors and captives united and moved on in search of the male guides. A little later, 'Near to the Arthur River [I] met . . . Jack, Timmy and Dick. They were heartily glad to see the natives and Jack his sister . . . These people express the strongest desire to go to the island.' But 'WOORRADY and MANNALARGENNA say that I shall never get the other natives: so they said before . . . I however . . . am resolved to persevere.'[20] On 17 March he arranged for the new captives to be marooned on Hunter Island.

Despite this success, Robinson's disquiet persisted. Potential new impediments were conceived.

> Few can imagine the anxiety of mind that I experienced relative as to the result of this enterprise. The natives on whom I depended had told me over and over again that I should not get them, that the natives had plenty of dogs and meant to go inland among the mountains and live on wombat ... I had strange forebodings and had almost desponded of success when I reflected on the vast extent of unlocated country extending from Cape Grim to Dentrecasteaux [sic] Channel, the difficulty of procuring supplies, the easy facility of escape to the natives, and the severe weather which is experienced on the coast ... Such were some of the feelings that pervaded my mind, oppressive hardly to be described ... .[21]

But his luck changed the day after that disconsolate entry. In heavy rain on 7 April he headed toward smoke seen rising near Sandy Cape 'and had the delightful and pleasing satisfaction to find that my people had been successful and that the natives was with them ... The moment the strangers caught sight of me they shouted vociferously. It was a shout of joy. We mutually advanced and shook hands.' The newcomers – four men, three women, and two children – included Heedeek, Loathdiddebope, and Lenergwin, men who had tried to kill him at Arthur River two years earlier. All were unapologetic about their attempt on his life.

> They had declared their intention was never to be subdued ... They had formed a plan to kill me and my aboriginal attendants by laying in ambush, and had stuck sharp pointed sticks in their pathways to wound the feet of my native attendants.[22]

Why such steely resisters had finally decided to capitulate is uncertain. Perhaps the size of Robinson's entourage intimidated them, perhaps the unrelenting doggedness of his pursuit was the deciding factor, or perhaps it was a sense of inevitability, of helplessness or hopelessness, as they traversed country now cleansed of clan and family, allies and friends. Whatever the cause, Heedeek and his little band submitted and were secured on Hunter Island before being shipped to Flinders Island on 24 April 1834 with the other recent captives. They were probably accompanied by Pagerly, Karnebutcher, and Nollahallaker, all of whom had been recent absconders and whose allegiance Robinson now distrusted.[23] The new captives' exiling was reported by a Hobart newspaper.

> Mr. Robinson has succeeded in capturing twenty one hostile natives; the whole of which party were brought up in the *Edward* . . . from Circular Head, on Saturday last [10 May], and were transmitted on board the government cutter *Charlotte*, and forwarded to the black establishment on Flinder's [*sic*] Island. The party taken consisted of seven men, five women . . . one male youth, and seven children.[24]

The writer saw nothing questionable about calling the 21 captives 'hostile natives' although 16 of them were children. Nor did he consider that their hostility was nothing more than a natural unwillingness to be rounded up and severed permanently from Country solely because colonists wanted them gone.

§

Ethnic cleansing was nearly complete. Only the Tommeginer band, whose Country was around Table Cape, remained to be rounded up and removed. End in sight, rewards nearly in hand, Robinson was resolute once again. He led the mission back over familiar ground to Circular Head and then to Emu Bay. By now the guides had settled into a fatalistic resignation, evincing little of the friction and refractory behaviour that had caused Robinson so much vexation and anxiety. As long as the mission went on, as long as there were Palawa to locate and conciliate (and as long as the guides did not try too hard to locate and conciliate them), they themselves would not be sent to Flinders Island, they believed, but could just keep travelling, safe in Robinson's service. They would be given rations and blankets and they could hunt and continue to lead something like traditional life as long as there were free

Palawa left to round up. So in this cone of relative contentment they did little to draw attention to themselves. Most of the guides were rarely mentioned by name in Robinson's journal during this period, although Trukanini, a perceptive and intelligent woman, shone on occasion.

> In a conversation with the domesticated aborigines [Robinson asked] whether they were willing to accompany me to England. Some of them said how long should they remain, three moons?, when they were immediately checked by TRUGERNANNA who said they were evidently under mistake, that England was not like Flinders Island, that they would have to remain a good many warm weathers.[25]

The mission left Emu Bay on 29 May, heading south-west toward Hampshire Hills. Rainy days followed and on 4 June the first severe frost formed. By 22 June Robinson could note 'Heavy falls of snow, and frost'; on the twenty-sixth, 'The natives' feet are sore from frost and unable to travel'; on the thirtieth, 'Last night so cold I could scarcely sleep'.

There were occasional diversions. One day Pevay noticed a thylacine hunting a kangaroo 'on the scent like a dog. He ran and speared him in the tail, and [his] dog caught him by the neck'.[26] And Trukanini again proved her worth when the hapless Teengerreenneener became detached from the mission and was lost and fireless in freezing conditions. Robinson sent the guides to search for him.

> About noon we were saluted by a screech or yell, repeated in quick succession from the opposite side of the river ... We ... was all glad to find it was Dick returned. One of the women, TRUGERNANNA, swum across and made him a fire. He was perishing with cold, and having warmed himself he swum across.[27]

Trukanini was unafraid of fast-flowing rivers and icy water. She had saved Robinson's life at Arthur River in 1832, and in April 1834, three months before rescuing Teengerreenneener, she had been Robinson's salvation a second time when he found himself in peril on a fragile raft, again at Arthur River.

Anxious to cross I ventured upon it. Wilkins [a servant] . . . ferried me across. The tide was ebbing fast and the current was carrying me out to the bar when a native female (TRUGERNANNA) rushed into the water and swum to the raft and towed it across.[28]

Two days after Teengerreenneener's rescue, the mission followed a *markenner*, a native road, to a mine on top of a hill that was part of the western spur of Toolumbunnerlunnerlinno (Gog Mountain), where the much-prized pigment red ochre was abundant. As they approached it, the guides became 'quite overjoyed at the sight' and the women immediately began to grub for the ochre and 'loaded themselves with large quantities of this colouring', Robinson wrote, 'packed up in kangaroo skins in separate bundles. [Planobeena] had a load as much as she could carry and would have been a load for a strong man.'[29]

But they did not find the Tommeginer. And although he knew a few Palawa were still at large, Robinson left the mission near Mole Creek on 29 July and set out for Launceston en route to Hobart. His role in the round-up was over, although his part in the annihilation of Palawa lives and culture was far from finished.

§

After Robinson's departure, the mission continued under the leadership of his sons Charles and George. When four Palawa were reported to have robbed huts in upper Derwent Valley near Hamilton on 11 August 1834, Robinson ordered Charles to lead the mission to Ouse River to search for them. Delayed by heavy rain that made river crossings impossible, they finally left on 24 August, but constant violent weather forced them to stay at Middlesex Plains, near Mole Creek, until 8 September, when they were at last able to strike out southward in the direction of the Ouse. It was not an easy journey.

> The route appears to have led them by way of Cradle Mountain first to the high plateau lying to the west of the Forth [River], thence south and south-east to the Mersey [River], which they crossed with

great difficulty, and on to the central plateau. During this trip they encountered very heavy snow and the travelling was so bad that the natives could scarcely be persuaded to proceed. Eventually, on 21 September, they reached Lake Echo, from where they made their way to the Ouse via Bashan Plain . . . the first recorded passage through the region.[30]

It was not until early October, 'after a most perilous and truly arduous journey . . . across an unknown and unexplored part of this territory', that they finally reached George Salter's stock hut in upper Derwent Valley between Wollerwerli (New Norfolk) and Hamilton, about 75 kilometres north-west of Hobart.[31] 'The fatigue the party have experienced during their journeyings . . . has been immense', a newspaper reported.[32] Another revealed that the trek had not been without casualties. 'The expedition . . . lost 2 men during the journey', the *Launceston Advertiser* noted. 'One man left two months ago on horseback with dispatches; and neither of them having been heard of since, the only reasonable conclusion is that they have perished.'[33]

For nearly three months the Robinsons based their mission in the Clyde region while they searched. The guides' presence was a constant provocation and concern to local settlers, who blamed them for the death of a valuable horse and accused them of scattering livestock. But on 28 December the party's persistence was finally rewarded when they sighted Palawa smoke near Central Plateau's Western Bluff. A day or two later Pevay and the other guides led the mission to what were believed to be the last free Palawa in Lutruwita: one man, four women, and three boys; two other men had died in recent weeks, one of them shot by a settler. The little band, coastal people used to a milder climate, had been ravaged by the isolation and harsh conditions of the Central Highlands and were 'in a sickly state originating in cold'.[34] They were ready to surrender. As George reported to his father, 'The moment those poor creatures saw our natives advancing, they run forward and embraced them in a most affectionate manner'.[35] They told him they had wanted to join the captives being sent to Flinders Island but were afraid because of previous mistreatment by colonists. Now it was time to accept the inevitable.

Their surrender was reported in a Launceston newspaper.

> They gave themselves up to Mr. Robinson's party about three days march from Middlesex Plains, 70 miles [112 kilometres] westward of this Town ... The captured mob having during this time visited the country as far to the southward as the head of the Derwent and a considerable distance westward, during the whole of which time the enterprising party under the Robinsons have followed closely upon their trail.[36]

The mission escorted the eight to Launceston, which they reached in mid-January 1835, and secured them in George Whitcomb's yard. As soon as he heard about his sons' success, Robinson hurried north to join them and to pack the new captives off to Flinders Island. Mission complete, the guides prepared to return to Hobart.

> The natives brought in by Mr. R.'s party last week, leave embarked on the brig *Isabella*, for the establishment at Flinder's [*sic*] island. The domesticated blacks who have been Mr. R.'s faithful attendants during his numerous arduous campaigns in the interior, leave this [town] for Hobart Town, overland, in a day or two.[37]

Once back in Hobart, a triumphant Robinson notified the colonial secretary that ethnic cleansing was now complete: 'the entire aboriginal population are now removed', he wrote.[38] It was 3 February 1835, five years to the day since he had led the first Friendly Mission from Recherche Bay into the wilderness.

§

Of the unnecessary round-up and removal of the entire Palawa population of western Tasmania, historian Lyndall Ryan has observed that:

Breakout!

By an odd irony the Van Diemen's Land Company ceased to graze sheep south of Cape Grim at the end of 1832, and in 1833 the penal station at Macquarie Harbour was transferred to Port Arthur [on the east coast]. After that the area attracted very few Europeans until the mining boom of the 1870s. So the western Aborigines would probably have survived if Robinson had not captured them.[39]

Part Two
Flinders Island

Sorrow like a ceaseless rain
Beats upon my heart with pain

Edna St Vincent Millay

9

'We don't want to live here'

Hobart in 1835 was a metropolis, a busy port with a population of 14,000. For most of that year the guides stayed there, housed in the annexe to Robinson's Elizabeth Street home – his so-called Aboriginal asylum – where they attracted little or no unfavourable attention. The town's newspapers made almost no reference to any of them during that time, which suggests their submissiveness. Even Robinson, a compulsive chronicler, wrote nothing about them except to report to the colonial secretary that their behaviour was 'beyond all praise and exceed[s] any eulogy that I can bestow on them'.[1] He kept busy trying to arrange rewards and public acclamation for himself and was working on a book about the round-up that he intended to write but never did. His silence about the guides, especially the refractory Pevay, during this period of major adjustment leaves a regrettable gap. Some record of how they accustomed themselves to urban life, of how they coped with eight months of an alien culture, circumscribed freedom, enforced idleness, involuntary church attendance, 'moral and religious inculcation', and British laws and manners would have been of interest.

A few were stricken by diseases of civilisation: Nollahallaker, Tanalipunya, and Pevay's brother Penderoin were said to have died, their deaths unrecorded, in Hobart's hospital during a measles epidemic that autumn.[2] But Nollahallaker did not die then; she was not even in Hobart. Robinson encountered her on Green Island later the same year, and he mentioned her again in his journal six weeks after that.[3]

And Tanalipunya's death in hospital was in fact recorded. She died on 1 May 1835.[4]

This sojourn was the last and longest of Pevay's and Timme's three stays in Hobart and therefore the most likely for them to have posed for Benjamin Duterrau. By the time they departed in October he had presented a sculpture of Timme to the Mechanics Institution, and six months later he gave Robinson a full–size painting of Wurati.[5] In August 1836, four months after that, he advertised for sale, at 30 shillings each, cedar-framed plaster casts of bas-relief heads of Manalakina, Tanalipunya, Wurati, and Trukanini, as well as of seven unnamed Palawa whose effigies were titled with 'various expressions of some particular passions . . . which Mr. Duterrau has carefully observed in these interesting people', including *Anger, Surprise,* and *Credulity.*[6] Since there were 11 guides in Hobart before Penderoin and Tanalipunya died, Duterrau presumably sculpted every one of them – the four named and the seven unidentified.

Additionally, Pevay and Timme posed for Duterrau paintings during that lengthy stopover – the last time he would ever encounter them – although it seems his life-size portraits, *Jack, a Tasmanian Aboriginal, holding a club* and *Timmy, a Tasmanian Aboriginal, throwing a spear*, were not realised immediately. When they were first noted in 1839, they were apparently recent enough to have been newsworthy.

> We have seen two paintings, executed by Mr. Duterrau, and representing the portraits, on a gigantic scale, of two Aboriginal Chiefs. One, that of *Timmy*, represents him in the act of throwing a spear, and is, certainly, a characteristic painting; the other, that of *Jack*, displays an athletic, well-formed Black, suddenly surprised, and wielding a waddy,–with 'full intent' to knock the first intruder most emphatically on the head. The figures are about six feet [1.83 metres] high . . . [and] are worthy of being placed, in the [Legislative] Council Room, by the side of those, already deposited there.[7]

Neither portrait is notably true to life. Their subjects' aggressive poses suggest Duterrau's eye was on commercial appeal rather than aesthetic excellence or ethnic accuracy.

§

Robinson was in no hurry to leave for Flinders Island to begin his new appointment as superintendent of Aborigines. He had been hoping instead for a long-touted more prestigious posting to one of the new mainland colonies. Almost three years previously, in November 1832, Lieutenant Governor Arthur had mooted his serving on the mainland as conciliator between Aborigines and colonists. That inflated Robinson's ego to the extent that he saw himself as the saviour of all Australia's Aborigines and the Flinders Island appointment as nothing more than a stepping-stone, one he was prepared to step right over in his eagerness to attain higher office. But in September 1835 Arthur ordered him to proceed immediately to Flinders Island in the brig *Tamar*. Robinson reluctantly boarded the ship on 1 October with his sons Charles and William, several convict servants, 50 women prisoners, and 'seventeen aborigines, nine adults and eight youths and children', and sailed the same day.[8] The eight youngsters were the only survivors of 16 who had been sent from Flinders Island to the Orphan School to be educated; the other eight had perished at the institution. The adult Palawa with Robinson were Pevay and Planobeena, Wurati and Trukanini, Timme and Numbloote (who were now a couple), Teengerreenneener, Prupilathina, and the recently widowed Manalakina.

Their voyage into exile was insalubrious. 'Passengers sick', Robinson noted soon after the *Tamar* put to sea, and their sickness continued. Four days later, when the crowded little brig anchored for the night off Swan Island, he noticed Manalakina suffering a sadder malady: great distress at being so unattainably close to Country. The old warrior 'gave evident signs of strong emotion. Here opposite to this island was his country . . . He paced the deck . . . took the spyglass and looked through it.'[9] It is a poignant image. Manalakina's life was near its end and he would never again set foot on Country. This was his final sight of it.

After the convict women had been disembarked at George Town on 8 October, Robinson allowed the guides ashore to camp overnight, noting that 'they were highly pleased with the change'. They caught several wallabies and held a corroboree, elated to be able to hunt and dance and be briefly free of seasickness, shipboard crowding, and British comestibles.

Two days later the *Tamar* set sail again and hove to off Green Island, the nearest safe anchorage to Wybalenna, the Flinders Island internment camp, on 13 October. A raging gale prevented an immediate landing, and the brig was damaged in the rough conditions. Despite the tempest, Robinson headed for shore in the ship's longboat with his sons and the guides. His former companions Draymuric and Nollahallaker and several other Flinders Island internees were on Green Island collecting muttonbirds. They watched with alarm the brig's difficulties. When they saw the longboat launched they waded out in the dark to guide its turbulent approach to shore.

> Notwithstanding the distance, parties of natives regardless of the boisterous weather were on the beach the whole of the day, watching with intense anxiety the perilous state of the vessel. When night set in they made fires on the shore and several of the women waded in the water with lighted torches . . . The night was dark and the conveyance perilous. Immediately the boat reached the shore the natives uttered a shriek and came to our assistance. They caught hold of my hands in the most affectionate manner and guided me across the beach to where they had made their fires. Seeing that I had got safe on shore their joy was unbounded . . . Never shall I forget the unsophisticated, the sincere and warm affections of those interesting people . . . DRAY and NOLLEHOLLICKER were the most conspicuous in their endeavour on the occasion and their conduct called forth my admiration and

gratitude . . . The natives were more intent upon saving me than their own preservation.[10]

On 17 October Robinson left his sons with the new internees from the *Tamar* on Green Island while he crossed to Flinders Island. He landed on a beach and strode through a tree-lined valley to Wybalenna, a kilometre inland. His journal recorded his first impressions of the settlement.

> The different cottages, which skirt a plain . . . had a village-like appearance. The buildings consist of commandant's quarters, doctor's quarters, catechist's quarters, storekeeper's quarters, coxswain's cottage, two cottages for military, hut for garden overseer and sawyer, hut for bricklayer and baker, boatcrew's hut, tailor's hut, men's hut, bakehouse, native store and nine double native huts, a large provision store and cultivated land . . . There were at least two dozen Cape Barren geese on the settlement who were completely domesticated . . . There was also a fine Indian deer named Bess which was quite tame and paid regular visits to the cottages . . . The settlement herd give a good supply of milk at present, so that we got butter and cream. There are good gardens on the settlement and no want of vegetables.[11]

At 1367 square kilometres Flinders is the largest of the 52 islands in the Furneaux Group in eastern Bass Strait. It spans 62 kilometres from north to south and is 37 kilometres wide at its broadest. Granite ridges extend from north to south, and about one-third of its total area is rugged and hilly. Although it has a mild oceanic climate, it is buffeted by the cold westerly gales known as the Roaring Forties that assail Bass Strait. The settlement was well established by the time Robinson stepped ashore. It had a staff of 46 Europeans, including a military officer and four soldiers with their families, a storekeeper, a catechist, a coxswain, a medical officer, and 16 convict servants. But little about it was as idyllic as his first observations suggested. The original settlement was moved in June 1831 from Gun Carriage Island to what proved to be an unsuitable site at the Lagoons, in the south-west of Flinders

Island. In 1833 it had to be moved again, to Pea Jacket Point (now Settlement Point), on the island's west coast, about 30 kilometres from the Lagoons, and was then given the name Wybalenna. Supplying it was problematic, and the superintendent always had many issues to deal with besides the internees, including constant squabbles among civilians and military and frequent convict misdemeanours.

Soon after his arrival Robinson requested a report on the internees' health from resident surgeon James Allen, a two-year veteran of the settlement. Allen's assessment was bleak. Morale was poor. Settlement life was disagreeable to nomadic people. Their yearning to return to Country was deep and abiding. Their huts were not weatherproof and were exposed to the icy westerlies. Clean water was wanting, food supplies were irregular and inadequate for the half of each year that muttonbirds were unavailable, and the male internees were angry about the frequent sexual liaisons with their women by staff and visiting sealers.[12] Robinson reported the shortcomings to the colonial secretary and recommended that all the internees be transferred to the coast of the Australian mainland.[13]

After he had been at Wybalenna for two months Robinson set down in his journal an extraordinarily frank and heartfelt meditation on conditions there, its recent history, human rights, and the melancholy status quo. Deep in his mercenary heart Robinson understood that the ethnic cleansing of Lutruwita had been unconscionable.

> The whites say they are sure the government do not care for the blacks or they would be more attentive to their wants. There have been frequent famines on the settlement; their ration is not sufficient for them . . . The people have been frequently destitute of clothing and of blankets, and which is the case at the present time. The natives complain and say why keep us here to starve. We don't want to live here. Let us go to our own country and we can live. There is plenty of kangaroo in our own country. Again, the absurdity of placing the native huts in exposed situations is so opposite to what ought to have

been the case, and so contrary to what they had been accustomed that any person endowed with the least discernment would not have so acted. It has been admitted by the medical men who have attended them that the prevailing diseases of the aborigines are catarrh, inflammation of the lung, etc, which originates in undue exposure to cold. Then why place them in bleak situations exposed to the prevailing winds? It is certainly the very height of inconsistency and folly, and may add cruelty and injustice. Had the people been left to themselves they would have selected warm and sheltered situations, but it is very evident they had no choice in the matter and it would seem they were considered as bondmen* . . . whereas they are or ought to be free men of the highest order, patricians not plebeians for they and not us are the legitimate proprietors of the soil. They are the lawful owners, not us. We are usurpers. We hold by might, not by right.[14]

Thoroughly agitated, Robinson concluded with the same searing honesty. 'We have desolated them, despoiled them of their country, the land of their forefathers, and having placed them on an isolated spot the least we ought to do is to abundantly supply their wants.'[15] He had come to believe, as he admitted during the first year of the Friendly Mission, that Palawa were 'equal if not superior to ourselves'.[16]

The internees' accommodation especially troubled him and he wrote of taking prompt action to remedy several deficiencies, including arranging for comfortable brick houses to be built, each with a fireplace and a brick or timber floor. New houses were certainly built, but the truth of many of his claims has been challenged. One historian has opined that 'Robinson's reports were usually part aspiration and part imagination', and it has also been observed that a typical Robinson report 'runs into many pages, is much exaggerated and in places even untrue'.[17] But although he regularised food shipments to the island and instigated measures to protect Palawa women from the sexual predacity of whites, he did nothing to improve the water supply, even after vice-regal prodding.

---

*   Here meaning convicts.

Breakout!

Especially concerning him were the number of deaths resulting from prevailing conditions: 28 internees had died in the previous two years. When the young Big River man Nooerer succumbed on Christmas Day 1835, Robinson mused that 'it is an appalling sight to view the mounds of earth now before us where the people are buried as they are in single graves . . . [and] no white men lie here'.[18] His absurd and insensitive response was to acknowledge the need to accelerate the internees' Christian indoctrination because 'death was making very rapid inroads among the people and no time should be lost'.[19] It would be less trouble to save their souls than their lives.

Morale had been bad from the outset in the 'world's first concentration camp'.[20] As early as 1 March 1832, while he was still afield with the Friendly Mission, Robinson had pointed out to the colonial secretary that having armed military guards on the island was one of several detrimental factors.

> The arming of the whites from the supposition that the natives were going to spear them, the placing sentinels over the natives, the transporting the aborigines to isolated situations . . . and the sealers in the straits still continuing to cohabit with the native women contrary to the wish of many of those females whose relatives are living at this Establishment, have conjointly tended to create in the minds of these poor creatures the most dire apprehensions.[21]

The existence of so many problems was not a promising basis for Robinson's administration. Whatever he might do to improve the internees' physical and spiritual welfare, constantly worsening morale would always be a problem. Palawa did not want to be confined on alien Country, constrained by armed guards, and subjected to an unwanted and bewildering process intended to expunge all trace of their culture. Although they had committed no crime, they were prisoners for life. The inescapability of their unjustified incarceration would for ever be a dark and ineradicable cloud on their horizon, a source of bitterness and sorrow – and, for a few, of rage.

10

'Too much dead man'

Charles Robinson and the new internees followed Robinson to the settlement on a wild and squally 1 November 1835. Pevay was still mourning the death in Hobart of his brother Penderoin, but if he had been expecting a happy reunion on Flinders Island with Wymurrick, another brother whose capture and removal he was responsible for, he must have been shattered to learn that he too was dead, although Wymurrick's young son Timemernidic was among the familiar faces who greeted the new arrivals.[1] Pintawtawa, another of Pevay's brothers, and Pintawtawa's new wife Larmoderic were also there. So too was Pevay's old friend Nikaminik; they had not seen each other since August 1830. Timme also had cause for delight: his parents Rolepa and Luggenemeener were there to greet him and his putative brother or half-brother Walter George Arthur, one of the eight youngsters from the Orphan School who had arrived in the *Tamar*. Another with cause for elation was Planobeena, whose brother Moultehelargener was at Wybalenna with his wife and daughter, as were at least one and probably two of her putative sisters, Pierrapplener and Woretermoteteyer (Margaret), who, like her, had been *tyrelore*. Even the recently widowed Manalakina had his spirits lifted as soon as he set foot on the island: his son Neerhepeereminer was there, a captive since 1831. Also to Manalakina's liking was his first sight of a woman named Pangum. He immediately attempted to seduce her but she flew to the parson for protection.

A few days after the newcomers arrived, Robinson invited all the internees – more than 100 of them – to what he called 'a grand fete' to farewell Henry Nickolls, the retiring superintendent.

> A convenient spot was selected in the bush where tables were laid for the whole of the aborigines. They partook of an excellent dinner consisting of fresh mutton, plum pudding and rice pudding. They also had wine allowed them . . . They were waited upon at dinner by the whole of the civil officers . . . In the afternoon the natives amused themselves with the game of cricket and other gymnastic exercises. In the afternoon the aborigines and officers took tea and in the evening there was a splendid display of fireworks . . . The happiness of those truly kind people was great, and the good order and decorum preserved by them would have done honour to any civilised assembly.[2]

Light-heartedness was subsequently offset by labour. Soon after the grand fete, Robinson asked the internees to cut a private road from behind his quarters through a tea-tree forest to the landing place at the beach. To his surprise and delight the task took them only three-quarters of a day, whereas 'white men would have required seven or eight days to accomplish the same', he wrote, noting that the internees had been eager to start the work and had performed it cheerfully.[3]

Yet such remarks mask their burgeoning discontent and its causes. During the Friendly Mission he had ensnared some Palawa with lies, telling them that:

> if the natives would desist from their wonted outrages upon the whites, they would be allowed to remain in their respective districts and would have flour, tea and sugar, clothes &c given them; that a good white man would dwell with them who would take care of them and would not allow any bad white man to shoot them, and he would go with them about the bush like myself and they could hunt.[4]

Those who had been Robinson's guides thought they had a special place in his affection. They also believed he had promised that they alone would be allowed to return to Country after the others were interned.

George Augustus Robinson
(*Courtesy Libraries Tasmania*)

Trukanini
(Benjamin Law; National Portrait
Gallery, public domain via
Wikimedia Commons)

Robinson in bush dress
(Benjamin Duterrau; courtesy Libraries
Tasmania)

Pevay
(Thomas Bock; collection Tasmanian
Museum and Art Gallery)

Wurati
(Thomas Bock; unknown collection, public domain via Wikimedia Commons)

The Friendly Mission ascending the Black Bluff Range
(GAR sketch, A7026 File 4 GAR journal Van Diemen's Land 19 August 1830 p. 89 e02639_0092, courtesy State Library of NSW)

Planobeena
(*Thomas Bock; collection Tasmanian Museum and Art Gallery*)

Timme (*Thomas Bock; collection Tasmanian Museum and Art Gallery*)

Manalakina (*Thomas Bock; collection Tasmanian Museum and Art Gallery*)

Robinson's mission crossing Arthur River by raft
(*GAR sketch, public domain via Wikimedia Commons*)

Anthony Cottrell
(*Courtesy State Library of Victoria*)

Macquarie Harbour penal settlement 1830s
(*Pretyman Collection, courtesy Libraries Tasmania*)

Towterer
(*Willim Buelow Gould; Journals of George Augustus Robinson and the State Library of NSW, public domain via Wikimedia Commons*)

Grummet Island
(*Pretyman Collection, courtesy Libraries Tasmania*)

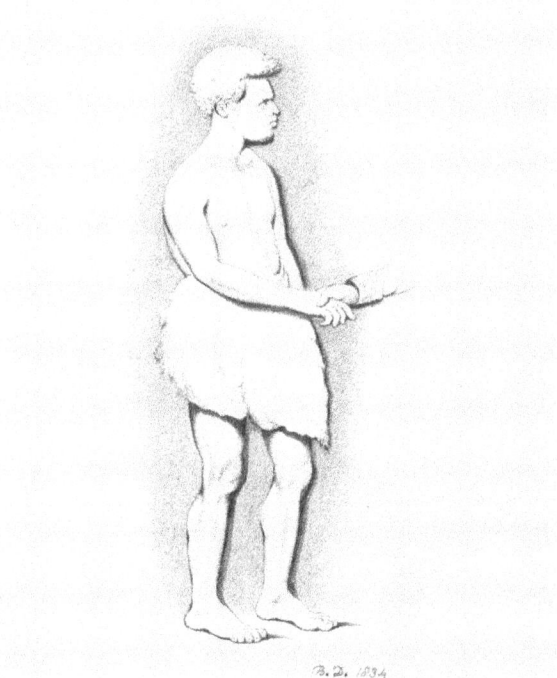

'Timmy, a wild native, address'd in a friendly
manner by Mr. G.A. Robinson'
(*Benjamin Duterrau; courtesy State Library of NSW*)

Teengerreenneener
(*Francis Guillemard Simpkinson De Wesselow [1819–1906], Cranky Dick (1845), pencil and watercolour and chinese white highlights. Presented to the Royal Society of Tasmania by the artist, 1900. Tasmanian Museum and Art Gallery*)

George Robinson junior
(*Courtesy Libraries Tasmania*)

Hobart c.1835–1840
(*E. Buchner; courtesy Libraries Tasmania*)

'Jack [Pevay], a Tasmanian Aboriginal, holding a club'
(*Benjamin Duterrau; Art Gallery of South Australia, public domain via Wikimedia Commons*)

'Timmy, a Tasmanian Aboriginal, throwing a spear'
(*Benjamin Duterrau; Art Gallery of South Australia, public domain via Wikimedia Commons*)

Wybalenna as it was
(*John Skinner Prout; National Gallery of Victoria,
public domain via Wikimedia Commons*)

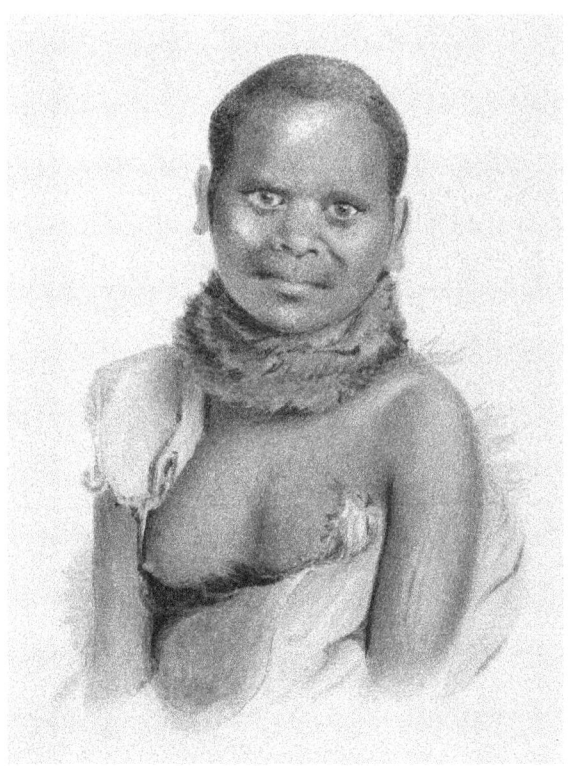

Numbloote
(*Thomas Bock; collection Tasmanian Museum and
Art Gallery*)

Wybalenna now (*Benjamin Cox*)

Wybalenna cemetery now (*Benjamin Cox*)

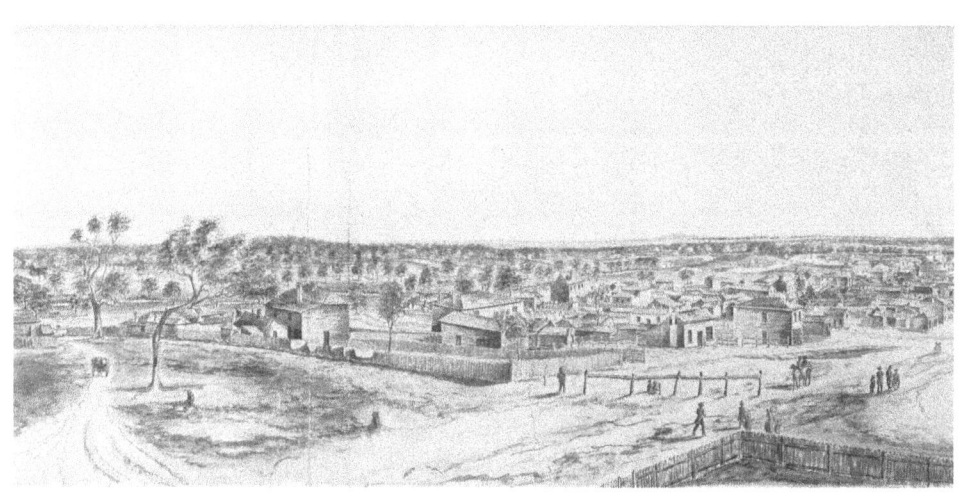

Melbourne, 1841 (*Courtesy State Library of Victoria*)

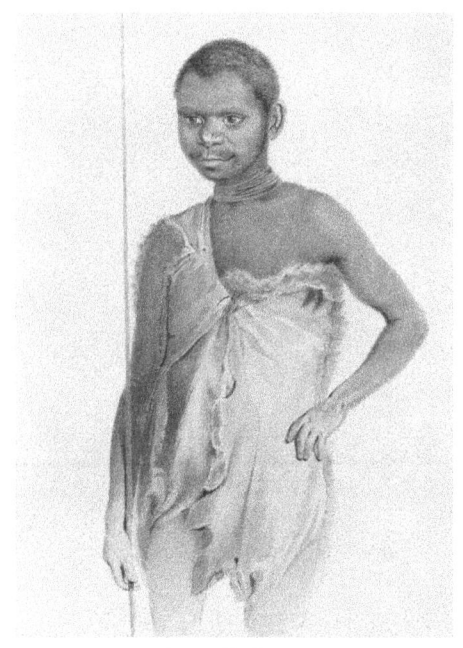

Prupilathina
(*Thomas Bock; collection Tasmanian Museum and Art Gallery*)

C.J. La Trobe
(*Courtesy State Library of Victoria*)

Robert Massie
(*Courtesy State Library of Victoria*)

Frederick Armand Powlett
(*Courtesy State Library of Victoria*)

Believed to be
Judge John Walpole Willis
(*Courtesy State Library of Victoria*)

Redmond Barry
(*Courtesy State Library of Victoria*)

William Thomas
(*Courtesy State Library of Victoria*)

Trukanini in old age
(*Courtesy Libraries Tasmania*)

'Too much dead man'

He had certainly pledged something of the sort, admitting in an 1838 report that 'in the stipulations made to the aborigines it was guaranteed by me on behalf of the government that . . . as far as practicable they were in the summer months *under proper protection* to occasionally *visit their native districts*'.[5] No such parole was ever granted, and well before 1838 it was clear to them that it never would be. If Robinson suspected their bitterness at his perfidy, he ignored it or at least did not note their rancour He admitted only that 'the non-fulfilment of the excursions to the main[land] . . . is an occasional source of complaint'.[6] It was a serious misjudgment of the intensity of their longing for Country, which was so deep and enduring that its denial would always be a source of profound and irremediable sorrow for them. Some colonists did recognise it. One, a senior civil servant and former editor of the *Hobart Town Gazette*, remembered 'the numerous statements of persons on Flinders Island who on seeing on a clear day the coast of Tasmania and the summit of the snow capped Ben Lomond . . . shed tears. "There my home, there my country".'[7]

Robinson was too busy either to notice or to care. Having been appointed a justice of the peace, he was now Flinders Island's resident magistrate as well as its commandant. His days brimmed with administrative and magisterial tasks. He now afforded little space in his journal to the actions and concerns of individual internees, instead concerning himself chiefly with the activities of the Europeans under his command. Even his most trusted guides, most of whom he had undoubted affection for, faded anonymously into the overall picture. Occasionally one of them was mentioned by name, as when 'Dr Allen said TRUGGERNANNA had trod on a snake at Green Island and thought she had been bit, and was greatly terrified. The doctor was there and assured her nothing of the kind had taken place.'[8] And when Manalakina, aged about 60, died in early December 1835 only a month after arriving, Robinson considered the event noteworthy, for Manalakina had been a respected and important veteran of his mission for more than four years.[9] Yet he did not record Manalakina's brief partnering with Meemelunneener in the month before he died. Nor did he document Pagerly's death, probably in the same year, although she had been his guide since the beginning of 1830, longer than Manalakina, and had been the widow of Kikatapula, another of his most important companions.[10]

§

His primary task at Wybalenna, Robinson believed, was to convert the internees into Europeanised peasant farmers and good Christians. Erasing their aboriginality was the necessary first step, although it would be a another breach of faith and another major and mendacious about-face. As he admitted to the colonial secretary, he had promised them that in exile they would be allowed to retain unchanged their customs and culture.

> [I]n my conferences with them I have been scrupulously tenacious in keeping my word. The tribes knew[,] when in their own districts[,] they would be sent to an island, where they would be secure from the attack of the depraved portion of the white population and where they would enjoy uninterrupted tranquility [*sic*] in the society of their kindred and friends, their wants and necessities were to be amply supplied in addition to which they were to enjoy their native amusements. Moreover their customs were to be respected, and not broken into by any rash or misguided interference.[11]

Such promises had served to bait his hook, but at Wybalenna he sloughed them as heedlessly as a snake sheds its skin or an autumn tree its leaves. He even managed to erase them from his own memory, later asserting that 'I never deceived them'.[12] Conscience clear, he proceeded with cultural genocide. Within weeks of first setting foot on Flinders Island he replaced their natal names with trite and sometimes bizarre nicknames, even supplanting existing English sobriquets (although in his journal confusingly continuing to use a mixture of all three). 'I gave names to some of the aborigines, their [existing] adopted names being some of the most barbarous and uncouth that can be well imagined', he noted on 15 January 1836.[13] Pevay (already nicknamed Cape Grim Jack or just Jack) became Napoleon; Timme (already known as Jemmy) became Robert or Bob; Rolepa was crowned King George; Trukanini (alias Lydgugee) was encumbered with Lalla Rookh; Wurati was dubbed Count Alpha; Prupilathina (aka Lacklay and Jemmy) was thereafter known as Isaac; and Numbloote (at that time called Sydney or Jenny) became Semiramis. Others fared no better. Although Robinson claimed they were pleased with their new names, the more perceptive internees surely felt unease at the unnecessary severance of this fundamental link to selfhood, family, and culture. First their Country had been stolen from them, now their very identities were being replaced.

More effacement followed. Despite his promise that their customs would be respected, Robinson reneged by forbidding or discouraging three fundamentals of Palawa culture: hunting, dancing, and the much-loved use of red ochre for bodily decoration. However, he soon found that hunting was essential to their general good health, something his predecessor Henry Nickolls had already observed. Nickolls had informed the colonial secretary early in 1835 that 'Dr Allen has . . . stated that frequent hunting occasions as necessary to counteract the constant living upon Salt Provisions'.[14] Palawa disliked salt meat, but when fresh meat was unavailable, as it often was, the internees' daily diet comprised a brackish pottage of salt beef or pork, turnips, and cabbage (supplemented with damper and small daily allowances of tea, sugar, and tobacco). The concoction was neither appetising nor nutritionally sound. Nickolls had further noted that although 'full rations had always been drawn by the natives . . . that had been found insufficient as they possess enormous appetites'.[15] Hunting alone provided enough meat to satisfy them.

After reaching the same conclusion, Robinson allowed the internees to resume hunting. Many did. They seized with pleasure the dole of freedom it afforded, to the extent that about half of them were 'frequently absent on hunting excursions for weeks together'.[16]

Robinson was never happy about their hunting trips being so protracted but knew there was no danger of abscondence. No matter how far from the settlement the hunters roamed, there was no escaping their island prison.

Their dancing annoyed Robinson and he did not long tolerate it, in part because he thought some of their dances were obscene. The frequency of their corroborees was also irritating; so too was their duration, for they sometimes danced well into the early morning. 'This evening the natives continued their hilarity till a late hour 10 pm', Robinson complained one sultry summer night in 1835, 'and I was obliged to go to them and stop them or they would have continued it till 12 o'clock for aught I knew'.[17] So he proscribed the activity, as he did the use of red ochre. A rationale for banning corroborees – one specious enough to have been written by Robinson himself – appeared in a Launceston newspaper, praising him for achieving:

> another very desirable effect in superseding the evening *corrobories* [sic] which used to injure their health very materially, as well as to encroach on their regular and moral habits. Their hideous yells on these occasions, their excessive exertion in dancing, and distortion of limbs and features, and their practice of taking large draughts of cold water, while thus overheated, are all replaced by exercises of a far more rational and satisfactory description.[18]

The internees responded by hoarding red ochre, decorating themselves in secret, and holding clandestine corroborees. Robinson had to relent and allow dancing to resume, although his intolerance was little diminished. In August 1837, having finished one day's corroboree, the internees resumed dancing the next, but consecutive days' terpsichore was too much for the commandant. 'I went and dispersed them', he wrote. He also ordered his Palawa constables to confiscate the red ochre and blacklead used by the dancers to paint their bodies.[19]

In March 1836 Major Thomas Ryan, who was commandant in Launceston, arrived at Wybalenna with instructions from Lieutenant

'Too much dead man'

Governor Arthur to report on conditions there. Ryan's account was as grim as James Allen's had been five months earlier. He wrote that it was difficult not to conclude that the internees were being deliberately exterminated in a manner involving considerable pain and suffering, citing, among other factors, their 'damp, poorly ventilated huts with impure water and inadequate provisions'.[20] Arthur ordered immediate rectification of the shortcomings. Robinson did arrange for new houses to be built for them, warmer and more comfortable and better situated for protection from the worst weather, but the aqueduct Arthur ordered to supply fresh water to the settlement from nearby hills was never built and the fresh meat supplies he ordered to be regularised stayed sporadic and unreliable until 1838.

Practical improvements might have been slow to be implemented or too difficult to contemplate, but Robinson's broadbrush deculturising continued to be applied without pause or impediment. Not only were all internees required to answer to their new names, they had to be clothed like civilised Britons. The men's everyday outfit was 'Maria Island cloth frocks [smocks]', but on Sundays they wore duck frocks and trousers. For the women, it was dresses made of Maria Island cloth six days a week and, on Sundays, 'cotton chemise, flannel and stuff petticoats, fustian stays, plaid cotton bed gowns, check aprons and coloured cotton handkerchiefs for their heads, and occasionally shoes and stockings'.[21]

As a further civilising measure, Robinson cloistered the children he had retrieved from Hobart's Orphan School. Not permitted to live with their parents lest their civilising be tainted by proximity to lingering Palawa culture, they were accommodated at catechist Clark's house despite his known physical and verbal abusiveness.

Robinson himself, for all his regulation and control of internees' lives and activities, never used physical force or corporal punishment on them as he did with offending Europeans. Instead he applied 'moral and coercive force with devastating results. He isolated groups, denied rations to others, prevented some from hunting, and encouraged spying – all the usual forms of behaviour that the superintendent of any asylum or institution can resort to in his need to keep control'.[22]

One compulsion was for all internees, adults and children, to attend classes in reading, writing, and arithmetic, but 'catechismal teaching of Christianity took up a very large part of the school curriculum'.[23] Indeed, it was relentless. Although Robinson's predecessor Henry Nickolls had come to understand that Palawa had 'a perfect horror of everything connected with religious instruction', Robinson's proselytising never let up.[24] He believed that 'if a man is christianised he is seen to be civilised'.[25] And he was convinced that 'The best and surest mode of imparting instructions to the aborigines is by single ideas often repeated'.[26] So everything was taught by rote – at least to those who bothered to attend classes. Pevay chose not to, evidence of his continuing alienation from and defiance of Robinson and his aims. Reproving him for his absenteeism made no difference; he remained defiant. 'This native attends school but very seldom', it was reported, 'and is not improving. Mr. Dove [the chaplain] addressed him very feelingly on his neglect of instruction.'[27] The clergyman's impassioned dressing-down must merely have hardened Pevay's obstinacy and would hardly have sat well with a proud and resentful young man accumulating grievances.

To religious instruction Robinson applied the same blinkered pedagogy he used in literacy classes. He 'force-fed them with the only sort of Christianity he knew, a meaningless catechism rather than the thoughtfulness for others which is the basis of Christ's teaching'.[28] Neither literacy nor religion germinated. The internees attended classes, appeared to listen, memorised what they were told to memorise, and regurgitated it on demand, but they were stonewalling. They feigned attention but did not absorb. Their eyes glazed over with incomprehension and boredom. During one prolix Sunday harangue by the catechist, Robinson observed that 'Nearly all the natives were asleep'.[29]

One Sabbath rigmarole must have seemed in equal parts pointless and stultifying.

On Sunday mornings at half-past ten all the men and women stood outside their huts to await Robinson's inspection. The women wore checked gingham petticoats with handkerchiefs about their necks and heads and the men wore canvas trousers with tall coats buttoned to the waist. After breakfast they proceeded to chapel from eleven o'clock to one o'clock. After lunch they had hymn singing.[30]

However, as Robinson had noted in Hobart years before, they always behaved decorously in church and were often enchanted by the music they heard there.[31]

In September 1836 the civilising process began to be supplemented by publication of a weekly newspaper, the *Flinders Island Weekly Chronicle*, a half sheet of foolscap priced at twopence. Its editors were two literate survivors of the Orphan School, Thomas Brune, aged about 14, and Timme's putative sibling Walter George Arthur (named in the journal's prospectus as Walter Juba Martin), who was estimated to be 17. The *Chronicle*'s stated aims were 'to promote christianity civilization and Learning amongst the Aboriginal Inhabitants at Flinders Island' in whom it was hoped to 'induce Emmulation [sic] in writing[,] excite a desire for useful knowledge and promote Learning generally'.[32] It was also intended to remind the internees of their great fortune at being under Robinson's tutelage and protection – he was sometimes adulated in its pages as 'our beloved father' – even if life at Wybalenna might be thought to have strained the notion's credibility. With Robinson exercising strict editorial oversight, the journal's content was a smorgasbord of propaganda, news, religious indoctrination, and moralising about internees' failings and misdeeds. And any efficacy it might have had as a re-education tool was severely limited by a lack of readers, for most internees remained steadfastly illiterate.

Although its publication ceased after a few months, the *Chronicle* opened a window on the internees' demeanour. It showed that they mostly demonstrated little more than lip service to Robinson's rules and regulations, indulged in brinkmanship, and frequently did whatever they pleased while managing to achieve a workable balance between compliance and defiance. Snippets from its pages illustrate their resistance to being purged of culture. 'I seen the Native men playing at spears to day' and 'Some of the people love to put on Red ochre and grease[,] yet is very bad work', the journal tut-tutted on 9 November 1837, toeing the Robinson line.[33]

For despite Robinson's best efforts to expunge it, Palawa culture survived. The men continued to exchange or discard wives, a practice the puritanical commandant abhorred and reprehended them for (notwithstanding his own adulterous dalliances, one with the wife of the island's storekeeper, the other with Trukanini).[34] Timme was one such offender. In late 1835 he 'put away' Numbloote and was living alone. Perhaps as a marital restorative, Robinson allotted him a hut and 'desired him to fence in a yard and garden, which he was anxious to do'.[35] Within a fortnight Timme had 'dug up a piece of ground in the rear of his hut for a garden and fenced it in; also enclosed a yard'.[36] This diligence might well have encouraged conjugal reunion with Numbloote, for, as Robinson noted, the Ben Lomond leader Woreternattelargener 'is anxious that Jenny [Numbloote] should live again with Timmy ... It is what I [too] am anxious for.'[37] Timme himself was now as keen to resume connubiality as his friends were to aid its resumption. When by faint firelight that night Robinson saw some Ben Lomond men taking away Numbloote and Pangum, who lived with them but had been dancing with the Big River people, he asked why. Because 'Timmy wanted to have Jenny again', they told him. Delighted, Robinson ordered Numbloote brought back to Timmy.[38] They reunited and were to remain a devoted couple until her early death in 1839.

§

Within weeks of the new internees' arrival at Wybalenna, many began to show signs of deteriorating health. The causes were a variety of climatic, dietary, and spiritual factors exacerbated by inadequate rations, clothing, accommodation, and sanitation. Respiratory infections were common, dysentery recurrent. On Christmas Day in 1835 Planobeena rated a rare mention in Robinson's journal when he noted that she was ill. He did not say what ailed her, but early in the new year the notably robust former *tyrelore* was reported to be convalescing.[39] However, another disorder had already begun to affect the internees and only a month later was epidemic. 'The whole of the aborigines have been afflicted for some time with ophthalmia', Robinson wrote on 21 January 1836. The following month Timme sprained his knee while performing the kangaroo dance with the Big River people and 'had it bandaged with human bones and a skull of a child. These were intended to charm away the pain.'[40] The treatment proved so effective that he was soon able to endure another prolonged footslogging mission in mainland Tasmania.

In those same early months of 1836 Trukanini heard rumour of imminent insurrection. She was the most loyal of Robinson's guides, as well as his lover, and had twice saved his life. Now she sought to protect him again. On 21 January she defied the day's gale-force wind and squalls and hurried to warn him that the Ben Lomond people were making waddies and intended to kill all the whites on the island.[41] If Robinson took the warning seriously – he made no comment about it in his journal or noted any preventive or defensive measures he might have taken – the threat somehow evaporated and he quickly forgot about it. Dealing daily with the internees' compounding health problems, staff squabbles, supply difficulties, administrative duties, and the persistent peccadillos of the civilians and convicts under his command occupied far more of his day than the internees' welfare or their smouldering disgruntlement, leaving him little time to concern himself with rumours of rebellion. But he did not forget Trukanini's fidelity. A month after she had warned him of the impending revolt he gave her and Wurati a new cottage, 'a warm, neat, convenient and dry habitation', where she 'reluctantly learned to keep house, cook damper and bread, and sew under the direction of the catechist's and storekeeper's wives'.[42] In reality she was able to enjoy her new home for only a month before she and Wurati left Wybalenna to join the recovering Timme and others in an unexpected new mission that took them away from Flinders Island for more than a year. Only when it was over were they able to live in their new cottage and perhaps enjoy the claimed calm domesticity.

Their long absence from Wybalenna was initiated three days after Robinson gave them the house. A letter from the colonial secretary had brought him news that ethnic cleansing was incomplete. Palawa had been reported in the north-west at Hampshire Hills and Surrey Hills and as far east as Westbury. There had been thefts and a stockkeeper was believed to have been slain.[43] Robinson, who had known all along that a few Palawa were still free, replied that he would send his son Charles with some trusted guides to capture the holdouts and incarcerate them on Flinders Island.[44]

Joined by Robinson's son George, the new mission left the island on 10 March 1836 with six men and three women as guides and the commandant accompanying them as far as Launceston. The guides were Wurati and Trukanini, Pevay and Planobeena, Timme and Numbloote, Prupilathina, the slow-witted Teengerreenneener, and a man named Leepunner (Edward) who was said to be the son of one of the holdouts they were to search for.[45] Robinson left them in Launceston and took a coach to Hobart, where he hoped to persuade his wife to join him at Wybalenna.

While the mission was preparing to leave Launceston, they were accommodated by Robinson's friend George Whitcomb. Word that some Palawa were still free and hostile had piqued the town's interest, so the mission's departure in early April was thought newsworthy.

> Mr. Robinson, junior, has . . . set out this week to the country beyond the Lakes and the Surry [*sic*] and Hampshire hills . . . [I]t appears that a native with his wife and child are still likely to be found alive in that neighbourhood. The man is known to Mr. G.A. Robinson, but . . .

not being seen for so long a period, it was conjectured that he had perished.[46]

Then the picture becomes hazy. Robinson's sons failed to keep adequate or intelligible notes of the expedition, so where they went and how much actual searching they did is unclear, although they were said to have been inactive at Mersey River for some months. Regardless, for a long time their quest was unsuccessful. On 4 November 1836, eight months after the mission left Wybalenna, Robinson wrote to Charles with the news that the government wanted the whole party to return to Flinders Island, although he might ignore the order if he were then in actual pursuit of his quarry. He wrote again 11 days later to say that the government had changed its mind and Charles was to continue searching, but neither letter reached its addressee.[47] It did not matter. On 20 November, near Cradle Mountain, the searchers finally located the last free Palawa: a man, his wife, and their four children. But the little family refused to go to Flinders Island and soon escaped into the bush (although decades later one of those children would feature again in history as Trukanini's last spouse).[48] Robinson put a positive spin on the incident. He reported to the colonial secretary that it was now certain that only the one family remained at large in all Tasmania. He also noted that although there had been some sickness among his sons' guides, none had died.[49]

It is a reasonable assumption that the guides were not very assiduous in their searching. Apart from a natural unwillingness to condemn any more of their people to a hated incarceration, they would have been delighting in the freedom of so many weeks in the wild, especially the total lack of Flinders Island regimentation and cultural effacement, and it would have been natural for them to prolong their absence for as long as possible. Led by such veteran recalcitrants as Pevay, they would have spent their days hunting while supposedly searching for signs that would lead them to their quarry. Since the three most senior men – Pevay, Timme, and Wurati – had their wives with them, they were not deprived of basic comforts and were probably not trying very hard to locate the lone family. When the mission finally found them, it was no accident that the holdouts escaped with remarkable ease despite the searchers' numerical superiority. A blind eye was surely turned to the getaway, and the guides' attempts, if any, to recapture them or follow their trail were unsuccessful and probably perfunctory.

In late November the mission returned empty-handed to Launceston, from which Charles sailed to Wyballena on 1 December.[50] When he left the island 10 days later to rejoin his brother and the guides, he took with him another internee, a young Macquarie Harbour man named Pennemorenoke or Pennemorehenudic (aka Benjamin).[51] A man Robinson esteemed, he appears to have been at Wybalenna since October 1835 and had come from the Orphan School, one of those who had embarked on the *Tamar* that month with Robinson and the guides.[52]

In January 1837 Robinson's sons set out from Launceston with the enlarged mission in a renewed quest for the fugitive family. During this leg Pennemorenoke taught the other guides the Lord's Prayer, but despite such devotions their mission was unsuccessful. In midwinter they gave up, blaming extreme weather for their decision.[53] Sixteen months had passed since their departure from Flinders Island and when they returned to Wybalenna on 21 July 1837 the guides took with them supplies of the much-prized red ochre. They were greeted joyously by the other internees. Welcoming them back, Robinson was impressed by how robust they all looked.[54] He himself was unwell and so were many of those who had remained at Wybalenna. Others had not survived to see the guides return. During the mission's absence 19 internees had been buried in the settlement cemetery, 17 of them in the previous six months.[55] Timme learned with sorrow that mother Luggenemeener was one; she had died on 22 March. Even the robust and prayerful Pennemorenoke survived his return to Wybalenna by only five months.[56]

Despite the mission's failure, Robinson was glad to see his sons and the guides back, especially Trukanini, with whom he soon resumed the physical liaison that had reportedly begun during the first Friendly Mission.[57] A week after her return he recorded a sexual encounter with her, cautiously using a Palawa noun to disguise it. 'Had a PARGENER at LYGUDGE's', he wrote.[58] The word he rendered as *pargener* is probably *paganer* (kiss or caress), but 'There is an association . . . perhaps between *paganer* (kiss) and *poangha* (intercourse)'.[59]

Among the internees who gathered that winter day to greet the returning guides was a newcomer, a woman named Mathabelianna or Mayterpueminner (aka Maria but Wybalenna-renamed Matilda). Said to be a Swanport woman born *circa* 1805, she had spent most of her life as a *tyrelore* on Gun Carriage Island. Sealers had subsequently left her on Flinders Island, where she was found by Big River internees on a hunting expedition. They took her to Wybalenna on 4 May 1836.

She soon proved useful to Robinson.[60] Some years earlier, while a *tyrelore*, she had been an involuntary participant in a slaving raid at Port Phillip.[61] When the lieutenant governor belatedly heard about the raid, in which local Aboriginal women had been abducted by the Tasmanian slaver George Meredith, he asked Robinson to investigate, and on 23 December 1836, while his sons and their guides were still in Launceston preparing to start their mission, he and Mathabelianna and three male internees – Pannabuke, Dowwunggi, and Manalakina's son Neerhepeereminer – had sailed from Flinders Island in the *Eliza*.[62] Ashore at Port Phillip three days later, Mathabelianna 'pointed out the spot a few miles down the harbour at Point Nepean where she said Meredith and his crew of sealers stole the native women', who were then sold to sealers on Bass Strait islands.[63] Her role had been that of enticer, she explained to Robinson, who reported the details to the colonial secretary.

The Statement of [blank] alias Maria alias Matilda

Says she has been for a long time with the Sealers. That she was in George Meredith's Schooner when he went to Port Phillip. That the

Vessel anchored within the entrance of the Port under Point Nepean. That there was a tribe of Natives on the Point hunting kangaroo, that they the Sealer's Men went on Shore in their Boats and enticed the Natives, and told her to do the same. After fixing upon the best looking women and Girls [they] did at a preconceived sign seize upon and tie them with cords, and then conveyed them on board the Schooner and proceeded on a Sealing Voyage to King's Island and the Hunter Islands and thence to the Furneaux Islands were [sic] they were left by Meredith. This woman having accompanied me to Port Phillip pointed out the spot and described these proceedings.[64]

Robinson noted that 'Matilda said the sealers did not shoot the blacks, nor did the blacks spear the whites; both parties were afraid to commence hostilities; but the sealers tied the women's hands with rope and put them in the boat'.[65]

After spending some days evaluating the pecuniary potential of the new colony, Robinson returned to Flinders Island with Mathabelianna and the others on 10 January 1837. Six months later she was in the crowd that greeted the guides when they returned from their unsuccessful mainland mission. As a new face and an unattached woman she quickly caught the eye of one of the returned guides. On 2 August Prupilathina, now aged about 19, 'called at my private office', Robinson wrote. 'I spoke and advised him to get married and he told me he was willing to marry Matilda [Mathabelianna]. I consented and urged them to consummate the nuptials. I also went to the natives and conferred with them and the woman. She acquiesced, as did the other natives.'[66] A day later he noted that 'On visiting the native cottages this morning I found that Isaac [Prupilathina] was married to Matilda'. A formal ceremony took place on 10 August. Robinson visited the schoolhouse that evening to witness their marriage by the catechist. Within eight days, however, Mathabelianna had abandoned her husband, provoking a rebuke from Robinson. She was still separated from Prupilathina in October, and the following January Robinson referred to her as a single woman. Nevertheless, on 6 October 'it was agreed by the natives themselves that Isaac should have Matilda. He had sighed long for her' and they were then reconciled. Only his youthful disappearance and rumoured death three years later would end their union. It would also trigger the revenge raid that cost four men their lives.

§

By the time the guides returned from their mainland quest in midwinter 1837, Timme, now aged about 22, had achieved some standing. 'This evening [I] appointed two fresh constables, Robert [Timme] and Washington [Maccamee], making in all six constables', Robinson noted little more than a fortnight after they came back.[67] Although constables were appointed after consultation with the internees, the commandant wielded considerable influence, and probably the power of veto, so the selection confirmed Timme's growing stature within the community and with Robinson himself.[68] Four weeks later Robinson's opinion of Timme was affirmed when the young man asked him for a pair of boots. The request delighted Robinson. Timme's desire to be shod, he opined, was evidence of 'a striking circumstance of the advance of civilised improvement'.[69]

Despite such noteworthy progress, Timme, like his friend Pevay and most of the other internees, remained in the firm embrace of traditional culture. Hunting was at its heart. It preserved their culture, provided their preferred foods, and gave them welcome periods of relative freedom away from the settlement. Sometimes it was also a show of defiance. Going off to hunt without Robinson's permission allowed them to thumb their noses at him and his strictures. Walter George Arthur, writing in the *Chronicle*, was the voice of official umbrage at these displays of independence. '[T]he Native men they go out into the Bush without asking the Commandant first[;] you ask the Commandant may I go out in the bush to hunt . . . you should not go away any where at all without asking the Commandant first', he wrote.[70]

Robinson was especially displeased when hunting expeditions lasted more than a day or two. Because native wildlife close to Wybalenna had long been exhausted, hunters had to venture far afield to be successful and they needed to stay away longer. Extended absences were especially popular when sickness engulfed Wybalenna. Even those too sick to hunt preferred to go into the bush to recover, perceiving that their maladies originated in settlement life.

That gloomy situation prevailed in the last few months of 1837. It had been a lethal year of recurring illnesses, moving Robinson to complain that even women were staying in the bush for 10 or more days at a time without his permission, and they were encouraging others to do the same. They had good reason. Wybalenna had no worse year for fatalities than 1837, and October, when five internees died, was especially deadly. The frequent sad processions to the cemetery led Trukanini to observe bitterly that soon 'there would be no blackfellows to live in the new houses'.[71] Her concern was universal. Even an anxious Thomas Brune, the day after her remark, briefly let his mask slip to editorialise on the subject in the *Chronicle*. 'And now my friends I am telling you . . . that we must all die in a short time . . . When I was standing at Mr Clark's house I saw coffin carrying along the settlement[;] we will all be like that', he wrote.[72] He continued in the same gloomy vein in the following issue. 'On the 16th October I saw two coffins carryied [sic] one by prisoner and one by the Natives and were put into the grave.'[73] The grieving survivors did not suppress their sorrow. '[W]hen a relative dies, they give themselves up to grief', Robinson wrote. 'They break their spears and necklace, throw away kangaroo skins, cut their baskets, don't red ochre themselves, are quite neglectful and mourn.'[74]

In that milieu of morbidity and death, unafflicted internees needed little encouragement to absent themselves for extended periods, but their long truancies exasperated Robinson. On 3 October he questioned Planobeena's brother Moultehelargener, who had just returned from a hunting trip, about why so many stayed away so long.

'Too much dead man'

Moultehelargener replied that 'blackfellow VIDER, PUDEYER come back, too much MONATIA at Flinders at Pea Jacket, too much dead man, VIBER frightened, like to CRACKENNY bush', meaning 'Blackfellow no come back. Too much sickness at Pea Jacket Point [Wybalenna]. Too much dead man. Blackman frightened, like to stay in bush'.[75]

Among those who prolonged an absence that pestilent spring were Pevay and Timme. On 27 September they left Cottage 9, the house they and their wives shared, to go on a hunting trip. They stayed away for more than a fortnight, to Robinson's expressed disapproval. It was not until a cold bleak afternoon in mid-October that Wurati announced their imminent return. He told Robinson they were 'walking along the sandy beach and coming towards the settlement' and were not far off. They arrived soon afterward with news that Robinson, who was riled at their long absence, refused to heed.

> They said that several of the natives were sick, Philip, King George's wife and another ... They had left them at Killiecrankie Point and had come for flour and sugar.[76]

Timme's concern was personal. King George was Rolepa, his father, and Phillip was not a male but Pillah his stepmother, Rolepa's wife. Robinson refused to give them supplies. Instead he admonished Pevay and Timme for their protracted absence and told them 'they should have come [back] to the settlement long since [ago] as the Governor was expected daily'.[77] Ten days later Pillah died of pneumonia.

Robinson's good opinion of Timme enabled him to overlook such peccadillos, but similar tolerance was denied Pevay, whom he continued to dislike and distrust. The Parperloinnher's rare appearances in Robinson's journal were invariably negative; even a trivial incident was enough to engender a disapproving note.

> I witnessed a thing done which if anything more than another was wanting to prove that the people was still in a state of barbarism ... Napoleon, i.e. Jack [Pevay], deliberately went to the dogs belonging

to the Big River people in the upper houses and threw a waddy at a dog and wounded it, probably broke its leg and ribs, and then threw at another dog but missed. The first dog ran into the bush howling. The owner of the dog (Alexander) then walked down with two waddies and struck one of Napoleon's dogs on the head, and here the fracas ended.[78]

The incident was so inconsequential that it is surprising Robinson thought it was worth recording. But it reinforced his opinion that Pevay, with his uncertain loyalty and defiant refusal to attend classes, was one internee who was still in a state of barbarism, a judgment that was never to improve. It was to intensify only a month later when the Parperloinnher mutinied against him at Pot Boiling Lagoons. Pevay 'never proved so faithful or so docile' as Timme, a newspaper reported years later, echoing Robinson's long-held opinion.[79]

§

By October's end all surviving internees were deemed convalescent, and in early November the *Chronicle* assured its readers that joy and godliness were again universal at Wybalenna.

> [T]he Native men was playing and singing about God and Jesus Christ and they were singing bout there [*sic*] own country song and some of the Native people was shooting swans and Duck and Pelilcans [*sic*] . . . And Native men was singing Godly song.[80]

Soon afterward, however, dysentery recurred. Three more internees perished. Morale slumped further. In mid-November Robinson admitted that 'Much gloom and melancholy appear to hang over the aborigines' dwellings'.[81] It caused more cracks to appear in the *Chronicle*'s official crust of joyous Christianity, one on the day of Robinson's comment, although an emollient smokescreen of all's-well-at-Wybalenna propaganda prudently came first.

> Now my friends you see that the Commandant is so kind to you he gives you everything that you want[;] when you were in the bush the Commandant had to leave his friends and go into the bush and he brought you out of the bush because he felt for you[;] he knowed the white man was shooting you and now he has brought you to Flinders Island where you get every things and when you are ill tell the Doctor immediately and you get relief.[82]

But immediately following that mimetic ballyhoo, and in direct contradiction of it, appeared a fleeting wail of anguish that had somehow escaped Robinson's censorious eye.

> Let us hope . . . that something may be done for us poor people. They are dying away. The Bible says some of us shall be saved but I am much afraid none of us will be alive by and by, as there is nothing but sickness among us. Why don't these black fellows pray to the king to get us away from this place.[83]

This third cry of despair and dissent in five weeks from the teenage Thomas Brune's pen did not pass unnoticed. Perhaps coincidentally, he was sentenced the following month to two hours in the stocks, and soon after that the *Flinders Island Weekly Chronicle* ceased publication.[84]

On 1 December Robinson wrote in his journal that 'Natives in tolerable good health', but he was being disingenuous. Sickness continued to beset them and the healthy ones continued to fret about it and to distrust the available medical treatment. When Robinson asked Drunamellyer (Caroline) for the bundle of ashes she carried close to her, 'she refused and said I had plenty and if she gave me that she had nothing left to put away the MANARTIC sickness. I said that the doctor would do that.' Druemerterpunner, her husband, scoffed at the notion. 'Doctor no good', he declared. 'He kill plenty blackfellow.'[85]

In this dour climate of death, distrust, and hopelessness Robinson opted to take 17 unafflicted internees on an excursion, their departure reported by Thomas Brune in the *Chronicle*: 'The people of Van

Diemen,s [sic] land is gone in the bush with Commandant the other side of the island'.[86] Among those chosen were Pevay, Planobeena, Timme, Numbloote, Wurati, and Trukanini.[87] Walter, just released from a week in jail for misconduct, also went. '[M]y object in taking him on this journey,' Robinson wrote, 'was as much to punish him by making him carry a pack as well as to keep him out of further mischief in my absence'.[88]

They left on 12 December for what was to be a five-day round trip to Pot Boiling Lagoons (now Logan Lagoon), a coastal wetland. Despite unusually hot weather and the weight of their packs, they found the walking easy at first, the landscape being benign. But when they shouldered their knapsacks again after a noontime halt, they encountered a far more challenging terrain. Their progress through it in the afternoon heat was troublesome and temper-testing.

> The latter part of this day the travelling was exceeding irksome, it being for the most part through thick scrub intermixed with prickly mimosa, honeysuckle, long cutting grass etc. of a very bad description and anon through lagoons up to our knees and often to our middle in water . . . This was a long and wearisome journey.[89]

Game was plentiful so far from the settlement. When some internees doffed their knapsacks so they could hunt, the others had to shoulder the extra burdens as the party trudged on. The heat was withering. Several of them, including Robinson, suffered nosebleeds. He noted that 'My head was dizzy and ached exceedingly[,] the effect of the heat' as they tramped through the taxing topography. He complained of 'many a stumble and fall to myself and people' because 'Burnt stumps and bushes made it difficult to travel'. Teengerreenneener, who had lagged in the rear with Walter, became 'very sulky because he fell down so often over the dead wood' and almost drowned while crossing a river. He said he would sooner go to jail than participate in another such expedition.

Continuing heat and more hard country made the second day's hike similarly gruelling. 'Our route was very devious and circuitous on account of the impervious scrub and deep lagoons', Robinson wrote. Despite the hardship, being in the bush meant revived traditional customs. 'The natives burnt the scrub, and during the afternoon some of the natives hunted and brought game which in those parts are not so scarce as at the settlement.' Late in the day the party waded more than two kilometres across Sellars Lagoon to make camp on the far shore, where Teengerreenneener suffered a fit or collapse. It was not the day's only tribulation. A cryptic note in Robinson's journal implied a serious incident. 'The natives burnt off the bush and my jacket was burnt also trousers, the natives' clothes and some knapsacks', he wrote. Although not impossible, fire accidentally spreading from bush-burning seems unlikely. Palawa knew how to manage fire. They habitually burnt country they were passing through (a practice known as firestick-farming or cultural burning). The incident angered Robinson and although he did not mention reprimanding those responsible, it would have been unlike him to let such an incident pass unrebuked even had it been inadvertent. Being admonished for something accidental – the result of a sudden wind shift, perhaps – would have been an added source of the surly opposition to him that Robinson would note next day. It was soon to worsen.

They moved on. 'The travelling was exceedingly heavy and laborious' was his summary of the third morning's long tramp through more torrid heat and a testing landscape 'abounding in lagoons and belts of forest of impervious description'. But the foraging was rewarding. 'Ducks, swans and gulls were in abundance', Robinson documented, and the hunters 'returned loaded with eggs. They afforded us a good repast.'[90] Late in the day, after a scorching afternoon's hike, they reached their destination and prepared for a recuperative evening. Instead, three days of travail and mounting tension ballooned into rebellion. Antagonism became apartheid. Twelve defiant Palawa distanced themselves from Robinson by refusing to help him or give him any of their food. As he sat famished and unfed, tormented by the

Breakout!

aroma of meat roasting on their fires, he admitted that a serious rift not only existed but had been building for some time.

> The natives during the time I have been with them have been very inattentive to my wants, but tonight they were worse than heretofore. They had four swans, an abundance of kangaroos, ducks, teal, etc. and never prepared me a morsel nor made me a shelter wherein to sleep nor made my tea nor damper bread. These I did for myself. I was exceedingly displeased at their negligence, at their careless indifference and their ingratitude.[91]

Only Prupilathina, Wowee, Leepunner, Teengerreenneener, and Walter sided with Robinson and for their loyalty were shunned and bullied by the outnumbering militants. 'Richard [Teengerreenneener] had a swan', the *Chronicle* reported, 'and [Wurati] took it away from him and . . . put it on the fire and roast it and he give Richard only bone of the swan'.[92] As the night wore on and the campfires burned low, Robinson's indignation was undimmed. At daybreak it blazed.

> This morning the natives evinced the same careless indifference to my comfort nor did they offer me either kangaroo meat or ducks. I therefore made my breakfast of dry bread and tea, and they would not allow the five natives who returned [to Wybalenna] with me any sugar. Reprehended the natives for their greediness, and then set off on our journey.[93]

As Robinson and the ostracised five started toward Wybalenna, the rebels, who included Pevay, Planobeena, Timme, Numbloote, Wurati, and Trukanini, went their own way. Staying out was an irresistible opportunity to demonstrate defiance, and the excellent hunting in this remote place was not to be readily relinquished. For the past three days they had enjoyed a cornucopia of traditional fare: 'wallaby, kangaroo, opossum, rats, bandicoots, little birds, porcupines or anteaters, eggs, etc.', Robinson logged – an abundance too good to be forgone too soon.[94] And they were in no hurry to return to a settlement rife with disease and despondency. They would choose their own route back and the time of their return.

Trudging homeward, Robinson and his compliant quintet endured two further days of blistering heat that did nothing to cool his lividity. When they reached the settlement late on 16 December he announced his dudgeon to all and sundry. 'I expressed to the natives on the settlement my displeasure at the greedy and ungrateful conduct of those natives who had been my companions', he wrote.[95] He was still festering when the rebels returned to Wybalenna three days later and he quickly let them know. 'I reprehended the natives who had returned to the settlement for their negligence and ingratitude to me in the bush', he declared.[96] Next day, anger unassuaged, he berated them again, and the *Chronicle* duly echoed his indignation. '[W]hy dident [*sic*] you give the Commandant a piece of kangaroo', it chided. 'No you would not because you was so greedy you was like hogs eating away as fast as you could[,] you threw it on the fire as quick as you can in case that the Commandant should wanted a piece of it . . .'[97]

Although Robinson never gave a precise reason for the rift, its causes were manifest. Foremost was the internees' resentment at being immured in a regulated island prison where their families and clansmen were sickening and dying at an alarming rate. Out in the bush, however, where Robinson was unsupported by armed military, they could demonstrate defiance of him and his regime. If the immediate trigger was perhaps an unrecorded Robinson scolding after the fire, underlying it all was a volatile mix of antipathies that included sickness, hopelessness, despair, broken promises, and a growing fear that death would be their only escape. Thirty internees perished that year, a frightening leap from the previous year's four.[98] Oblivion loomed, they sensed it, and the recurrent appearance of fresh graves in the Wybalenna cemetery was a relentless reminder of it, each new mound a raw wound in the sad earth. During Flinders Island's time as a prototypical concentration camp from 1830 to 1842, a total of

244 Palawa are believed to have been incarcerated there.[99] But when Robinson took a census of internees in January 1836, three months after he arrived, only 113 were left, to which two newcomers were added in the following two years. Of those 115 internees, nearly one-third – 37 men, women, and children – died in the two years after the census – that is, by the time of Robinson's excursion to Pot Boiling Lagoons and the truculent mutiny of 12 of his old companions. The calculation is as obvious as it is ominous. In 1837 there were probably only 78 Palawa remaining, a catastrophic and irreversible plunge from the estimated 5000 who had been living in 1803 – a mere generation earlier – when the first British invaders took their guns and diseases and genocidal land-lust ashore in Lutruwita, and they too were fast disappearing under Robinson's stewardship. When Wybalenna was finally abandoned in 1847, there were just 47 survivors, and soon enough they too were gone.

Too much dead man . . . Robinson shrugged it off. He had made clear from his earliest days at Wybalenna that responsibility for Palawa deaths was not his but God's. George Augustus Robinson was doing no more than giving poor savages a safe place to die and making their last days comfortable.

> The sad mortality which has happened among them . . . is a cause for regret but after all it is the will of providence and better they died here where they are kindly treated than shot at and humanly destroyed by the depraved portion of the white community.[100]

It was as adroit a piece of rationalisation as Robinson the chronic rationaliser ever contrived.

§

Early in 1838 Wybalenna was visited by distinguished personages: the new lieutenant governor Sir John Franklin with his wife and entourage. Although Robinson had assured Franklin that corroborees were no longer permitted, he ordered the internees to perform one – 'their war dance, kangaroo ditto, emu ditto, horse ditto and a variety of others' – for His Excellency's entertainment.[101] The following day another prohibition was briefly lifted to enable the amusements to continue. Robinson assembled the men 'armed with ... small sticks instead of spears' and ordered them to stage a mock battle.

> The men were divested of their upper garments and had a warlike appearance. They entered the grass plot in front of my quarters by different routes and shouting their warwhoop, and then formed into two ranks and commenced the sham fight. It afforded the Governor and company great amusement . . .[102]

For more than two years Robinson had been attempting to purge or discourage dancing and every other aspect of Palawa culture, beliefs, and practices in order 'to root out everything Aboriginal and substitute a peasant Christianity'.[103] He encouraged only practices he considered to be civilising, and they did not include corroborees or battles, sham or otherwise. Now, after two years of having their culture suppressed and forbidden, the internees must have been perplexed that a brief regression was not merely allowed but commanded, only to be proscribed again immediately afterward, although not before they had been rewarded with gifts of beads, knives, handkerchiefs, harmonicas, scissors, and marbles from the hands of Sir John and Lady Franklin themselves. After accepting this largesse, the performers 'withdrew to the grass plots to amuse themselves with rounders and marbles', perhaps also to puzzle over the fickleness of their jailers.

§

Despite the uncertainties blighting internees' lives, one feature was virtually inescapable: compulsory Christianising. Although in official reports Robinson noted that 'The schools and religious services are still maintained' and dubiously claimed that 'the Natives are constant and regular in their attendance', it is unlikely that he ever believed his involuntary neophytes truly understood or embraced Christianity.[104] But it was essential to his missionary self-esteem that they publicly exhibited at least a superficial knowledge of the subject, which he could then report to the colonial secretary to add gloss to his self-laudatory accounts of his achievements.

In a typical such demonstration, heard on 21 April 1838 during a service at the school, the preachers included several who had not previously spoken. Pevay was one – it was his only known oration – but its brevity shows he was as resistant to evangelising as he was to learning literacy, with a concomitant reluctance to participate then and later. 'Blackmen, Blackwoman – Why do you fight God? Jesus Christ came into the world to save sinners.'* He then put to various internees such rote-learned doctrinal queries as 'What shall we do to be saved?', which he directed to Wottecowwidyer (Harriet). His delivery was in 'the languages generally spoken on the Settlement'.[105] No English for Pevay, although he was known to speak the language 'tolerable well'.

Timme also preached that night, but his ministry, in 'tolerably good English', was unlike his friend's. It demonstrated that the supposed religious instruction at Wybalenna was chiefly about white supremacy, for his sermon had nothing to do with Christian creed. Although, as Pevay had, Timme directed rote queries about faith to the women, his address made obvious his own susceptibility to Robinson's cultural remoulding. Philippic rather than homily, it also highlighted the difference in the two men's personalities and their divergent attitudes to indoctrination. Whereas Pevay's brief discourse suggested reticence based on sullen resistance, Timme's pointed to his acceptance of what he had been taught. He enthusiastically hectored the Palawa congregation about how inferior they were to their white masters.

> You knew nothing in your own country but to fight plenty. You learn plenty of good things from the white man. You could not make a

---

*   Punctuation added to original text.

house no you made a breakwind not a warm house. The Commandant make fine house for blackmen – you can't make glass for a window. You [are] wild people all every one. When you came here you know nothing[,] you went about naked but you kill kangaroo you no make stone houses[,] you only make breakwind all round.[106]

Whatever their doctrinal shortcomings, both men's speeches were compliant enough to have satisfied Robinson. Yet although in his journal he praised the disquisitions of Timme and five other internees who preached that night, he chose not to mention Pevay or his ministry. He appears to have understood that the tokenism of Pevay's discourse demonstrated all too clearly his resistance to forced Christianising and that his failure to publicly endorse the many advantages of white culture signified his entrenched defiance – his barbarism.

Some, however, were more easily persuaded of Pevay's piety. That year Wybalenna's new chaplain, Rev. Thomas Dove, examined the internees about their religious understanding. The 25 questions he asked Pevay revealed 'a broad, basic knowledge of the key ideas presented to VDL people at Wybalenna. He is the only person who, when asked "Who was the strongest man?", replied "Samson".'[107] It was enough to satisfy Dove. Yet it is noteworthy and surprising that although Wybalenna had obligatory religious education from the outset and a resident clergyman from 1837, neither Pevay nor Timme was baptised there. Whereas some from the Orphan School appear to have shown a superficial grasp of Christianity, it never became a force or a concern or a motivation in the others' lives. On a typical Sunday in 1838, significantly while Robinson was away and unable to enforce attendance, the settlement's office journal noted that 'Divine service was this day but thinly attended[,] most of the natives being out hunting'.[108] Robinson himself was under no illusion about the efficacy of his proselytising or the depth of the internees' religious understanding. During a visit to Sydney later the same year he was asked if Palawa still believed in spirits and whether they understood the doctrines they had been taught. His reply was equivocal: 'they respond to the forms, I can say no more'.[109] When his son George, who briefly succeeded him as superintendent, was interrogated on the same subject the following year, he was franker. He said 'he did not believe that any of the aborigines male or female have any knowledge of religion or that their conduct is in any degree influenced by religious motives'.[110] That lack of conviction, of genuine understanding of what they were parroting, was obvious to others too, notably to a priest in Melbourne in 1842. Ministering to the two condemned Palawa shortly before their execution, he refused to baptise Timme – baptising Pevay was apparently not even contemplated – because 'he had no knowledge of the notion of the [religious] instructions, although he said he knew the fundamental principle Jesus Christ came into this world to save sinners; Jesus Christ was the Son of God; he died for our sins'.[111] That it was meaningless catechism born of compulsory rote-learning and nothing but mimicry was all too evident. The lack of genuine understanding and the true nature of the supposed religious instruction at Wybalenna were further (and tellingly) demonstrated by Wurati's son Myyungge when he corrected a woman who thought Eve was God. 'God . . . is a not a woman', he chided. 'God is a white man.'[112]

Robinson himself would damningly affirm his doubts about their religious understanding when he testified during their trial that Pevay and Timme had 'a basic knowledge of the existence of a Supreme Being and know right from wrong' but would say nothing more.[113] His testimony suggested they had no more than the thinnest veneer of Christianity, yet that veneer helped to hang them. On the morning of their execution Robinson noted (perhaps with satisfaction, perhaps in self-exculpation) that 'They prayed fervently'.[114] At least they appeared to be praying. Or perhaps his brief sketch of desperate last-minute supplications, of distressed clutching at spiritual straws, was created to appease his own missionary conscience. For Pevay was noted to be 'evidently sceptical of the simplest truths of Christianity, and doggedly retained his firmness to the moment of death'.[115] The years of cultural brainwashing had failed. Pevay remained defiantly and rebelliously Palawa to the end.

§

As years passed it was no secret that the internee population of Wybalenna was being relentlessly eroded by sickness, although it was of general unconcern to the outside world. Occasionally, however, a newspaper remembered them and their plight and voiced disquiet at the death rate and its tragic ramifications.

> The aborigines imprisoned on Flinders Island continue to die at the rate of 20%, without any births to supply their loss. Ninety are now the sum total that remain of all the various and large tribes of Van Diemen's Land, so that the utter extinction of the race is hastily approaching.[116]

Two months later, in the early winter of 1838, the same journal reprised its sympathy for the internees and their suffering, pinpointing the reason with compassion and percipience.

> We do not pretend to be quite correct in stating, that the original number of the legitimate proprietors of the soil of this Island, two or three years ago – upon the forming the Flinder's Island Bastile [sic], exceeded 400, – the number might have been at that time a few more or less. It is enough for us to know that we are correct in stating that their numbers now do not amount to 90 – and, that it is decreasing very rapidly, in consequence of a disease prevalent among the poor kidnapped blacks, vulgarly called a broken heart.[117]

For Pevay the broken heart recurred again and again. He had already lost his brothers Penderoin and Wymurrick to diseases of colonisation, and in 1838 his family shrank to nought. His brother Pintawtawa's wife Larmoderic died on 3 March, followed by Pintawtawa himself on 4 August and their young son Robert on 2 September; his sister

Pordeboic also died at Wybalenna.[118] The following January Pevay's last known relation, his orphaned nephew Timemernidic, son of Wymurrick, was taken away on a whim by Lady Franklin, the lieutenant governor's wife, who had decided to adopt a Palawa boy.[119] Pevay was not consulted and he never saw his nephew again.

Some of 1838's deaths had an especially profound and haunting significance. On 30 June Robinson saw Planobeena in deep mourning outside a house where Timme's half-sister, a child known only as Eliza Robinson, had just died. Planobeena was 'seated in the little yard in front, weeping bitterly'.[120] Although deaths were hardly rare – 14 more internees succumbed that year – her grief was well founded. Because there were few children left at the settlement and births were now non-existent, a child's dying presaged a far greater tragedy – the death of a race's future.

§

For some of the surviving few a future had already been mapped. On 10 August 1838 a gleeful Robinson wrote in his journal that 'A *Hobart Town Gazette* extraordinary arrived, and made me acquainted with the intentions of the home government to remove the Flinders Island aborigines to Port Phillip, and of the offer to me of the appointment of Chief Protector of Aborigines in New South Wales' (of which colony present-day Victoria was still part). Next morning he 'interrogated all the natives about their willingness to go to Port Phillip, to which they most cheerfully consented'. Pevay and Timme were among 21 internees, all males, who purportedly signed with their marks a statement affirming their willingness; other ostensible signatories included Prupilathina, Nikaminik, and Rolepa.[121] Their eagerness is undoubted. To escape from Flinders Island, with its ever-expanding graveyard and its miasma of distress, sickness, and death, was to grasp at hope.[122]

But death had not yet finished with the Bass Strait gulag. Influenza, which was epidemic in Hobart, reached Flinders Island well before the selected internees' departure, and it quickly engulfed Wybalenna. Of the 10 deaths recorded in 1839, eight were attributed to influenza. On 21 February Robinson recorded that 'Three part of the aborigines are afflicted, several dangerously so, among whom is Semiramis [Numbloote]'. Three days later, impatient to take up his new post, he struck out with eight of the chosen to walk to the old settlement at the Lagoons, where they would embark for Port Phillip. When they halted for the night they found 13 internees camped nearby, eight of them severely ill with influenza. But there could be no delay, onward was upward, and at first light Robinson moved onward. With Pevay, Wurati, Trukanini, Walter George Arthur, Myyungge, and Thomas Thompson, he boarded the cutter *Vansittart*, which sailed for Port Phillip on 25 February 1839. Left behind, too sick even to go aboard, were Timme and Numbloote. She survived only three more days, dying on 28 February. The sorrowing Timme recovered but was not able to leave Flinders Island until 30 March, when he sailed for Port Phillip with Robinson's wife Maria and some other internees, including Planobeena, Mathabelianna, and Prupilathina.

The farewells sank abyssally the spirits of those left behind. Their despair was summarised with stark honesty by Robinson's son George.

> It would be impossible to describe the gloom which prevails . . . from the bereavement of so large a portion of their kindred and friends, and the anxiety they evince to leave a spot which occasions such painful reminiscences is hourly increasing . . . the island has been a charnel house for them.[123]

For those who had just escaped the charnel house a new and different chapter was starting. By early April 1839 all the Tasmanians who were to terrorise Port Phillip were together in that colony.

Part Three
Port Phillip

Earthgrip holds them – gone, long gone,
    fast in gravesgrasp

From an Old English poem (anon.)

11

'Get plenty of guns ready'

By the time the Port Phillip Heads came into view on 27 February 1839, *Vansittart*'s passengers, including Robinson and all six Palawa, were themselves beset with influenza. Two days passed before Robinson could send them ashore at Hobsons Bay, although he had to remain on board, too sick to disembark. When he finally stepped ashore on 5 March he was 'Greatly astonished at the rapid improvement in the settlement since my last visit'.[1] In a letter a few days later he shared his enthusiasm with his wife, who was preparing to move from Flinders Island to Melbourne with their children and nine more internees.

> The Town of Melbourne is on the banks of the Yarra Yarra – and without exaggeration is a delightful spot. The river is deep and quiet and excellent water [–] what a contrast to Flinders[;] the climate is beautiful.[2]

Robinson's motives for shipping some of the 68 surviving Palawa to his new posting appear, as with many of his endeavours, to have been a mix of altruism and self-interest. Purportedly he hoped removing some of them from the moribund Flinders Island establishment would ensure their survival; he also believed that the selected Palawa, with their alleged Christian civilising, would help him to conciliate the Kulin people of Port Phillip.[3] But James Stephen, the secretary of the Colonial Office in London, dismissed the notion with a damning assessment of Robinson's real intention. He wrote that it 'was not the hope of arresting their mortality, which he regarded as inevitable, but rather the wish to throw a veil over an event which he thought it desirable to withdraw from the knowledge of mankind'.[4] Stephen's censorious opinion was based on the report of a board of inquiry, set up a month after Robinson left Wybalenna, to examine the 'appearance of improper doings' at Flinders Island and to 'direct a thorough investigation into all the accounts'. Its findings were wholly pejorative. Among others, there were serious irregularities in finances and stores, and the official records of the settlement were nowhere to be found – Robinson had taken them to Port Phillip. Lieutenant Governor Franklin demanded their return but Robinson did not comply. When Franklin pressed him for an explanation, he wrote a long and ramblingly incomprehensible reply, blaming everything on Dove, the chaplain.

His fraudulence extended to the number of internees he transferred to Port Phillip. Before embarkation he was given official permission to take one family of Palawa with him to be his personal servants.[5]

> The Governor said . . . that Mr. Robinson, the Protector, had applied to him for permission to bring [to Melbourne] with him some [Palawa] as personal attendants. Accordingly, he had given Mr. Robinson permission to bring one family with him. Mr. Robinson, had taken advantage of his permission, and had introduced a regular Scotch family, consisting of all the kith and kin of the family, while he had meant only a father and mother and their progeny.[6]

In typically duplicitous fashion Robinson transferred a total of 15 internees to Port Phillip. Few ever returned to Lutruwita.

§

Robinson's first action at Port Phillip was to dump the first six transplanted internees with Victorian Aborigines at a reserve that is now the site of Melbourne Botanical Gardens. What they saw and experienced there that autumn was graphically described by one of Robinson's assistant protectors when he visited a Yarra camp.

> A scene truly appalling presented itself, five [Aborigines] were in the last stages of dysentery, [it was] a piercingly cold night and . . . not a blanket to cover them. [The following day a doctor came and said that] in his whole experience of eighteen months . . . he never visited them in such a diseased and wretched state of want and disease, that five or six have already died and that five or six more are at the verge of death, and that unless something is done to relieve their wants, speedy extinction must soon take place.[7]

This was even worse than Wybalenna. Submission evidently meant degradation.

On his first day ashore in Melbourne Robinson visited them at the assistant protectors' camp, a makeshift tent town. Now with the title chief protector of Aborigines, he had four assistant protectors: Charles Sievwright, Edward Parker, William Thomas, and James Dredge (who was replaced in June 1840 by William Le Soeuf). He was impressed by none of them, nor by what he described as their constant bickering among themselves.

> In the beginning of March, I arrived at Port Phillip and found the Aboriginal natives congregated in the environs of the township in considerable numbers. As it was intended to employ the Van Diemen's Land natives as mediators and instructors to those people, I took an early opportunity of introducing them to each other. Their reception was of the utmost friendly character, and has continued so to the present moment.[8]

Peaceful integration of or coexistence between the two groups there was, but the Palawa were rarely used as emissaries or conciliators, as Robinson had mooted. In ensuing months they were left mainly to their own devices or used as free labour for Robinson and his sons, in which roles they were rarely noticed in his journal. No more than general glimpses of them survive in its pages for the first year or so, mainly brief notes of his occasional attempts to keep them entertained or occupied: a visit to a Kulin corroboree; a boating excursion; attendance at a fete he staged; attendance at a prayer meeting he had arranged.[9]

On 2 April 1839 their numbers swelled when Maria Robinson arrived from Flinders Island in the *Vansittart* with her children and nine more internees. Among them were Pevay's wife Planobeena and his now-widowed friend Timme, as well as Mathabelianna, Prupilathina, Droyyerloinne, Meeterlatteenner (Rebecca), Thomas Brune, and Charlotte, a South Australian Aborigine taken to Wybalenna after being rescued from Bass Strait sealers, who brought her son Johnny Franklin, aged about 11, with her. There were now 15 former Flinders Island internees at Port Phillip, as well as two Palawa males – Rolepana (aka Ben Lomond) and Batman's Jack (aka Jack Allen) – who had been taken there by John Batman. Rolepana was said to be a son of Rolepa and therefore Timme's and Walter George Arthur's sibling.[10]

Robinson continued to have little time or occupation for any of them. Their infrequent and innocuous appearances in his journal suggest their purposelessness: Timme killing a platypus in Yarra River; several Palawa going with Robinson and some Kulin on an excursion that ended in a corroboree; Palawa helping to build a house for Robinson's clerk William Lansdown.[11] His alleged intention that they would help conciliate the Kulin came to nothing, and he found little to occupy them. Given the now-public mess he had made of his Flinders Island administration and the multitude of challenges facing him with Port Phillip's large and squabbling Kulin population – as well as his own land-seeking and empire-building – Robinson turned his back on the transplants. Instead he spent many hours setting up a personal fiefdom, settling his family, pacifying truculent Kulin, and fudging answers to Franklin's insistent demands for explanations about Flinders Island irregularities.

Vigorous young people thus left idle and unsupervised quickly became bored which soon led to trouble. When Rolepana, aged about 12, absconded in early May 1839, the chief protector, who now had responsibility for the boy, made no attempt to find him. Months later Rolepana was returned to Robinson in Melbourne – he had been located working in a Geelong public house – and was then found employment with a settler, but he absconded again in August. Although he eventually returned to Melbourne, Robinson quickly shunted him off into the care of Assistant Protector Thomas.[12]

Perhaps Rolepana's August abscondence precipitated Trukanini's first Melbourne escapade. 'The VDL native Lallah Rhook [sic] went with Sharlotte [sic] last night to the Port Phillip native men', Robinson wrote on 7 August.[13] It caused him no great concern because he was otherwise occupied and had lost interest in Trukanini, who had lost interest in her ageing husband Wurati, although she had not lost interest in men. She would continue to strain against Robinson-imposed shackles, geographical as well as moral, and others would increasingly do the same. The results would ultimately be tragic.

§

Robinson's asset-building aspiration suffered a blow within months of his taking up office at Port Phillip when he was informed that the government of Van Diemen's Land would give him rations for only four of the 15 internees at Port Phillip; the others, and his own large family, would have to be maintained from his own pocket. It was an unexpected and unwanted liability. Amassing wealth was essential to improving status, and this would be a serious impediment. He cast about for paid employment for the Flinders Islanders.[14] Because they were the most tractable, Timme and Walter George Arthur were the first to be put to work; Pevay was apparently not considered suitable. On 10 August 1839, with Robinson's son William, Timme and Walter left Port Phillip in the employ of Alfred Langhorne, part of a droving team overlanding 800 cattle to Adelaide, about 700 kilometres distant.[15] The purpose, Robinson told Charles La Trobe, superintendent of the Port Phillip District, was for Timme to become 'personally acquainted with the Country[,] intending hereafter to employ him as a Guide in the service of the Department'.[16]

On 21 October, six weeks into the drive, Langhorne's drovers had just crossed Rufus River with their cattle when they were attacked by a large Aboriginal mob who had driven away 300 of a settler's sheep. Most of the animals had been recovered and left in charge of Langhorne's men when the Aborigines assailed them, starting a desperate battle that was reported in an Adelaide newspaper.

> Shortly after, the blacks mustered to the number of at least two hundred, and advanced towards Mr Langhorne's party. They were warned to keep away, and some shots were fired over their head to frighten them, but without effect. The party was therefore obliged to fire a few shots in self defence, and some of the blacks were wounded but none of them killed. Mr. Fletcher then mounted a horse and charged the main body upon which they fled, but rallied again shortly after; and it was not till he had charged them a second time that the party was allowed to collect their cattle and sheep uninterrupted.[17]

The report was standard Empire-stirring stuff: a plucky Briton saving his outnumbered comrades by single-handedly repelling the savage hordes. As such, it made no mention of another of Langhorne's drovers, a man who saved Langhorne's own life during the attack and was crucial to the others' survival. But Timme was black and therefore unsuitable for public acclamation as the saviour of beleaguered white men. Langhorne himself admitted to Robinson that Timme's actions were what had saved him and the other drovers during the attack.[18] Yet it seems Timme and Walter were never paid for their 19 weeks of working for Langhorne, an omission that would continue to rankle and eventually have lethal consequences.[19]

Timme's long slow weeks in the saddle, as Robinson had predicted to La Trobe, acquainted him with the vast expanses of landscape that lay beyond the settlement at Port Phillip – good country where a black man might spend his days hunting. Plenty much country, plenty few *num*. Shared with Pevay, such information had ramifications.

§

At Port Phillip, meanwhile, the other Palawa were having a more mundane time: helping build a stockyard one day, hunting with one of Robinson's sons on others, or going off alone to shoot ducks.[20] The general inactivity perhaps drove Pevay in search of diversion. On 5 September Robinson tut-tutted in his journal that 'Mr C. Robinson informed me that Napoleon had contracted the venereal'. Perhaps, like Trukanini, Pevay had been alleviating his ennui by visiting the Kulin camp, where syphilis was rife.

Two days later Robinson showed his distaste for Pevay and his affliction by leaving him and Planobeena behind when he took Wurati, Trukanini, Prupilathina, and Mathabelianna on a three-day excursion to Mornington Peninsula. They hunted unsuccessfully the following day, amused themselves shooting birds the next, and then camped at a lagoon near the coast. Like Timme's, Trukanini's and Mathabelianna's horizons were expanded at the sight of so much sparsely settled country in the south-east. It was a tantalising introduction to Mornington Peninsula and the Western Port area. Two years later a dramatic and dangerous chapter in their lives would be played out there.

Pevay's affliction did not affect his relationship with Robinson's sons or his usefulness to them. (In fact the infection might have been cured by a strong decoction of wattle bark applied to the afflicted organ, a remedy one European noted as successfully used by Victorian Aborigines for the purpose.[21]) In October, when Robinson's son Charles found what he thought was a suitable tract to settle on, Pevay was one of the Palawa he took with him to help build a hut, but five days later they returned to Melbourne after finding the water supply was inadequate.[22] But the short trip away served another purpose: it showed Pevay, as Timme's droving showed him, the appealing extent of wild country beyond the settlement. When Timme returned from his Adelaide trip a week before Christmas 1839 after nearly 19 weeks away, the two friends and their women had much to discuss and information to exchange about the vast landscapes each had encountered. The enticement was strong and would grow stronger. As Pevay was heard to comment, at Port Phillip the Palawa 'were not cooped up in an Island, they had unlimited bush to roam over at their will'.[23]

Only a few days after Timme's return, another Flinders Islander succumbed to the allure of freedom. On 5 January 1840 Johnny Franklin was found to have run away and had to be brought back, only to abscond again later the same day. It was obvious to the Palawa that they were still prisoners even without the sea confining them as it had on Flinders Island. They were denied their Country, denied their freedom. Their lives were circumscribed by white men.

§

For much of the period between 1830 and 1835 Robinson's former Friendly Mission guides had placed great reliance on him as their protector. Although few of them had played any part in the Black War in Lutruwita, they had all been affected by it and the fear and uncertainty it imposed on their lives. Robinson had come to represent protection and a kind of assurance for them through the upheaval. If his failings had become clear to them during his stewardship of Wybalenna, he remained a known quantity after their removal to Port Phillip. With all his faults, he was something of a father figure and a shield against white men of uncertain goodwill. Feeling their way in this alien place, they needed the security his familiar presence provided.

But when he departed from Melbourne on 9 January 1840 to explore Assistant Protector Parker's district from Gippsland to Twofold Bay more than 500 kilometres distant, he left them behind to cope alone. His nine-week absence dissolved their certainty. The relative steadiness his presence imparted began to unravel. Because his departure was only four days after Johnny Franklin absconded, the synchronism of the two events may have been catalytic, and it can be inferred from an ambiguous Robinson journal entry – see below – that some Palawa immediately went bush with a Wurundjeri mob led by Jaggy Jaggy, as a result of which their firearms were confiscated. Robinson learnt of the confiscation when he returned from Twofold Bay on 12 March. The confiscation was triggered by a skirmish at William Ryrie's station at Yering, about 40 kilometres north-east of Melbourne, between Jaggy Jaggy's mob and a police party led by Commissioner for Crown Lands Henry Fysshe Gisborne. Ineffectual shots had been exchanged; the confiscation had followed.[24] Writing months later about the skirmish and the seizure, Robinson vaguely recorded that 'It was at this time that they took away the guns from my VDL natives at the same station'.[25] Presumably 'the same station' was Ryrie's, which suggests that Palawa had left Melbourne with Jaggy Jaggy during Robinson's absence, were present at the so-called Battle of Yering, and had lost their firearms as a result. Always protective of his own authority, Robinson complained to La Trobe about the confiscation, a clear admission that he knew they had firearms and was unconcerned about it.[26] As long ago as the Friendly Mission he had allowed Palawa to hunt with guns, yet when questioned later by Governor Gipps he denied having provided the weapons, although he certainly knew they had them. A footnote to his journal entry for 11 March 1840, the day before he returned to Melbourne from Twofold Bay, stated 'Guns of the VDL, two, a musket from Flinders Island and one lent by Sawyer'.

Robinson's first long separation from the Port Phillip Palawa proved to be a stimulus for subsequent breakouts. The Palawa had been disenchanted by his abandoning them for two months in a still-alien place, and when the first long absence was followed less than a month later by another, it sparked a chain reaction. La Trobe had ordered Robinson to go on another journey, this one to the Goulburn district, a round trip of several hundred kilometres, 'to investigate some outrages by the Goulburn blacks'. He was away from 2 April to 4 June, more than two months, and he went alone.[27] The Flinders Islanders watched him leave, unrest rising in his wake like the dust of his departure. He was hardly out of sight before they began to disperse.

> Informed that my natives had left the day after I went [that is, on 3 April] . . . but had returned here brought back during my absence. Lallarook [sic] had however left a second time and had taken away Sharlotte [sic].[28]

Although Robinson did not name the absconders, his brief note suggests there were several, but who they were and where they went are unclear. Two who together either absconded a second time or were not returned after the 3 April getaway were Timme and Prupilathina (Isaac), who said he was leaving because of inadequate rations.[29] In late April or early May they parted. Timme was sighted soon afterward camping with Aborigines at Tuerong, the Aboriginal Protectorate Station on Mornington Peninsula.[30] He was still there in May, his presence confirmed in a report by Assistant Protector Thomas, after which he and the Aborigines moved to Hyatt's or Highett's run at Mt Eliza, about 25 kilometres from Tuerong.[31] In June he was back in Melbourne, either assisting two of Robinson's sons – they might have been in quest of Trukanin and Charlotte, who absconded again on 2 June (see below) – or as he was himself being escorted back (with Walter George Arthur) by them after a long truancy; Robinson's journal note is ambiguous: 'Mr G and C Robinson, Robert and Walter, natives, returned from the country'.[32]

After separating from Timme, Prupilathina camped in Gippsland with the Kurnai clans, a numerous people who had suffered grievously at the hands of settlers. During his time sitting at their campfires he plausibly heard Kurnai planning revenge raids. As one of the more Europeanised Palawa, he felt obliged to warn settlers, and when Thomas learnt of his whereabouts and what he was doing, he reported the warnings to higher authority on 14 May.

> When last in this part of the country (only two days ago) it was reported to me that a Van Diemen's Land Black from Flinders Island had been traversing over this district. He met with a good reception from the settlers having, as he stated, come to tell them that the Five Fold Blackfellows were coming down – and bid them get plenty of guns ready.[33]

The unnamed Palawa was undoubtedly Prupilathina. Even the odd English phrase 'Five Fold Blackfellows', presumably meaning 'a great many', points to him, for he was Orphan School-educated and semi-literate. Because his alarm-raising preceded by 16 months the five-Palawa breakout in September the following year, he was clearly warning colonists about something more immediate and of far greater magnitude.

After Trukanini and Charlotte escaped Melbourne on 2 June, they were free for weeks.[34] Their abscondence was explained by Assistant Protector Thomas in an undated note almost certainly written at this time: 'I am informed by the Blacks who in general are correct in reports of this kind that the two Van Diemen's Land women are gone to Western Port after Isaac'. The Flinders Islanders obviously knew Prupilathina was at Western Port, so his identification as the Palawa who was warning settlers there is affirmed.[35] But after that he was not heard of again.[36] In due course his disappearance became the trigger for the violent deaths of four men, two of them at the nervous hands of a novice hangman.

On 23 June it was reported to Thomas that the two women were still at large in his protectorate, but it was not until the end of the month that Robinson's son George found them living with white shepherds at Point Nepean, on Mornington Peninsula more than 100 kilometres south of Melbourne.[37] He persuaded or forced them to go back but the women escaped from him a few kilometres from Melbourne. George Robinson and Timme began a renewed search for them on 3 July but were unsuccessful. Twelve days later Robinson senior was informed that the women were still on Mornington Peninsula, but now at Arthurs Seat, about 85 kilometres from Melbourne. After being returned on an unrecorded date, Trukanini absconded again, and on 26 August Robinson despatched Timme and some colonists to find her and bring her back.

Such manpower-wasting escapades exasperated the chief protector. Although minor, they were increasingly frequent and he yearned to be rid of the troublemakers. In a discussion about the cost of keeping them he told La Trobe that he wanted them all returned to Flinders Island. La Trobe dismissed his request, saying they could be made useful to the assistant protectors instead.[38] But Robinson was determined to send them back, although he soon had more pressing problems to deal with. In August, Aborigines attacked a squatter named George Mackay on Ovens River. Some were said to have been carrying firearms, a report that concerned Governor Gipps. He asked Robinson whether it were true that he had given firearms to Aborigines, but Robinson denied the charge. Gipps decided to legislate to forbid Aborigines having guns, and in support of the proposed law he told the Legislative Council of the denial.

> A report has been spread abroad that the blacks had got fire arms from the protectors, which he (the Governor) did not give credit to, as he did not believe they would so far abuse their duty; but as the report had been made to him, he thought it necessary to call on the protectors for an explanation, and he had received an explicit declaration from Mr. Robinson, that the charge was entirely groundless, and that neither he nor his assistants had ever given any arms to the blacks.[39]

During the second reading a fortnight later the councillors discussed the unwanted and unwelcome Palawa presence at Port Phillip. After Bishop Broughton explained that everything possible had been done to prevent Robinson from bringing them in the first place, the debate continued.

> The Colonial Secretary said he did not think that much mischief or inconvenience could result to the colony from the blacks who had been brought from Flinder's [sic] Island by Mr. Robinson, as those blacks had always been kept under the immediate superintendence of Mr. Robinson, and had always been reported as being very well conducted.
>
> The Governor said, that if Mr. Robinson had permitted the Van Diemen's Land blacks to ramble about the country, he had acted directly in opposition to the orders he had received and must be held responsible for it.[40]

Robinson had indeed allowed them to ramble about the country – or was increasingly powerless to prevent their doing so, especially during his absences on protectorate business, when they were no longer under his immediate superintendence. At a meeting with La Trobe later in the month he found the superintendent was not concerned about the Flinders Islanders and still did not share his desire to be rid of them, much to the chief protector's irritation.

> Spoke to His Honor about the VDL natives and begged they might be sent back to VDL or Flinders Island. He said it was a mistake about VDL natives being engaged [in the] Mackay affray and he had written in favour of the VDL natives and had spoken highly of their general good conduct, and that he had not a single complaint against them. I said I had made up my mind to have the VDL natives removed from me.[41]

He renewed his efforts to find employment for them, especially for the most troublesome. At the beginning of November 1840 he attached Pevay to a droving team going to Goulburn River, about 150 kilometres away. They returned many days later with a mob of cattle.[42] But while droving temporarily kept Pevay occupied and out of trouble, Trukanini was more footloose than ever, determined to be free. 'Allen called and brought Lalla Rhook [sic]', Robinson wrote in his journal a few days after Pevay had returned from Goulburn River. 'She and Matilda [Mathabelianna] had gone to Allen's station [in the Dandenong area]. Matilda is at Allen's still and I said for the present she could remain. Sent Lalla Rhook [sic] to the [Robinson] farm.'[43] Six days later, when Mathabelianna joined her at Robinson's farm, Trukanini was threatening to abscond again and then did.[44]

The unrest soon extended to Batman's Jack, who had acquired a gun, and to Thomas Brune. The two men had absconded with Trukanini and Mathabelianna and were at Ruffy's run at Cranbourne, about 40 kilometres south-east of Melbourne. In late November Charles Robinson and Timme were sent to retrieve them but on 3 December, after a week away, they returned without the runaways.[45] Robinson sent them back out, and again they were unsuccessful. 'Charles and Robert arrived', Robinson wrote on 20 December, 'out in rain all last night, lost their way'.[46] From Pevay he had further news of the fugitives the same day. 'Jack, Napolean [sic], came to the farm and said Brune and Batman Jack and two women were at Ruffies', he noted.[47] On Christmas Eve a man named Nowland, returning from the country, told him the four absconders had moved to Arthurs Seat. They did not linger there, however, and Thomas Brune had not long to live. He died early in the new year at a Yallock Creek run, 60 kilometres from Arthurs Seat. It was 3 January 1841, two days after he had broken his back in a fall from a tree, which he had climbed to hunt possums.[48]

As the Flinders Islanders became more annoying and uncontrollable, the chief protector became more determined to be rid of them. They were a burden and a nuisance and a substantial personal expense. Yet nothing he wrote in his journal gave any indication that he was aware of the cause of their unrest or that he cared about their poor morale or that he realised the uncertainty his prolonged absences caused. When he left for a three-week trip to Ovens River on 4 February 1841, taking with him three Kulin but no Palawa, his rejection of them was further highlighted. Whatever remained of their binds to him fell away. On 22 February Pevay decamped, 'went away to Allan', one day before Robinson returned to Melbourne.⁴⁹ He was gone for several weeks.⁵⁰ Robinson did not note how and when he managed to get the fugitive back, but forcibly curtailed freedom was always a cause for further resentment.

With Robinson now under orders to leave on a long mission to the Western District, Pevay's rebelliousness became a pressing problem. Robinson discussed with La Trobe how they might prevent further instability while he was away. La Trobe wanted to place all the Flinders Islanders under Assistant Protector Thomas's supervision, but Robinson demurred, insisting that they would refuse to go.⁵¹ He decided to take Pevay, 'the leader of the malcontents', with him, thereby removing him as a spark for instability at Port Phillip.⁵² As they travelled Robinson might find an opportunity to rid himself of the troublesome Parperloinnher, preferably somewhere far from Melbourne.

Ambivalent but cool even as they prepared to leave, their relationship would deteriorate by the time they returned five months later. For Pevay the long mission would be a turning point. As Robinson had noted, Pevay 'spoke the English language tolerable well', and during this extensive excursion he would hear many settlers boast of having massacred Aborigines. Those stories, and what he himself saw and experienced, were to mobilise Pevay. He would return to Melbourne less than ever an ersatz Englishman. Instead he would be a black man again – and an angry one.

12

'It was a big big country'

Robinson's task for this mission was to investigate complaints against squatters in the Western District and their reported slaughters of Aborigines. As he would discover, the record is shameful. Many settlers in the new colony had simply arrogated vast acreages by dislodging the traditional owners and then defending their usurpations with gunfire. An aspiring pastoralist named Niel Black put in writing what he had learnt about becoming a colonial land baron at Port Phillip.

> The best way is to go outside [into the country] and take up a new run, provided that the conscience is sufficiently seared to enable him without remorse to slaughter natives right and left. It is universally and distinctly understood that the chances are very small of a person taking up a new run being able to maintain possession without having recourse to such means . . . killing the Aborigines seems to be little thought of here . . .[1]

Although Robinson knew the value of black emissaries when travelling into frontier country, his mistrust of Pevay had never diminished, and now the Parperloinnher was even further out of favour because of his recent abscondence. Pevay was hardly unaware of why he alone had been chosen from all the Palawa and Kulin at Port Phillip to go with Robinson. He undoubtedly understood it was intended to prevent his absconding again or causing unrest in Melbourne. Accompanying Robinson meant he would be under close daily supervision.

Their departure from Melbourne might paint in the mind's eye a pleasing picture. It is 21 March 1841, a sunny day in early autumn. Two men, old travel companions, are setting out on a long adventure into unknown country. Robinson is driving a cart amply packed with provisions for the many miles ahead and Pevay is riding one of the two horses in its shafts. But thereafter a melancholy shadow begins to cloud the sunlit image, for the same conveyance will soon afterward carry the rider and his friend Timme to their death on the scaffold and then bear their bodies to the grave.

Robinson and Pevay left town in the late forenoon and in fine weather trundled south-westerly along the Geelong road, both sides of which Robinson was surprised to find were strewn with empty bottles. After passing through Werribee, Corio, and Geelong they crossed Barwon River and went on to Lake Colac, Corangamite, and Lake Keilambete. Robinson made frequent journal notes about such natural phenomena as the profusion of scrub turkeys, but of Pevay he noted only trivialities such as their climbing Mt Shadwell on 29 March.[2]

Unspooling before them was a countryside shrivelled by drought. Waterholes were dry. 'Numerous holes where the natives had dug for water were met with in all parts of the sand', Robinson noted, 'and dead eels strewed the sand and banks. And at the old camping places of the natives, the dead eels lay in heaps; dead eels lay in mounds, thousands of dead eels, and large ones too, strewed the ground around the lake'.[3] Day after day he made copious observations about landscape and wildlife and weather and people he met, but of Pevay he wrote nothing consequential. Harmony of a sort – détente at least – must have prevailed on the road that April.

§

Back at Port Phillip, however, unrest continued to fester. Timme, who on an unrecorded date had partnered with Meeterlatteenner, was widowed for the second time in two years when she died on 29 April, aged about 30.[4] He soon found a willing replacement in the footloose Trukanini, who had renounced Wurati, her ailing husband.

Timme became infected by his new spouse's restlessness and they soon forsook Melbourne for the south-east, finding employment at farms and stations in the Dandenong area. In May Assistant Protector Thomas was surprised when he found them working for James Horsfall on Ballymarang station at Carrum Carrum Swamp, a coastal wetland about 50 kilometres south-east of Melbourne. Horsfall, who claimed to have a work agreement with Timme, protested at Thomas's attempts to coerce the two Palawa into returning with him to the Protection Station at Narre Narre Warren. They did not want to go but when Thomas insisted they promised him they would. But as soon as night fell they vanished into the darkness.[5]

§

Unaware of the unrest, Robinson and Pevay pressed westerly. Robinson's travel chronicles continued to be chiefly topographic and anthropological – Aborigines and their customs and languages interested him as much in 1841 as Palawa had a decade earlier – and at every opportunity he recorded their vocabulary. He noted too the reaction of Aborigines when they first encountered Pevay.

> VDL native: the Aborigines were greatly astonished at the VDL native when they first saw him. His woolyhead was a curiosity. At first introduction they offered him two widows. They call him moke. al.lum.be.[6]

It was a recurring theme. The following month, May, he noted that 'The VDL native is considered as a great curiosity with the native tribes'.[7] Colonists also considered Palawa to be 'obviously a different race of men from the Aborigines of New Holland', as a Melbourne newspaper opined; 'their colour is much deeper, and in the general characteristics of their appearance there is much more of the African feature'.[8]

The expedition pushed on through shortening days and cooler nights into what Robinson observed to be a complex Aboriginal landscape. At a creek they were preparing to ford they were astonished to see a huge weir, built by Aborigines. Robinson estimated the construction to be at least 100 metres long.

> I called to Pevay, my VDL attendant, who had passed it with one of the [local] Tcharcoate natives and pointed it out to him. He evinced surprise at it and the [Tcharcoate] native said it was made by black fellows for catching eels . . .[9]

A few days later they sighted another massive weir. Impressed by its scale, Robinson took a tape measure and found it to be 62 metres long and 1.5 metres high.[10]

Now six weeks into the journey, the chief protector had not yet noted in his journal anything adverse or unfavourable about Pevay. If their constant proximity had not fostered amity, at least the détente was holding. Pevay's compliance at this time was confirmed in a report Robinson sent to La Trobe the following year. In what amounted either to a posthumous whitewash or a rueful conscience-clearing, he praised the Parperloinnher's general usefulness and good conduct during the expedition, commenting that 'He was a general favourite with the Blacks'.[11] Yet he knew Pevay would remain a problem once they returned to Melbourne.

Toward the end of April, as they were nearing the westernmost point of their mission, Robinson seized an opportunity to rid himself of the troublemaker. It came during a stay at Merri River near Port Fairy, a daunting 280 kilometres from Melbourne, where Captain Alexander Campbell was part-owner of a vast run that extended from Hopkins River to Killarney. Campbell, a Scot, had originally settled in Lutruwita, farming at White Hills near Launceston, and had taken active part in the Black War and the Black Line before moving to the new colony on the other side of Bass Strait.[12] His selection was well populated with Aborigines – an estimated 300 to 400 of them whom Robinson called 'the wildest natives I have ever seen', lacking 'all and everything connected with white people ... all were pure, original'. He immediately sought to sully that by inflicting on them a farrago of unneeded new names, each listed in his journal alongside the person's natal name and estimated age. Bizarrely, the new cognomens included familiar Palawa names or mutilations thereof such as Pevay, Nattelargena, Mannerlargenner, Tunnerminwright, Lyjudjeje, Woorradedy, Truggermonner, Brune, Eumariah, Wymurric, and Tymemiddic. Equally bizarre, he renamed five of them Tommy.[13] 'I had some difficulty in inventing names for them', he admitted.[14] Since those Aborigines were not about to be interned or subjected to a civilising process, his efforts were without discernible point.

Robinson was accommodated in Campbell's house during their stay, while Pevay, with a convict servant named Joseph Myatt as his probable watchdog, was sent to camp with the Aborigines.[15] His experience there was inferably influential. Seen by his hosts not as a stranger but as a visiting distant cousin, he assimilated so naturally that they gave him a tribal name, which Robinson rendered as 'Paddy my land'.[16] They were cheerful and healthy, unlike so many of their counterparts in the Port Phillip reserves. If their culture were not exactly Pevay's own, it was far closer to remembered Parperloinnher life than was incarceration at Wybalenna or containment in Melbourne. And they lived on Country just as his own people once had, and they were free to come and go at will, while he was denied both his Country and his freedom. The contrast between their life and his, between their freedom and his subjugation, was stark. It could only rankle.

Even while the experience was stirring metamorphosis in Pevay, his protector was concluding a deal to be rid of him. Campbell offered Robinson a work contract that would take the restive Parperloinnher off his hands. He would employ Pevay at £30 a year, plus board and lodging, if Robinson would provide a written agreement. To clinch the deal, and to ensure Pevay was not tempted to return to Melbourne, Robinson arranged for Campbell to employ Planobeena too.[17]

Such a deal could hardly have been agreeable to Pevay. Throughout his adult life he had been constrained and controlled by white men. White men would always order his future and he wanted freedom. He had many reasons not to trust white men, most recently some consequential Port Phillip experiences that he would later recount to Robinson.[18] Now, too, he had undergone whatever renaissance had been fostered by his brief re-exposure to traditional life. If he were not already considering seizing his liberty, a final impetus would soon be forthcoming.

On the last day of April the chief protector and his Palawa companion left Campbell's and moved on. As their cart juddered across the miles, freedom's enduring allure was further enhanced by the arresting countryside unfolding before them. Near the present-day town of Hamilton, about 260 kilometres from Melbourne, Pevay was stirred by the Arcadian landscape, which Robinson described as 'a beautiful undulating country covered with dwarf banksias, gums, cherry tree and well grassed' and 'A vast champaign country' that 'resembled one vast park'. Pevay, he observed, 'was in rapture. He exclaimed it was a big big country . . . like a big garden'.[19] Country where a man might for ever roam free like his forefathers.

Suddenly he was shot at. It happened the same day, just after he had crossed the dry bed of Lake Linlithgow with the rest of Robinson's party, which included eight Aborigines. They were bound for a station called Darlington to reunite with Robinson, who had gone ahead. As he waited, Robinson witnessed the unprovoked attack.

> I had not been in many minutes before a shepherd came running to the home station. He had a gun in his hand and reported that a shepherd . . . had been chased by the blacks . . . The sub-overseer took his gun and I went with the man. Several shots were being fired and, as I guessed . . . it was my party the man had seen. But so far from their chasing him, they were a long way from him and in charge of my two white men and VDL native . . . The whole was a gross

fabrication. The natives, eight in number, were quietly walking along with my men and belonged to my party. What the fate of these natives would have been if I had not been there may be guessed.[20]

From Darlington, with Pevay doubtlessly shaken by the experience, they headed toward Portland, a coastal whaling settlement about 350 kilometres from Melbourne. The landscape continued to delight them. 'It is a very fine country', Robinson wrote, 'and the scenery very beautiful'.[21] He remained reticent about Pevay, noting only that the 'VDL native is considered as a great curiosity' to the Aborigines they encountered and that Pevay was greatly amused at the ignorance of those Aborigines about the delights of drinking tea.[22] They trundled on toward Portland.

Robinson's attitude to Pevay at this time appears to have been equivocal. If he had noted nothing adverse about the Parperloinnher since leaving Melbourne, neither had he recorded anything praiseworthy or even cordial. Anodyne tolerance prevailed as they neared Portland. Three kilometres east of the town, at the junction of the road with the beach, was a place called Double Corner. They made camp there on 14 May, and the following day he and Pevay rode into the town. Both were bemused by the number of prepubescent Aboriginal girls they saw who appeared to be pregnant.

> I observed the native females, quite girls with their abdomen protruding to such an extent that it was mistaken for pregnancy by some of my people. The VDL native was astonished at it and said, got a piccaninny and no whiskers.[23]

Robinson knew better. The girls' bulging abdomens, he decided, were 'occasioned by the food they eat, a great deal of which consists of fungus'.[24]

Given various tasks, Pevay returned to Portland several times on following days. Four days later, after Robinson had left camp on a recreational ride in the opposite direction, Pevay again walked into the town. On the foreshore he encountered Superintendent La Trobe and some of his retinue, who had arrived that afternoon for a brief visit. Pevay spoke with La Trobe but purportedly did not recognise him. He also failed to tell Robinson about his casual encounter on the sands.

Next day, as he and Robinson were proceeding into Portland to buy supplies, they chanced to meet one of La Trobe's entourage, a man named Ross, who surprised Robinson by telling him the superintendent was in town. La Trobe had received laudatory reports from settlers about Robinson's successes with local Aborigines, Ross said. Robinson's ears pricked up; he was always eager to hear approbation. But his pleasure died aborning when he learnt Pevay was already aware that La Trobe was there and had failed to tell him — moreover, that La Trobe had asked Pevay about him and had then continued on to Double Corner looking for him. Robinson was furious.

> VDL Jack said he had met some gentlemen on the beach who enquired for Mr Robinson and that they had gone on to the camp. But this stupid man although he had often seen Mr La Trobe did not know [recognise] him.[25]

Whether or not Pevay did recognise La Trobe that day is immaterial. The forelock-tugging demands of the British class system were unknown to him, so his failure was likely no more than an innocent lapse — in real terms, a trifling oversight. But not to Robinson. Old misgivings about treachery recrudesced as he farewelled Ross and hurried into Portland to find La Trobe. He wanted to hear from the superintendent himself about settlers' praise of him, which he then augmented with an equally exalted account of his own. During the eight weeks he had been away, he told La Trobe, he had 'conferred with near 800 natives south of the Grampians personally and communicated with every tribe in that range of country'.[26]

The Portland incident cast further Robinsonian doubts on Pevay's trustworthiness. If the Parperloinnher were perplexed by Robinson's anger, he must also have been offended by his rebuke, although he continued dutiful and compliant as they broke camp. Robinson's umbrage, however, was undimmed. At the end of May, four days after leaving Portland, they encountered a stranded dray in charge of two men whose bullocks had strayed. One of the two had gone to borrow another team, leaving his companion to guard their load. Robinson saw the danger. 'They could not have stopped in a worse place', he wrote, 'as the natives are numerous and a loaded dray with only one man was sufficient to excite their cupidity'. He sent Pevay and an Aborigine named Benniwongham to search for the missing animals. Benniwongham soon gave up and returned alone while Pevay continued to search. It took him all day but he located the missing bullocks and drove them back to the stranded cart. The grateful draymen wanted to reward him for his effort, but Robinson, in a display of petty malice, refused to allow it.[27]

§

In Melbourne meanwhile, the chief protector's long absence had fomented further Palawa restlessness. In June, as Robinson and Pevay were beginning their return journey near present-day Coleraine, Timme and Trukanini again absconded and began free-ranging on Mornington Peninsula. Assistant Protector Thomas discovered them at Pallarangun, a sprawling acreage owned by John Hyatt where Timme had worked the previous June and where Prupilathina had also been employed. Trukanini tried to hide from Thomas when she saw him, as she had the previous month when he located her and Timme at Ballymarang. Thomas made them promise they would leave and go straight to the Protectorate Station at Narre Narre Warren. But they had no intention of curtailing their freedom. Instead they found sanctuary on a run at Tuerong, about 55 kilometres south-east of Melbourne, that belonged to Thomas's son William.[28] There they remained until September, when Pevay, just back from his western journey and beginning his breakout, would come with Planobeena and

Mathabelianna to retrieve them. It was to be a fateful reunion. When the five left Tuerong, they would do so as rebels determined to seize their liberty. And they would leave with a gun.

§

That June, as Robinson progressed through the wintry Koroit region, a few kilometres north of Warrnambool, he observed how dramatically the Aboriginal population had shrunk since the first seeds of colonisation were sown. 'The numerous native fires, as seen by [explorer Thomas] Mitchell, no longer darkened the air with smoke', he wrote, 'not a solitary smoke of a native fire was to be seen. Nor does the original inhabitant roam in freedom and at will over the green hills and valleys of the Wannon as recorded by that traveller'.[29] Mitchell himself had begun the eradication when he passed through only five years before Robinson. He had slaughtered dozens of Aborigines at Mt Dispersion, setting a bloody precedent for the settlers who followed. Pevay understood the prevalent ethos of violent extermination only too well. At every stage of their western journey he and Robinson heard stories of five years of murders and massacres of Aborigines by colonists. Alexander Campbell had boasted to Robinson of slaughtering 20 Aborigines in retaliation for the killing of a single stockman.[30] Tales of bloodshed reverberated with Pevay and troubled Robinson, as did the profusion of firearms he saw in the hands of settlers and their often-disreputable employees. 'It is distressing to see the arms and ammunition at the different stations and appalling to see the double[-barrel] guns . . . placed in the hands of the white savages', he wrote.[31] Some stations even mounted swivel guns – small cannons. Pevay saw the guns and listened in silence to the tales of carnage. They echoed his experiences and the grim stories his own people told of whites stealing black land and defending their thefts with slaughter. Yet in that big big country of Port Phillip he had seen that there was abundant space where Palawa might roam free like the Aborigines and avoid murderous whites.

Breakout!

As the party made its slow way back toward Melbourne, Pevay began to feature more often in Robinson's writing, but now, after Portland, the entries were jaundiced. Only Pevay's mishaps, misunderstandings, and other shortcomings, and the reprimands they engendered, flowed sourly from his pen. Now he rarely trusted Pevay to go off alone. If he himself did not go as escort, he sent Myatt in his place, although he had already characterised the convict as 'useless, almost an incumbrance [sic]'.[32] But Myatt's company became for Pevay a second discordant partnership. Despite his own lowly standing in colonial society, Myatt racially disparaged the Parperloinnher, habitually derogating him as 'a black bugger'.[33] Pevay was familiar with white men's invective. He understood the meaning of and the malice in Myatt's words. He knew they were meant as a rejection of him as Myatt's equal, as something lower than the lowliest of white men.

Despite this atmosphere of intolerance and mistrust, Pevay continued to be useful, helping Robinson locate Aboriginal tracks and campsites, although negative journal entries hint that his stoic accordance hid a rising tide of resentment and rebellion.[34] Its harbinger was a minor incident of defiance late on 4 July in the Grampians as he and Robinson were searching for Aboriginal signs. Finding none, Robinson 'proposed to VDL to ascend Mt Abrupt [826 metres] to look for smoke'. He began the climb, leaving Pevay to follow him after tethering the horses. Instead 'VDL lay down and did not follow'.[35] Five days later, still in the Grampians, Robinson noted another act of insurrection, this one serious enough to trigger his outright wrath. The party's horses had strayed overnight, so he sent Pevay and Myatt in heavy rain to find them. They were gone for some hours. As Robinson was sitting in his tent making notes in his journal, he was startled to hear a gunshot. When Pevay and Myatt returned with the missing horses soon afterward, he questioned them about the shot. Pevay was responsible, Myatt said. He had fired his pistol at a kangaroo. Suspecting subversion, Robinson was furious. 'I reprehended the man for his conduct', he thundered, 'that we had not come so far to shoot kangaroo but to communicate with the natives, and their firing off that shot might so alarm them as [to] prevent my communicating with them – and frustrate my plans. And it was with reluctance I consented to his having the pistol.'[36]

A tighter rein was needed. Later that day Robinson felt compelled to take Pevay with him when he rode out of camp to procure meat from a settler named Thomson a few kilometres away. They found the station but it was deserted; Aboriginal raids had forced Thomson to abandon it. The nearest settler from whom meat might be obtained, Robinson learnt from two travellers, was Richard Bunbury, whose selection was at the foot of Mt William about 13 kilometres farther on. Robinson's frustration at the news was tempered by the discovery nearby of another enormous eel-catching edifice 'resembling the work of civilized man', he opined. He was impressed and fascinated.

> A specimen of art of the same extent I had not before seen and therefore required some time to inspect it ... These trenches are hundreds of yards in length. I measured at one place in one continuous trepple [sic] line for the distance of 500 yards [462 metres]. These treble watercourses led to other ramified and extensive trenches of a most tortuous form. An area of at least 15 acres [six hectares] was thus traced over ... On first seeing these works ... the VDL native was struck with amazement and exclaimed 'Tar le winem paner wrongwaly wornaddud' – 'Oh dear, look at that! Black fellow never tired'.[37]

But they needed meat, not distraction. After giving Pevay his own mount, which was faster than Pevay's, to speed his return, Robinson ordered him to ride back 'to the camp and bring forward the van ... I should wait there until he came'.[38] While he waited at Thomson's he amused himself by examining the eel trap. Time passed; nobody came. By nightfall Robinson was worried. 'My mind was racked to account for the cause of their non-arrival', he wrote. His distrust of Pevay ballooned. All the man had to do was deliver his message to Robinson's party and then lead them back to Thomson's, where

Breakout!

Robinson was waiting. It was not far. It should not have taken long. Where was Pevay? Had he deserted, still smarting from the Portland reprimand and that morning's rebuke?

Nightfall, damp and midwinter frigid, deepened his concern. Even after building a crude shelter he was unable to sleep, fearing attack by Aborigines and unnerved by howling dingoes. He decided not to wait for the cart. When the rising moon provided enough light he rode off on Pevay's horse, leaving at his campsite at Thomson's a note explaining that he had 'gone to cattle station, 8 miles north'. He reached Bunbury's mid-morning but was surprised to find that, despite the note he had left, his cart was not already there waiting for him (a seemingly impossible expectation in the circumstances). For the rest of the day he rode anxiously around Bunbury's 15,000-hectare run, searching without success for his missing party. Next morning the weather worsened, bringing cold wind and rain, further souring his mood until, at 11 o'clock, Myatt rode up. He vindicated Pevay, telling Robinson that the Parperloinnher had complied with his instructions: he had led the party to where Robinson had said he would wait and told them Robinson said they were to wait there for him. When he did not appear, they first assumed he had been slain by Aborigines, but after finding his rough campsite and his note they trailed him to Bunbury's. Relief at the cart's arrival later that day stilled Robinson's perturbation. 'Vexed as I had been', he wrote, 'I was glad nothing had happened'.[39] Yet he made no journal entry clearing his Palawa companion of suspected wrongdoing or praising his faithful compliance with instructions. Nor did he relinquish his adverse view of the man, especially when another display of Pevay's rebelliousness stoked his ire only four days after they left Bunbury's.

> Soon after day light the messenger started for Boloke accompanied by Pevay . . . About noon the messenger returned and said Pevay rode on and would not stop for him. I was, I thought, doomed to disappointment.[40]

'It was a big big country'

That sentence – 'I was, I thought, doomed to disappointment' – encapsulated Robinson's attitude. He was wholly disdainful of Pevay, to whom he had never warmed as he had to Timme. After more than a decade of close daily association he characterised him as a man who could never be trusted to act in a predictable way – a man irretrievably beyond civilising. Furious, fearing the Parperloinnher had absconded, he ordered Myatt and the unnamed messenger to ride out, find Pevay, and bring him back. It proved unnecessary.

> Soon after they left they met Pevay returning who said he had seen some blacks on a creek and they ran from him. He called and showed them damper but they would not stop ... He also said there were natives at a shepherd's hut close by. He spoke to them (in English) but they would not come with him.[41]

The explanation was wasted on Robinson. He let fly. 'Had Pevay, instead of riding on, frightening the natives, bawling in broken English ... which they did not understand[,] taken the messenger [with him]', he fumed, 'a communication would have been open'.[42]

Trailing clouds of antipathy, they moved on. If Robinson made no adverse comment about his Palawa guide during the fortnight that followed, neither did his journal note any thaw. As the travel-weary party approached Burrumbeep, William Kirk's station south of present-day Ararat about 200 kilometres from Melbourne, Robinson, who was mounted, seized an opportunity to needle Pevay, who was on foot.

> I was amused at VDL who had a difficulty to keep pace with the [Aboriginal] guide; he [Pevay] said he was a big one tired. I was glad of the opportunity of drilling him as he is a lazy fellow ... I cantered my horse when near the camp and the native guide kept pace with the horse. The guide amused himself with VDL; he saw he did not know where he was and he kept saying, 'big one tired, VDL; no pickerninny

way, a long way [to] Mr. Kirk . . .' Jack assented to this arrangement and was not a little surprised to find he was at Burrumbeep.⁴³

Laziness was not a trait Robinson had previously noted in Pevay, who in general had served him dutifully. And he should have known better than to humiliate a proud man with whom he had an abrasive and deteriorating relationship. Pevay suffered the chief protector's mockery, as he had his rebukes and Myatt's insults, in stoic silence. But he had a long memory. Robinson himself had commented a decade earlier that 'though slow to enrage [Palawa] never forget an injury', and Pevay forgot no wound – neither insult nor reproof, slight nor humiliation.⁴⁴ They accrued, they compounded. The 'fine stout young man' once cited as good-natured and facetious had changed during 11 years of curtailed independence and white mistreatment. A dourer mien had supplanted the cheerful expression that Thomas Bock's hand had captured a decade earlier. He had become taciturn and resentful – 'sullen, but daring', a newspaper called him.⁴⁵ He had also become a storm about to break.

§

When Robinson and Pevay reached Melbourne in mid-August they found the fraying Palawa fabric further shredded. Timme's spouse Meeterlatteenner had died while they were away and his sibling Rolepana, for whom Robinson had become responsible after John Batman's death in 1839 and who had been living at Point Nepean, was near death. Other Flinders Island internees had scattered, driven by fear of forced return to Wybalenna. Most of them understood some English and, like all prisoners, they were covert eavesdroppers on their captors' conversations, from which pertinent intelligence might be gleaned. Since Robinson had made no secret of his determination to send them back to Flinders Island, talk of being returned to that despised place with its grim remembered graveyard probably spurred their diaspora, and Robinson's long absence had provided ample opportunity for them to seek distant sanctuary. Johnny Franklin was at Colac. Wurati and one son, Droyyerloinne, had gone to Dr Allen's station; his other son, Myyungge, was believed to be working at Point Nepean. Thomas Thompson had found employment with Michael Solomon at Moodie Yallo. Timme and Trukanini, having resisted efforts to return them to the reserve, remained with William Thomas's son at Tuerong. Planobeena and Mathabelianna were still at Narre Narre Warren. Apprised of all this and having no intention of returning to Port Fairy to work for Alexander Campbell, Pevay found nothing to keep him in Melbourne. After five months' separation he was eager to reunite with Planobeena, so his pathway was clear. 'He left Mr. Robinson for the purpose of joining the rest of his family at the Protectorate Station under Mr. Thomas', a newspaper reported, 'and [was not] heard of again until named as the ringleader of the outrages at Western Port'.[46] He travelled first to the Narre Narre Warren Protectorate Station to reunite with his feisty wife, then took her and Mathabelianna to Tuerong to collect Timme and Trukanini. In the warming days of early spring the five Palawa set out from there to search for their missing friend Prupilathina.

Robinson too on his return saw that much had changed during his absence. Because the dispersed Palawa now seemed beyond his control, he ignored them in his journal. From 24 August until 14 October 1841, every entry about his Flinders Island charges and Batman's Palawa related only to two of them. He noted the illness, treatment, and death of Rolepana and he recorded that Johnny Franklin, Charlotte's young son, was living with a settler at Colac.[47] As to the others, he shrugged, washed his hands of them, remained obdurate about them and where they were and what they were doing, and for two months he maintained that studied and impotent indifference.

But in October something happened that was impossible for him to ignore. 'Received letter from His Honor of the murder of two white men by two VDL natives.'[48]

13

'Now was the time for revenge'

The killings should not have been a surprise. William Thomas junior, son of the homonymous assistant protector, was one who was expecting trouble. Timme and Trukanini had complained to him of their discontent, and Pevay, after reaching Tuerong with Planobeena and Mathabelianna at the end of August, also let his anger erupt. He raged to Thomas about his animosity to whites, his intention to reclaim his freedom, his thirst for revenge.

> At length they tired of the monotony [of] not being allowed to go about at their will. There was a man among them, a man superior in every respect to the others. He . . . was the leader of the malcontents here – his name was Napoleon [Pevay]. He talked about what they had suffered at the hands of the white man, how many of their tribe had been slain, how they had been hunted down in Tasmania – now was the time for revenge, they were not cooped up in an Island, they had unlimited bush to roam over at their will . . .[1]

Pevay's mind was a midden of grievances, some especially painful. Among the people he knew he had betrayed were four of his siblings – Pintawtawa, Wymurrick, Penderoin, and Pordeboic – as well as Pintawtawa's wives Laweric and Larmoderic and son Robert. All had died in and of captivity. A rage for revenge to expiate his guilt would have found favour with the three women, each of whom had suffered grievously at white men's hands, and Planobeena had once threatened to 'teach the black fellows to kill plenty of white men'.[2] As events would soon prove, an angry Trukanini also craved vengeance.

And there was more. Late in their lives Pevay and Timme told Robinson about a particular iniquity that had alienated them so profoundly that they blamed it for their breakout. They would never have taken to the bush, they said, 'only that the settler did not give them their wages and the stockmen bounced them'.³ Alfred Langhorne, for one, had reportedly defrauded Walter and Timme after their 1839 drove, and 'bounce', in slang of the eighteenth and nineteenth centuries, meant 'beat' or 'bully'.⁴ Neither of the charges, which have invariably been overlooked or undervalued, was innocuous. Although the Palawa had dutifully worked like and with white men, they had been defrauded and mistreated – unmistakably a climactic message of absolute rejection, like Myatt's racist taunts. Pevay and Timme had been compliant, spoken white men's language, worn white men's clothing, and worked alongside white men at white men's jobs, yet they were not accepted as white men's equals. They were victims of a vile attitude they had no word for – racism. They could see they would never find an agreeable place in a world dominated by white men who disparaged them and forbade them to be Palawa on Country yet refused them the freedom that Aborigines enjoyed. Helpless in that claustral limbo, they could see only one exit. They would have to forge an independent existence somewhere on the outer reaches of acceptability and they would have to be willing to fight to keep it. Better to die in a bold bid for liberty than to endure lives for ever ordered and controlled by racist white men.

Such a powder keg of wrath and resolve needed only a spark to ignite it, and one was quickly struck. Soon after seizing their freedom, they were given a motive to become killers.

§

After fetching Planobeena and Mathabelianna from Narre Narre Warren, Pevay led them to Tuerong to get Timme and Trukanini. Mathabelianna was eager to locate Prupilathina, her missing husband, last heard of 15 months earlier at Western Port. So at the beginning of September 1841 the five of them left Tuerong to search for him, stealing a gun, ammunition, and some clothing as they departed. On 4 September they arrived at Ballymarang station on the eastern shore of Port Phillip, near present-day Cranbourne.[5] Their stay was brief. Timme and Trukanini knew Ballymarang's overseer James Horsfall, for whom they had worked a few months earlier. They asked him what he knew of Prupilathina's whereabouts and he gave them shattering news. Their friend was dead, Horsfall said, shot by William Watson, overseer at a Cape Paterson coal mine about 100 kilometres further south in Western Port.[6] Why he told them that is unknown. Watson had undoubtedly never set eyes on Prupilathina, who had last been heard of at Western Port in May 1840, a full year before Watson moved there from Geelong.[7] Perhaps Horsfall intended to punish Timme and Trukanini, who had angered him when they abruptly quit his employ in May, by sending them on a futile hike to distant Cape Paterson. It matters little. What he told them was untrue, but it put a match to the powder keg and the ensuing detonation cost four men their lives.

Fired by Horsfall's allegation, they stole his shotgun and headed toward Cape Paterson, possibly robbing Robert Innes Allen's Balla Balla station as they passed through. Two days after leaving Ballymarang they were spotted and the sighting was reported to Assistant Protector Thomas.

> My Son calls & informs me that Robert and Lalarook left their employ & robb'd Station of Gun powder, shot & sundry clothes. Captn Mantuan calls & states that several Van Diemens Land Blacks are at Station by Western Port.[8]

The latter station was Thomas Rutherford's on Rutherfords Inlet at the head of Western Port. Thomas guessed they were on their way to Western Port to look for Prupilathina.[9] He was right about their destination but not about their purpose. They were no longer looking for Prupilathina. Now they were seeking the man they were told had killed him, and they were seeking revenge.

To skirt the Great Swamp at the head of Western Port they clung to the coast, travelling southward through the forested, miry, and sparsely settled country along the eastern shoreline of Western Port toward Cape Paterson and William Watson. In early September, supposedly after plundering Robert Jamieson's hut on Yallock Creek, they continued in that direction.[10] On 15 September Robert Massie and Samuel Anderson discovered the five Palawa camped on their Bass River farm, then known as Old Settlement Station, close to the coast near present-day Bass. Although the rebels carried firearms, the two squatters were not alarmed. Both had worked for the Van Diemen's Land Company at Circular Head and knew Pevay and probably Timme, Trukanini, and Planobeena. After giving the visitors flour, Massie observed that 'They must have plundered some other hut before arriving at my station as they brought a large quantity of tea and sugar with them'.[11]

At first the Palawa seemed in no hurry to move on. For an uneventful fortnight they remained at Bass River without causing concern. Anderson evidently knew Watson, so it was probably he who precipitated their departure by telling them where to find the miner's hut.[12] On 29 September they broke camp and headed straight to Cape Paterson. Even burdened with weapons, ammunition, and food, they took hardly a day to travel the final 30 kilometres. When they located Watson they approached him amiably, careful not to cause alarm, and then set up camp 'in the most friendly manner' near a temporary hut he had built for himself, his wife Mary, his daughter Elizabeth, and his son-in-law William Ginman. The rebels gave the family no cause for concern, instead biding their time 'for three or four days, from a Wednesday [29 September] to a Saturday [2 October]', Watson recalled.[13] At daybreak on that Saturday he and Ginman left to fetch supplies from their main hut some kilometres distant. It was the opportunity the rebels wanted. They waited until the two men were out of sight, then made their move. Mary Watson recalled what happened.

The five came to our hut, or within twenty yards of it, and dallied about the grounds until I gave them tea and sugar; they then went to their mia-mias,* and boiled their tea kettle which I had lent them; after having done this they brought the tea kettle back, and the women began packing up their things, the men never left the hut; shortly after this Jackey [Pevay] went into the bedroom and insisted on taking my husband's guns; Bob [Timme] then came to me and took me by the shoulders, and insisted upon me and my daughter going to their mia-mias, which we positively refused to do; with this Bob laid hold of me, and Jackey Jackey brought the muzzle of the piece to my head, and said he would shoot me if we did not go, we walked then towards the mia-mias, and they called the women back who took hold of us; two of these women I can identify as Matilda and Truganini; the women then took us on their backs and carried us across the creek** . . . We asked the women when we got across to let us hide in the scrub; they did so and we made our way into the bush, and heard the sea roaring and knew we were in the right track, we kept on forward until we came to a road that lead [sic] us to Mr. Anderson's station.[14]

Meanwhile, Pevay and Timme had stripped the hut before torching it. As flames consumed the building they moved away into nearby sandhills, where they were joined by their women. All then settled down to wait. It was evening before the unsuspecting Watson and Ginman came into view, heading for home. From afar they could see the waiting rebels, who had not bothered to conceal themselves, although twilight and distance obscured their identities. 'We saw three persons there', Watson remembered. 'I could not tell whether they were black or white men . . .'[15] Suddenly Pevay and Timme fired at the two miners, wounding Watson in the foot and elbow and Ginman in the calf.[16] Both unarmed, they bolted for the security of the hut, only

---

*   Bark huts or shelters.
** Tarwin River.

to find it a pile of embers and their wives and weapons gone. Their only option was to flee through the gathering darkness to Massie and Anderson's, where they had a relieved reunion with their wives. Massie issued firearms to Watson and two of his own men and sent them back to Cape Paterson to search for the attackers.[17] Next morning, 3 October, he dispatched a boat to Melbourne to notify authorities of the attack. He also named the culprits.

> The party consist of two men and three women. The men are named Bob, alias Jamie [sic], and Jack, the latter a stout man and I believe a native of Cape Grim, Van Diemen's Land. The women are named Truganini, Matilda and Fanny.[18]

Robert Jamieson had already set out to report the raid on his Yallock Creek hut, and on 4 October, two days after Watson and Ginman were ambushed, he arrived in Melbourne with a note to inform La Trobe that his run had been attacked and robbed by 'a large party of Aborigines'.[19] He needed help, his note said, because he expected them to attack him again.[20] La Trobe responded by ordering Ensign Samuel Rawson, second-in-command of a Port Phillip detachment of the Sydney-based 28th Regiment, to proceed to Yallock Creek. Rawson was Jamieson's partner, a 22-year-old English gentleman whose rank and background are important to this account. Born in Elland, near Halifax, Yorkshire, in 1819, he was a scion of a prominent family – his father was a doctor of laws and a justice of the peace – and he had come to the colony about two years earlier, bringing substantial capital with him.[21] Soon after arriving he had been offered and had accepted a commission in the 28th Regiment. He had also paid £1000 for a share in Jamieson's run, about 80 kilometres from Melbourne, where he was now headed in response to La Trobe's order. He reached Yallock Creek on 8 October.

§

After wounding Watson and Ginman the Palawa rebels had lurked around Cape Paterson, the implacable Pevay being determined to kill Watson if he came back. Watson did return, but he had Massie and Anderson's two farmhands in support, and all three were armed. Pursuers and pursued had a brief skirmish late on 5 October, when Watson's men spotted Timme on a sandhill. They fired at him but missed, after which the rebels disappeared in the scrubby dunes.[22]

The next day a third group appeared at Cape Paterson, unaware of the prevailing strife. Six men – Thomas Robins, William Cook, Samuel Evans, and others recorded only as Howard, Ned, and Yankee from the Lady Bay whaling station on Wilsons Promontory – were hiking along the coastline toward Melbourne to buy supplies. Before reaching the mine they encountered the rebels, who demanded to know if it were they who had fired at Timme the previous evening and put a bullet hole in his jacket. The whalers said they had not and then moved on.[23]

At the mine the whalers found Watson's main hut unoccupied and decided to rest there. When they noticed several people 200 or 300 metres distant, too far away to identify, they assumed them to be the absent miners, so Cook and Yankee went out to make contact. A few minutes later those in the hut heard two shots fired close together. Evans went outside to investigate but saw nothing to alarm him, as he later deposed.

> I saw four or five persons who had dogs with them running down towards the beach. We still thought they were the miners and I said they must be shooting birds or kangaroo.[24]

Evans returned to the hut, stretched out, and slept for more than an hour. When he awoke and found Cook and Yankee had not yet returned, he decided to investigate. About 300 metres from the hut he encountered Watson with Massie and Anderson's two men.

> I held up my hands for fear they would fire at me: one of them fired over my head. I asked them if they had fired any shots lately. Mr Watson said 'No'. I then informed him that there had been two shots

fired and that our two mates had been absent for about an hour and a half. Mr Watson said it must be the blacks and asked us whether we had seen them: a man of Anderson's called Patrick said he would go and endeavour to find our mates.

In less than 10 minutes he returned and said the men were shot and both dead close to the beach.[25]

The whalers' bodies were slumped on bloodied sand about 300 metres from the hut. From concealment behind a sand hummock 30 metres away Pevay had shot Yankee and Timme had shot Cook. While Planobeena and Mathabelianna stayed on the hummock, Trukanini and the two men had then run down to their victims and been shocked to discover they had shot the wrong men – not Watson and Ginman but two of the whalers they had spoken to earlier that day. Timme later said that he had 'thought it was Mr. Watson; that was the reason why he shot them'.[26] Yankee was dead but Cook was still alive and 'able to run . . . about twenty yards . . . where he immediately fell upon his knees, and begged hard for his life, but . . . Truckanniny . . . and Jack, came up with two roots of a tree, and beat his brains out'.[27]

The four shocked whalers went out with Watson and his two companions to view the bodies. Yankee had died instantly. 'There was a hole in each ear', Thomas Robins deposed. 'He had been bleeding in each ear, blood upon the sand and on his clothes.' Cook had 'blood issuing from his side. His head looked as if it had been knocked about with sticks. Four pieces of stick lay near the body, thick as my wrist.' Watson added that 'Cook was lying on his back, shot through the side. A hole right through perforated the body and came out at the back, and his head was dreadfully cut with clubs or sticks.'

Toward evening, watched by four not-quite-identifiable figures about 400 metres away, Watson and the whalers buried the corpses in a sand gully above the highwater mark. Watson said the watchers were blacks; Robins said they were carrying what looked like guns. He told Massie that 'The Blacks were at this time on an adjacent hill making gestures. The men went in pursuit of them . . . but were unsuccessful in capturing any of them . . .'[28] He later recalled how the rebels evaded and frustrated their pursuers.

> [W]e went in pursuit of them, and got a view of them as follows: Now we would see two of them, and then three and four, and so on, but never obtained a view of the five together; these were seen in various ways, such as on their knees, sometimes behind trees, &c., and last time we saw them they were crawling on their knees, and they got out of our sight.[29]

Thwarted and with darkness encroaching, they gave up the chase and returned to Massie and Anderson's, trailed at a distance by the rebels. Next day, 7 October, Watson and Ginman, with their wives and the four surviving whalers, borrowed Anderson's boat to sail to Melbourne to report the attacks, but three days later they had progressed only as far as Rawson and Jamieson's station at Yallock Creek. Rawson, who had arrived two days before, was surprised to see them and alarmed by their news.

> At about 5.00 p.m. a large party, consisting of two coal miners and wives, and four whalers arrived from Massie and Anderson's in a boat with the intelligence of the murder of two of their party by some V.D.L. blacks who are now at liberty in that neighbourhood – the murders had taken place near Cape Paterson but the blacks are supposed to be near Massie and Anderson's.[30]

By himself Rawson could do nothing. Next day, however, unexpected reinforcements arrived by boat: Commissioner of Crown Lands Frederick Armand Powlett and two policemen, there to oversee land sales to squatters.[31] Powlett was a police magistrate, so his duty when he heard the news was clear: find the culprits and bring them to justice as quicky as possible. Three days later neither he nor Rawson had moved from Yallock Creek.

§

Jamieson's note, delivered to La Trobe on 5 October, had given the superintendent his first news of trouble at Western Port. A week later, word reached him that the Palawa rebels had killed two whalers. He informed Robinson by letter of the killings and named those responsible.[32] Although that day's *Port Phillip Patriot* also reported that the 'horrible outrages' had been committed by 'two of the Van Diemen's Land blacks brought over here by Mr. Robinson', the chief protector of Aborigines was moved to neither action nor written comment.[33] Not until 17 days later did he 'proceed to Dandenong in quest of the two VDL blacks', and then only after a presumably testy order from La Trobe spurred him into motion.[34] By then there had been more attacks, more robberies, more bloodshed.

§

Under cover of darkness on the day of the killings the rebels had trailed Watson as he made his way back to Massie and Anderson's with the four whalers. The Palawa made camp near there, at Settlement Point, after which a stealthy foray to Massie and Anderson's – likely looking for Watson – enabled them to purloin two bullet moulds. Killing Watson remained their objective, so from their hideout they might have watched with frustration as he and the others climbed aboard Anderson's boat and pushed off for Melbourne on 7 October.

Even with their quarry gone, the five were in no hurry to move on. The following day Pevay and Timme appeared at John Hawdon's run, adjacent to Massie and Anderson's. Hawdon's employee John Langham encountered them about five kilometres from his hut. His brief recounting of the meeting sounds innocuous, suggesting he was unaware of the killings. 'I saw the two men . . . they were well armed', Langham said. 'I had a long conversation with them'.[35] Four days later he would encounter them a second time, but amiable colloquy was not to be a feature of that meeting.

Breakout!

The rebels returned to Hawdon's run on 12 October and approached the hut. Langham and a workmate named John Bourke, having become aware of the killings by then, barricaded themselves inside, warily observing the visitors through a keyhole. When the rebels saw they were being watched they fired shots into the door and then tried to set the hut alight by shooting into the thatched roof. Langham later described the ensuing firefight.

> On looking out of the hut I saw two gins* crossing the creek; I told John Bourke that they were there, and shortly after [that] the blacks fired, the ball came through the reeds of the hut and out of the thatch; we fired and they returned the fire, I then fired two shots and they returned us, we fired six altogether and they fired three, after that the dogs barked in the direction the blacks were, we then ran away to Mr. Jamieson's station [at Yallock Creek] being short of ammunition . . .[36]

They had to force a slab off the hut wall to escape. Once the attackers realised the two men had fled, they broke in and helped themselves to Hawdon's provisions and a pair of Langham's trousers before moving on.[37] Nearby was the 3100-hectare tract selected by Thomas Armstrong and George Westaway. More supplies could be had there.

Meanwhile Langham and Bourke had burst breathlessly into Jamieson's hut to beg for help. Inside were Ensign Rawson, Commissioner Powlett, and the two Border Police. They had been there, inactive, for three days with Fitzherbert Mundy, a bibulous local squatter from the selection he'd named Red Bluff. Seven men – a considerable armed force – were now gathered at Jamieson's. Powlett's response should have been to lead them all straight to Hawdon's, where the hostile Palawa had so recently been and might be still. Instead, he gave the shaken Langham and Bourke ammunition and sent them back alone. They made a wary return to Hawdon's, approaching the hut with weapons primed and ready, but the rebels had disappeared. Six pairs of blankets and 90 kilograms of flour had disappeared with them.

---

* An often-derogatory term for Aboriginal women.

Powlett's decision not to support their return is curious to say the least. He chose instead a strangely inappropriate action: to immediately resume sailing toward Cape Paterson — a dereliction of obvious duty, it might be thought — away from where the culprits were known to be. Mundy offered to assist by riding along the coast and lighting a clifftop fire to guide the boat to a suitable landing place. Although daylight was fast fading, Rawson, Powlett, and the police pushed off in the boat in such haste that they neglected to load provisions. Sail was quickly hoisted but the evening was windless. They were forced to row.

> We started and we pulled for about three hours without seeing any light. We fired several shots to give notice [to Mundy] that we were near, but all to no purpose, and, after pulling till eleven o'clock, the tide having run out considerably, we were forced to land. The place where we landed was an open, reedy plain, not an ounce of [fire]wood within a mile of us. I had luckily put a bottle of brandy in the boat of which I gave a glass to all hands. We had no water and nothing to eat, so we had nothing to do but to lay down and go to sleep which we did after smoking our pipes. I slept soundly till morning, when I awoke stiff and cold, wet through with a heavy dew.[38]

Their oarsmanship had taken them no great distance, and Mundy, who had failed to light a signal fire because he had lost his way in the dark, had also been forced to sleep in the open. At sunrise both parties found their way to Red Bluff, where they breakfasted on damper and tea before returning to Massie and Anderson's. There they were given embarrassing news. Not only were the culprits still nearby, they had made a second raid the previous day, 12 October, soon after attacking Hawdon's. They had gone to Armstrong and Westaway's neighbouring run and, without being seen, helped themselves to provisions and clothing. Although George Westaway was away from his camp at the time cutting bark, he claimed that he was never out of sight of his tent but saw nothing. By the time he discovered the theft, the rebels had moved on, vanished in the surrounding scrub. Powlett and

Breakout!

Rawson, perhaps chastened after their bizarre response to the attack on Hawdon's, decided to assemble all available men to comb Westaway's run the following day.

Conditions next morning were less than ideal. Cold, rain, and clammy mist combined to make visibility poor and men uncomfortable. Fourteen of them gathered to warm themselves at Westaway's campfire and check their weapons before they divided into two parties to scour the scrubby tract. Supporting Powlett, Rawson, Mundy, the police, and Westaway were local volunteers and some of Massie and Anderson's employees. They included John Buxton, Charles Bennett, John Ireland, and Thomas Bates, as well as others recorded only as Sparrow and Andrews. Buxton later described to a newspaper the alarms and excitement of a day spent as a Palawa-hunting special constable.

> Sometime after we had been out, we heard a shot; we then went to the spot whence the noise proceeded, and lay in ambush until we heard a second [shot]; we then got up and went to the spot whence the shots had been fired; we came to the conclusion that it was the blacks, for on searching the scrub we found a quantity of wearing apparel, flour, balls, caps, and some bread [Westaway's possessions]; we heard voices; we knew that they were not white people . . . we then lay in ambush , expecting that they would return; about two hours after[,] we thought we heard a rush, but at that time could not see anything, but concluded it was the blacks; shortly after[,] we heard a cooee; I believe it was a black's cooee; thinking we were discovered, we bundled the things up, took them to Mr. Westaway's . . .[39]

Specialised help was now thought necessary, so Rawson and Powlett immediately set sail for Melbourne to enlist blacktrackers, leaving the pursuers leaderless. As they all relaxed around Westaway's campfire that night, Buxton dozed off, but he was not long asleep.

> I went to sleep, being much fatigued; about nine o'clock Mr. Westaway cried out, 'I've been shot by the blacks'; I then heard another shot, which wounded Thomas Bates . . .[40]

Both men had been easy targets in the firelight. The rebels had shot Westaway through the lung and then seriously wounded Bates, blowing off part of his chin.[41] When Bennett saw the two bleeding men crawling away from the fire into the darkness, he groped frantically for his firearm but Buxton had already seized it. 'I went into the tent to look for another gun', Charles Bennett said, 'at last I got one and went down to the fire; the shots then commenced from behind the two trees'.[42] He and John Buxton fired back. 'I then retired and reloaded', Buxton recounted, 'and then perceived one flash, as if it were from a pistol or a gun; shortly after another flash in the same direction . . . I took a spade with me, fearing lest I should meet with the blacks.' He ducked into the tent, abandoned the spade after finding another firearm, and rejoined Bennett in the dark, both men taking care to stay clear of the firelight. 'I told Bennett not to fire, as they would perceive where we were', Buxton explained, 'but if they fired, it would give us the like chance'. A shot was then fired at them from behind two large trees 20 metres away, giving Bennett a target. He took quick aim and fired back. 'We concluded there was a black fellow behind each tree[;] the flash of the fire arms gave me a distinct view of a black fellow's face along the line of the barrel.'[43]

Having discharged their weapons (and probably lacking ammunition), Buxton and Bennett had little choice but to fade into the security of the darkness like the others. Because they had been deprived of the previous day's plunder, the rebels then rifled Westaway's camp for a second time. The spoils included £22 in currency, which Timme said Pevay later burnt – a gesture of contempt, perhaps, for the money-lust that maddened white men and moved them to cheat black stockmen of their wages.[44]

They then vanished into the night, not to reappear until month's end, far distant from the strife they had caused.

14

'They would fight to the last'

On 14 October news of the whalers' killing was published in Melbourne. 'Intelligence reached town yesterday of a horrible outrage committed at the Coal Mining Company's station at Cape Patterson [sic] by two of the Van Diemen's Land Aborigines, named Bob and Jack, brought over here by Mr. Robinson, the Chief Protector of Aborigines', the *Port Phillip Patriot* reported. A detailed account of the killings and their aftermath followed, but the *Patriot* assured its readers that Commissioner Powlett and a party of the Border Police were in quest of the murderers. In truth, Commissioner Powlett was at sea with Ensign Rawson, inexpertly sailing toward Melbourne and making numerous landfalls along the way. A fortnight would pass before he and Rawson could be said to be in active pursuit of the rebels.

The five Palawa, meantime, had moved northward to the Dandenong region, about 80 kilometres from Cape Paterson's bloodied ground. Wild rumours about them circulated. In late October Assistant Protector Thomas noted in his journal that he had been told the fugitives had killed three more men and robbed three huts, but in fact there had been no more killings.[1] Two days later Thomas, who had just left Melbourne with two police and a blacktracker, learnt that the rebels had been at Langhorne's station the previous day but had moved that evening to Michael Solomon's Moodie Yallo run, site now of Keysborough, a Melbourne suburb on Port Phillip well north-east of Western Port. He hurried straight there but reached Moodie Yallo too late: the rebels had decamped again. Thomas recorded in his journal what one of Solomon's employees told him of the fear and desperation the rebels had aroused.

> [Solomon] had laid a plan for capturing the whole, & . . . had taken Bob into his hut and being frightened had made a proposition for him [Timme] to bring him his plunder in 3 days and he would buy them of him, that [Solomon] had [then] gone to town to give information to Mr. Powlett – that I [Thomas] had better go immediately to town, stating further that they were in great fear & that they thought the Blacks were not far off[,] that [the rebels] had taken a VDL Boy who had the last few days . . . taken a quantity of damper and meet [*sic*] with him who he thought gave it to a Lubra who was said to be lame . . .²

Trukanini was the limping woman; she was suffering from swollen legs. The 'VDL Boy' was Thomas Thompson, the former Flinders Island internee whose value as a source of provisions and information had been one of Moodie Yallo's attractions. Timme too had once worked there, so his knowledge of the lie of the land, its water sources, and its secure camping places was another. When Solomon called him into his hut, Timme listened to the settler's proposal and appeared to acquiesce, but the rebels were not fooled. As soon as Solomon rode off toward Melbourne they abandoned Moodie Yallo, taking Thomas Thompson with them, and headed southward, back toward Western Port.³

By the time Solomon reached Melbourne, reports of the rebels' deeds were causing consternation far and wide, not least because they were being blamed for imagined offences and credited with improbable feats of mobility and geographical reach. The *Port Phillip Patriot* sounded a typical alarm.

> A private letter received yesterday says–'The Van Diemen's Land blacks are continuing to commit horrid outrages in the neighbourhood of Cape Schank, Western Port and Arthur's Seat, and being well armed, the settlers are kept in perpetual terror' . . . Since the above

Breakout!

was written we have received intelligence that the same bloodthirsty ruffians have attacked several stations in the neighbourhood of Dandenong, and have shot four white men. Two were killed at Mr. Ruffy's station. The Western Port settlers have applied to Mr. Powlett for the protection of the Border Police.[4]

The Ruffy brothers' station was probably the 12,500-hectare Mayune on Western Port – they had another run, Tomaque, adjoining it on the south-west – but no other report exists of a Palawa raid or any killings there. Next day another newspaper piled fuel on the fires of panic by accusing the rebels of atrocities.

> The daring party have extended their depredations to Dandenong and its vicinity, plundering Messrs Munday's, Westaway's and different other stations and committing unmentionable atrocities . . .[5]

It added that the 'three women . . . are as well skilled in the use of the firearms they possess as the males'. The 'unmentionable atrocities' were journalistic invention.

Nevertheless, blacks killing whites . . . indignation . . . outrage. A prompt punitive response was demanded. Rawson and Powlett had reached the town after several days' sailing from Westaway's, during which time they had called at various stations to warn squatters of the rebels' breakout, thereby heightening the general panic and 'putting them in a great state of alarm'. After reaching Melbourne their pursuit was further delayed by such obligations as attending a ball in Geelong, and it was not until 29 October that they rode out of Melbourne to resume the manhunt. At Dandenong they joined Thomas's posse, which now included six blacktrackers, six policemen, and a colonist named Airey.[6] Twelve of them were mounted and they were supported by a cartload of supplies, but Rawson was dubious about the participation of Thomas, whom he described as 'a harmless inoffensive man, and, tho' living all his life in the bush, yet knew little of its ways'.[7] Thomas, however, despite subsequent comical episodes, would prove to be the rebels' nemesis. A devout and humane man, he would also be the only person to make an effort to see that justice was done.

§

Having traversed Ballymarang, where Thomas Thompson left them, the rebels appeared on 30 October at Robert Innes Allen's Balla Balla station, adjoining Mayune. They concealed themselves to wait and watch until Allen and his four men went away to work. Planobeena and Mathabelianna then broke cover and approached the hut where a lone female servant was working. After asking for tea and sugar, they went inside with her, quickly followed by Pevay and Timme, who produced a gun and demanded she show them where Allen kept his firearms. The terrified servant obeyed. After taking Allen's firearms – two shotguns and two pistols – and all his ammunition, the rebels moved on, leaving the servant shaken but unharmed.[8] Perhaps it was she to whom they gave a message for relaying to the police: they would fight to the last rather than be taken alive.[9]

Unaware that Powlett and his men were not far behind – they had reached Balla Balla the day of the raid – the five Palawa continued slowly southward, their progress hampered by loot and Trukanini's lameness. The posse were trying to pick up the raiders' trail but they had disguised their passage by walking in cattle tracks. On 31 October they made camp in a carefully chosen location that was well screened by scrub while allowing them a clear view across the tracts of flat open country that surrounded their bivouac. There, secure, they relaxed.

Initially their track-concealing tactics had worked; Powlett's blacktrackers had lost the trail. But the direction the rebels had taken was clear enough for the posse to push on with some confidence. Soon they were rewarded with a sighting of the fugitives' camp. They halted a safe distance away, hidden by dense bush, and contemplated how best to proceed. It was not going to be easy; the rebels had chosen their campsite shrewdly. Rawson described the terrain and the problems it posed.

> [W]e saw some people about 200 yards off. We were on a small thickly wooded hill. Immediately in front of us was an open flat, about 150 yards wide and then a thick scrub, in which we could see our opponents. Behind them was the sea [Western Port].
>
> We dismounted and consulted how we should attack them. It was an awkward place for they could pick us off as we crossed the flat without our being able to see them. After reconnoitering [*sic*] we determined to charge across. Accordingly, at a given signal, we started from our shelter into the flat, and immediately every horse was floundering up to its girths, the flat being a swamp.[10]

The sudden charge by a dozen mounted men stunned the rebels, but their recovery was immediate. They seized their weapons and disappeared into the scrub as the posse struggled in the mire. Distressed horses plunged and whinnied. Riders cursed. After a difficult time spent extricating the animals, Powlett's men resumed pursuit, casting about for tracks. Around midday they sighted the rebels a kilometre away and spurred their mounts into another charge.

> We had a beautiful race, every horseman off as hard as he could go. But the villains took [to] a swamp which the horses could not cross. We had to go a mile [1.6 kilometres] to a crossing place, and then return. We now lost all tracks for about an hour, the natives searching most patiently [until] about 2 p.m. One of them gave the signal, and away we went, the tracks leading for my station now about seven miles [11 kilometres] off with four creeks intervening about halfway there. The natives pointed out a smoke rising amongst the trees . . .[11]

The posse's hour-long search for tracks had given the rebels time to escape to a secluded spot near the edge of the Great Swamp. They made camp, lit a fire, then rested, recuperating from their flight. But the blacktrackers sighted a wraith of their campfire smoke, impelling a third charge.

We galloped on, but the blacks were off. They had left almost everything. The bivouac was on the edge of an immense morass, in the middle of which we saw them, making for a thick scrub. Some horses refused to go in, and the others when they got in could not move . . . The water was about three feet [one metre] deep with long reeds and soft bottom. We all worked away . . . but could not get within shot before they reached the scrub, which was composed of tea tree, in which you could not see a yard either way. It was in the form of a triangle, each side about half a mile [800 metres] long.[12]

From their hiding places the Palawa watched Rawson and Powlett posting some men at strategic points around the scrubland before dividing the others into two parties and sending them in to search. It was a dangerous situation for the rebels. But, as they had at Cape Paterson, they deployed traditional tactics to confound and elude the searchers. '[I]t seems they must have separated, for their whistling was heard by the police while searching the scrub, making signals to one and other', a newspaper reported.[13] The frustrated pursuers combed the bush until waning light forced them to abandon their search, 'hungry, wet, tired and disappointed', as Rawson noted. 'It was no use stopping, as the place was too large to surround effectively after dark', he added, 'besides it was anything but comfortable, standing so long in the water'. During their flight the rebels had abandoned an array of stolen property, including ammunition, food, clothing, and a pocket compass, but not their firearms.[14] A newspaper reported that they made their getaway by sea after seizing Samuel Anderson's whaleboat.[15]

Safe for the moment, they concealed themselves on Rawson and Jamieson's Yallock Creek run. But they were hungry. Their escape from Powlett and Rawson had meant abandoning their provisions, so they were forced to hunt. Station hands heard their shooting and reported it to Rawson when the posse, after following tracks from the rebels' Great Swamp camp, arrived at Yallock Creek on 1 November. Although he had at his disposal about a dozen armed and mounted men, as well as fresh information that the rebels were nearby, Powlett decided reinforcements were needed. On the following day he set out for Melbourne with Thomas and Airey to seek help. When they reached Edwin Sawtell's station on the south-western fringe of the Great Swamp at the head of Western Port they encountered the chief protector of Aborigines.[16] Robinson had left Melbourne on 31 October after La Trobe ordered him to assist Powlett.[17] 'Received letter 5 p.m. from Mr. La Trobe', he wrote in his journal, 'to proceed to Dandenong in quest of the two VDL blacks. I started, slept at Clow's.'* Next day he rode to the Aboriginal station at Narre Narre Warren before travelling to Farquhar McCray's and then on to Henry Bacchus's, both in the Dandenong area, reporting that 'people much frightened'.[18] He visited various other squatters near Dandenong, which was as close as he would ever get to the manhunt. Only on 3 November and only by chance did his path and Powlett's converge at Sawtell's.

> Powlett and Thomas and Airy arrived. The natives had crossed to east side of the bay and a party was left to watch. Mr Powlett was returning to town and Airy. I ordered Thomas to cross the bay to Jamieson's and render what assistance he could. Rode around the bush looking for the plant [stashed supplies] of the natives. Powlett and Airy started [for Melbourne].[19]

The following day Robinson too set out for Melbourne, calling at Narre Narre Warren on the way. A fortnight later, as the breakout neared its climax, he headed in the opposite direction, on a westward tour that further widened the gap between him and the manhunt at Western Port.

§

Now in sole command of the posse, Rawson stayed at Yallock Creek for a few days after Powlett and the others left, but he was edgy, worried that the rebels were still in the area. Uncertain about what to

---
*   Thomas Clow's Glen Fern, 30 kilometres from Melbourne.

do, on 7 November he decided to follow Powlett's example and return to Melbourne, whereupon the posse disbanded and the manhunt stalled. After all the excitement of the chase and three tally-ho charges, everything was in stasis. The rebels were still free, their whereabouts uncertain. Their pursuers, at a loss, had ceased to pursue.

15

'By ¼ past 6 it was all over'

Fear was now widespread throughout the colony. Many stations were isolated and several remote runs at Western Port, including Hawdon's and Mundy's, had been abandoned in panic, their occupants having fled to the safety of Melbourne. A few chose not to flee but to arm themselves ready to fight. One Mornington Peninsula settler, Henry Meyrick of Colourt, had no intention of running away despite the danger. He wrote to his parents in England of the prevailing fear and the precautions he was taking.

> The whole neighbourhood has been thrown into the utmost confusion, as the newspapers would say, by three [sic] Van Diemen's Land blacks, who were brought over as servants by Robinson, the Chief Protector, and ran away, making common cause against all white men. They murdered four [sic] and robbed Allen's station which is ten miles [16 kilometres] from Colourt . . . Had they come to Colourt we would have robbed the hangman of his fee for we had guns loaded enough to have annihilated a whole tribe.[1]

Although pursuit had effectively ended and no reliable news of the rebels was heard for some time, one man had not given up. Sent by Robinson back to Yallock Creek, the intrepid Assistant Protector Thomas, in pain and on foot after falling from and then losing his horse, was scouting for the fugitives' trail. They had left the security offered by the scrubby swamplands in the northern part of Western Port and were moving again. On 5 November Thomas's blacktrackers – Lively, Poky Poky, and Buller Bullup – found their footprints about 10 kilometres south-east of Jamieson's run. Thomas immediately dispatched a message to Robinson, his boss, who had just arrived back in Melbourne after his brief sojourn in Dandenong, asking him to send urgent reinforcements. He told Robinson that 'the only way of capturing the parties will be at a station or by tracking, in which case more hands are needed, as stations have already been deserted and most of the parties fled to town. In consequence no assistance can be obtained now we have passed Mr Jamieson's station.'[2] No military man, Thomas was alone, outnumbered, outgunned, on foot, and a long way from help in that remote and now mainly deserted countryside. But the tracks were no more than a day old so he pressed on in expectation that the requested reinforcements would soon arrive.

Aware that they would be pursued, the rebels were moving south-easterly, more or less parallel to the Western Port coastline. About 8 November they slaughtered a calf at Massie and Anderson's and made camp in scrub near Settlement Point, feeling secure and in no hurry to move on, perhaps because of Trukanini's lameness. It was a serious mistake. Three days later Thomas and his blacktrackers located their hideout. Basing himself a few kilometres away at Westaway's, Thomas could do no more than keep the rebels under surveillance until help arrived. To speed the reinforcements, he sent another hastily scribbled note to Robinson with the news that he had located the fugitives. He stressed his need for urgent backup.

> Having but three blacks with me, I think it most prudent to let [the rebels] remain where they are, till the remainder of the [trackers] arrive. In fact, without more assistance in this scrubby part, I think it impossible to take them. I . . . am now near Westaway's as the station most likely to be attacked again.[3]

Robinson ignored the plea. His sole response was to complain to Thomas that the note had been written in pencil on a torn scrap of paper. Thomas responded that it was all the paper he had because all the official notepaper supplied for the assistant protectors had been kept by the chief protector for his own use.

§

Rawson reached Melbourne on 10 November after passing Powlett on the road. The rebels were still camped near his own station, he told Powlett, so they agreed to meet at Dandenong the following Friday to resume the manhunt. Rawson continued on to Melbourne, where he tried to persuade La Trobe to give him more help, but the superintendent refused to arm any Aborigines. That would be too dangerous, he said. Rawson then turned to the Aborigines camped by the Yarra. Robinson, who was readying himself to head west to the Loddon, said he had six of them willing to help in the hunt, but when Rawson went to the Aboriginal camp to collect them he found only one man prepared to go with him. He decided to send an urgent request to his commanding officer for military reinforcements.

On 12 November, as arranged, he rendezvoused with Powlett in Dandenong. The rebels, they were informed, were now at Western Port and raiding stations almost at will, although Thomas had their Settlement Point camp under surveillance. Prompt action was essential, but Powlett chose to delay until the military reinforcements arrived. As he waited he grew pessimistic about the likelihood of success. Even after the reinforcements – a corporal and eight soldiers – arrived on 16 November, he remained negative and sent a note to La Trobe to report his misgivings.

> If the blacks should continue in the scrub, I fear we shall have little chance of recapturing them; no robberies have been committed since the one at Mr. Allen's station but several cattle have been found shot on this and the adjoining run.[4]

The following day, 17 November, Powlett and Rawson and their reinforcements set out toward Massie and Anderson's run, recruiting civilian volunteers and two blacktrackers along the way. Powlett now commanded a substantial force. 'I had my border police – some mounted police . . . and eight soldiers of the 28th Regiment under my direction as a magistrate', he said.[5] In all, the posse comprised nine mounted police, the soldiers, '10 or 12' settler volunteers, four armed blacktrackers, and Powlett, Rawson, and Anderson.[6] Aiming to travel quickly, they took an inadequate single packhorse load of supplies, which were soon exhausted. They rode all day in unrelenting rain, finally arriving, wet and tired, at Westaway's at evening. Thomas greeted them with grim news. The rebels had attacked Old Settlement Station that day. A man had been seriously wounded, shot in the chest.

The rebels, needing food, guns, and ammunition, had indeed raided Massie and Anderson's that day, but there had been no shooting and no bloodshed. From concealment near the hut they had waited until the inhabitants finished lunch and Hugh Anderson, Samuel's brother, went with his men to work some distance away. As the watching Palawa hefted their weapons and approached the hut, a servant named Joseph Lonini emerged and spotted Pevay and Timme. He yelled a warning to Sarah London, who was washing dishes in the kitchen. She hurried outside to be told the blacks were in the hut, a separate building, at which she ran panic-stricken back into the kitchen to rescue her baby. But Pevay confronted her in the doorway. 'I begged of him to let me have my child', she said, '[but] he ordered me to go, and lifted one of the three guns he had on his arm towards me'. Although he assured her he would not harm the child, she ran toward the hut to seek help from Jennett Bailey the housekeeper, but Mrs Bailey had an intruder of her own to deal with – Timme.[7] '[H]e had a gun in his hand', she said; 'he pointed towards me, and then levelled his gun and said "Be off".' She did not argue. Outside she found Sarah 'in a great state of alarm' crying for her child. Lonini, who had hidden behind a tree when Pevay threatened him with a gun, now hustled the two women to safety across the creek, shouting for Hugh Anderson, as the rebels ransacked both buildings.[8] Anderson was already hurrying back, having heard Sarah's cries and Lonini and Bailey's yells, but he was unarmed. There was nothing he could except run two kilometres to get help from the adjacent station, John Thom's Hurdy Gurdy.

> I . . . went to Mr. Thom's station, where I expected to see [Assistant Protector] Thomas, who I understand had been down in the morning . . . Mr. Thomas . . . and several persons armed themselves, and accompanied me to the house; on reaching which, we found the place had been plundered of flour, sugar, tea, and many other things, amongst which were two double-barrelled guns . . . also a pistol with bayonet attached . . .[9]

Thomas had just eaten a meal at Thom's when Anderson 'came in almost exhausted saying the blacks were in his hut'. They all grabbed weapons and hastened to Massie and Anderson's where they found 'the 2 women were in a dreadful fright, Mrs Bayley could scarcely speak [sic]'.[10] But the rebels had gone, leaving no trace. They carried their pillage back to their Settlement Point camp, secure in the belief that it was well hidden. Despite the success of their raid, they had not finished with Old Settlement Station. That night they went back. Although armed men were now standing guard on the premises, the rebels had no difficulty robbing the poultry run of fowls and eggs and stealing potatoes.[11]

Safely back in their camp, they were satisfied with their efforts. As well as three additional firearms, they had gained substantial supplies of tea, sugar, flour, and potatoes, so they were well victualled and well armed. But their nocturnal sortie had also provided unwelcome intelligence: Rawson and Powlett's posse had arrived and there were now many more men and horses at Massie and Anderson's. Time to move on.

Next day Powlett's blacktrackers spent a long time examining the ground around Old Settlement Station, but when they finally found the tracks left by the long-departed rebels it was too late in the day to follow them. The following morning, 19 November, the posse took up the trail, noting that the tracks seemed to lead southward in the direction of Cape Paterson before veering more easterly toward the South Gippsland hills. Travelling apace in stifling heat, the posse paused only to refresh themselves and their horses at each creek they came to. At the second creek they discovered the fugitives' campsite from two nights earlier. Sensing that they were close, they pressed on after a brief pause and soon located the rebels' most recent campsite. It was a significant find. Abandoned around it was evidence that the five were tiring: a firearm, women's clothing, and – a stroke of luck for a famished posse with no more provisions – some potatoes, which they ate before resuming pursuit. Soon the blacktrackers found more evidence that fatigue was retarding the rebels' flight: two lines in the sand that they told Thomas were made by Timme's gun butts. The weight of the weapons was slowing him down, they said. Instead of carrying them he was dragging them along by their barrels with their butts furrowing the ground, one on either side of him. The discovery moved the trackers to perform a strange ceremony involving smoke and two mounds of earth. When Thomas asked what it meant, they explained that it symbolised the deaths and graves of Pevay and Timme.[12] They knew they were close to the end.

Six kilometres farther on they found a campfire burning. Next to it were a single bullet and some unused lead where the rebels had paused to mould more ammunition – a sign that they were preparing to fight. Hushed and tense, the searchers advanced. They were proceeding with caution through open forest when the sound of a shot stopped them dead. Nerves taut, weapons ready, hearts pounding, they waited, strained and silent. Long seconds passed. When nothing more was heard, they cautiously moved on.

Late that afternoon they came to a watercourse, thought to be Tarwin River, meandering through sandhills into the sea at Venus Bay. On the far side of the dunes was the beach, on the near side a lagoon – now named Anderson Inlet – about eight kilometres south of a ford in the river. They halted to reconnoitre, Rawson wrote, and to eat what remained of the rebels' abandoned potatoes.

> While some went by the creek, some of us went to the top of the [sand]hills, but the beach was all clear for some miles. It was now near four o'clock, so we halted and lighted a fire to roast our potatoes, as we could not do it after dark on account of being seen. We had one potato each, which we enjoyed exceedingly, and then commenced our march.[13]

Lately the rebels had changed course – their apparent veering toward the South Gippsland hills had perhaps been a feint – and they had doubled back and were moving in the direction they had come from, as though intending to return to Massie and Anderson's. If they expected the abrupt about-turn to thwart pursuit, the tactic failed. The posse stayed closely on their trail after crossing the river, hoping to catch up with the fugitives before dark, but fading light forced a halt after they had ridden about six kilometres.

> We encamped, that is to say, we laid down. Our tobacco was nearly finished, we having only about half a pipe full each, and nothing to eat, and only cold water to drink. No fire, a cold night, and having the same distance to go back that we had come before we could get anything, without [having] captured the blacks, anything but pleasant.[14]

Taking advantage of the darkness, they sent the blacktrackers ahead to scout. If the fugitives had made a campfire, the blacktrackers would locate it. They did.

> About 9.00 p.m. they returned, and to our great joy said they had seen their fire about a mile [1.6 kilometres] off, so Mr. Powlett and I immediately arranged our plans to march just before daylight, so as to come upon them at sunrise in hope of surprising them as blacks generally sleep late into the morning. Mr. Thomas wanted to go forward to negotiate with them, he being a man of peace, but that we would not allow.[15]

Debate ensued. The blacktrackers wanted to shoot the rebels but Powlett forbade it. He preferred to take them alive, Thomas noted in his journal, but the blacktrackers 'would not . . . attempt to take them alive [because] they [the blacktrackers] would [themselves] be shot'.[16] The posse was assuredly willing to use gunfire and discussed wounding the rebels in the legs to prevent their escape.[17] Then they slept.

Less than two kilometres away, near the mouth of Powlett River, the five rebels also slumbered through the chill night, unaware of their pursuers' proximity. Weary and well fed, the five slept soundly with a fire and a warm covering of stolen cloaks and blankets.

Their fireless and famished pursuers woke before dawn, numbed and damp. 'I don't know that I ever felt the Cold like it', Thomas recalled, 'all our teeth chatter'd. We just got lights to our pipes, & the [blacktrackers] are off . . . up to our knees in mud and water.' It was 20 November 1841. Pevay and Timme had just two months to live.

Rawson described the posse's stealthy advance.

> [We] arose about 4.00 a.m., a cold morning, heavy dew falling. Having examined our arms to see that all was right, we marched in silence in single file, the blacks leading to point out the way, which lay under a range of sand hills about half a mile [800 metres] from the sea. After advancing half a mile we had to cross a lagoon, water two feet [60 centimetres] deep, anything but pleasant on a cold morning with an empty stomach. We advanced some time, till we began to think the guides had lost their tracks, when just as the sun was rising, they pointed out the smoke of the fire, rising above a few shrubs about twenty or thirty yards below us. We were on a sand hill, at the bottom of which was the camp and immediately beyond that was a thick scrub, almost impassable for a black man, and quite so for a white man, and as they had dogs with them, I was afraid of their giving the alarm and giving them an opportunity of hiding in the scrub.[18]

For their surprise attack on the rebels' camp, which is said to have been at Wonthaggi between the dunes and Lake Lister, west of today's Rifle

Range Reserve, the posse was deployed in two parts.[19] '[W]e fell in, I and four blacks and Mr Powlett and party on right, Mr Rawson and party and three blacks on left', Thomas recalled. Rawson described their careful approach.

> I extended the men along the top of the hill, and then myself in the centre advanced in a kind of semicircle down upon them. Each man was six feet [1.8 metres] apart, with orders to take them alive if possible, but if they offered resistance or to escape to shoot them at once.

As they crept down the hill in the waxing light of daybreak they could see the recumbent forms of the sleeping rebels and their dogs around the campfire about 20 metres away. Despite their number, the posse managed to advance so quietly that their surprise was absolute. Then they all fired. Rawson said it happened when a policeman discharged his gun prematurely, but Thomas wrote that they 'all let fire at once'. The sudden fusillade shattered the dawn stillness. Chaos erupted. The rebels' dogs scattered and fled. Timme leapt up and ran into the adjacent bushland, abandoning his weapons. Pevay and Trukanini bolted into a different part of the scrub, but she fell when hit by one of Rawson's shots. He had 'fired both barrels, right and left, and I saw one drop', he said.[20] His ball hit Trukanini's head but 'ploughed through the scalp without fracturing the bone'.[21] Pevay meanwhile had disappeared, although those chasing him through the bush could hear underbrush snapping under his running feet. Rawson acted decisively to stop the two fleeing men.

> I immediately ordered the men to surround the scrub to prevent their escape, and then I went to reconnoitre the camp . . . [F]rom the heavy fire opened upon them, I concluded they must all be shot. While I was turning over the blankets with the end of my gun, I discovered a woman. I handed her over to a policeman to put handcuffs on her and a little further I discovered another.[22]

Like Planobeena and Mathabelianna, the stunned and bleeding

Trukanini was quickly secured. Rawson then used the women to force Pevay and Timme to surrender.

> After [the women] were secured I put a pistol to their heads and told [them] to call their companions out of the scrub if they were alive . . . Just now a man [Timme] was taken escaping from the other side of the scrub, and directly after, we saw the other haring across the country near half a mile off . . .[23]

Unencumbered and having a good start, Pevay might have escaped. But he was their comrade and their leader, and when Rawson forced the women to call out to him to surrender, he did. He stopped running and allowed himself to be seized by Corporal William Johnson and Trooper William Limont of the Border Police.[24] 'We thus had the whole party and to our astonishment only one [was] wounded . . . tho' . . . about thirty balls were sent at their heads', Rawson wrote in his journal. Thomas was more succinct. 'By ¼ past 6 it was all over.'[25]

After handcuffing the two men and fettering them with leg-irons, posse members made 'threats to kill them if they did not tell all about it – who they had killed', the women later asserted.[26] Captive but not cowed, Pevay smoked his pipe and the others also appeared unruffled as they answered questions put to them, allegedly confessing to nine robberies and four shootings, including those of Yankee and Cook. Powlett later testified that 'Bob seemed terrified slightly for a few Min's [sic]' and in his fright tried to exculpate himself by playing down his part in the killings.[27] He told Corporal Johnson that Pevay had fired the first shot at the whalers and then threatened to kill him if he did not also shoot.[28] It seems improbable. The whaler Thomas Robins swore there had been no appreciable pause between the shots fired at Cook and Yankee. 'I heard two shots fired as close together as they could be fired', he would testify at the trial.[29]

When the posse examined the rebels' camp they found 'six or seven double or single guns, and pistols', Rawson noted, 'also a large supply of ammunition'. The *Port Phillip Patriot* was more specific, reporting that the rebels had 'thirteen stand of firearms, three bags of shot and seven cannisters of powder'.[30] There was also much other heavy baggage: an assortment of cloaks and blankets, a mould for casting 50 bullets, nearly 30 kilograms of flour, a similar quantity of sugar, and several kilograms of tobacco. Although their flight had been a remarkable feat of strength and endurance, their fondness for damper and sweet tea had helped bring them down. The captured victuals were soon put to good use by the ravenous police party. They baked damper and brewed tea and shared both with their captives. In making dough for the damper, they discovered the flour contained so much spent lead shot from their opening salvo that Thomas likened it to a plum pudding.[31]

After they had all eaten, the posse divided into two parties for the first leg of the long trek to Melbourne and justice. Crucially, Rawson noted just who went where after they separated.

> Powlett took two of the prisoners and the police about 3 miles [five kilometres] further to examine the place where the two men had been murdered, while I with the soldiers and the other prisoners returned . . . [W]e reached Anderson's station about 3 p.m. where we were received with great joy, the women crying and looking upon us as their deliverers . . .[32]

Rawson's note about who went to the gravesite with Powlett and the police is very significant. Thomas too recorded in his journal what happened after the two parties diverged. He wrote that 'men Blks took us to the spot were [sic] killed 2 men', while 'Rawson and party took the women towards the station'.[33] With Pevay and Timme as guides, Powlett, with Thomas and the police, soon found the burial place. 'I had the grave opened', Powlett testified, saying he thought there were two bodies in it but 'the effluvia was so offensive I did not go close'. He reported that Pevay and Timme now 'appeared to disagree as to who fired the first shot; they seemed to accuse each other'. He asked them why they had killed the two whalers, to which 'they replied they thought it was Watson'.[34]

Meanwhile, Rawson's party, with the three Palawa women, had reached Massie and Anderson's, where Hugh Anderson, a former ship's surgeon, dressed Trukanini's wound while they waited for Powlett's group to rejoin them.[35] It did not take long. Late that afternoon the two parties were reunited at Old Settlement Station, whereupon a blacktracker known as Old Joe shook his fist at Pevay and offered £5 for a shot at him.[36]

After a day's rest they departed for Melbourne, the prisoners on foot with their escort of police and military. Rawson and Powlett chose to sail but fickle winds forced them to wade ashore and walk to Rawson's station, where they were joined soon after by the prisoners and their escort.

Four days later, shackled and handcuffed, Pevay and Timme and the three women were marched into Melbourne. It was Thursday 25 November 1841.[37] News of their arrival was picked up by the *Port Phillip Herald*, which published a long story about them, their breakout, and their arrest 'kindly given to us by one of the mounted police, who assisted at their capture, and, indeed, was the man who had the honor of first seizing one of the villains in his attempt to escape' – Corporal Johnson. The following excerpt from the story is believed to be an unadulterated account of the prisoners' first admissions to their captors. As the earliest to be recorded, it is probably the most authentic narrative of what the rebels confessed when first captured.

> The prisoners have told the police of all the depredations committed by them, and admitted that they had murdered the two sailors . . . thinking that they were Mr. Watson and his son-in-law, Mr. Jinman [sic] . . . 'Jack' told the party that he shot one of the sailors with a gun . . . and 'Bob' said that he fired at the second with slugs, and wounded him in three places . . . but one of the women, named Truckaninny (Bob's wife), and Jack, came up with two roots of a tree, and beat his brains out![38]

The chief protector of Aborigines, just back from the Loddon, noted in his journal that the rebels had been 'lodged in the watch-house and subsequently examined at p.m. I heard accidentally of their arrival and attended.'[39]

The five rebels had been at large for little more than six weeks after shooting Cook and Yankee. Pevay's reclamation of his freedom had lasted just three months.

16

'Shooting at Watson would hang them'

What awaited them in Melbourne proved not to be justice but ineluctable revenge, for baleful racial forces in unseen play had made 1841 a particularly inauspicious time for blacks to be facing murder charges in the colony of New South Wales. This singularity had emerged in April 1838 when Aborigines escaped unpunished after slaying eight stockkeepers at Benalla, north of Melbourne. The public wrath thus aroused had intensified eight months later when Governor Gipps and the Executive Council set a controversial precedent by approving the execution in Sydney of seven colonists convicted of massacring Aborigines at Myall Creek. The hangings caused a furore. Colonists angry that black killers of whites at Benalla had gone unpunished were further incensed that whites had been executed for murdering blacks at Myall Creek. Racial hatred intensified. After the executions 'settlers were more intent than ever on destroying the blacks', Assistant Protector Thomas observed, adding that poisoning Aborigines was widespread.[1] Despite the passage of three years since the Myall Creek executions, settler anger was undiminished. It would not do. White deaths must be avenged. Blacks must pay. So while most of Melbourne's population were making plans for Christmas, one official was scheming to ensure that the culprits would not escape retribution this time.

The fate of Pevay and Timme was thus ordained before they ever faced judge and jury.

Breakout!

§

One day after being lodged in the watchhouse, the five rebels were escorted into the police office for formal committal hearings. Pevay was wearing the patched trousers – John Langham's – he had taken from Hawdon's hut. Hearing their case was Major George Frederick St John, a notoriously corrupt and lazy magistrate whom Robinson called 'a troubled man'.[2] Witnesses testified about the attacks on Westaway's and Hawdon's stations but could not positively identify the prisoners as the perpetrators. William Watson, however, was untroubled by doubt. When the hearing resumed the following day, 27 November, he 'identified the prisoners as the persons by whom he was wounded', despite the attack having been in the fading light of evening.[3] Two days later he was reported to have told the hearing that 'we saw three persons ... I could not tell whether they were black or white men'.[4] When two firearms and an axe were produced, he identified them as those 'stolen from his hut by Jackey Jackey'.[5] His wife and daughter identified other stolen items and testified that the five accused were those who had robbed and burnt the family's hut and threatened their lives.[6]

Commissioner Powlett now strode forward to testify. Bible in hand, he swore to tell nothing but the truth. Then he unleashed the lies he intended to ensure the rebels' conviction. 'On the 20th October [sic = November]', he swore, 'I was shown the place where the men was murdered ... *the women* pointed it out to me [emphasis added]'. The last statement was untrue. As Rawson and Thomas had recorded in their respective journals, only Pevay and Timme had guided Powlett to the whalers' grave. No woman went with them.

Continuing in the same vein, Powlett refined his story as he testified. He swore that at the grave he saw 'several sticks or waddies ... which one of them said had been used for the purpose of finishing their victims, or words to the same effect; *she* further described that Bob had fired one shot and that it took effect, upon which the women beat out their brains with the sticks [emphasis added]'.[7] This statement too was perjury. The 'one of them' referred to was obviously a woman, evinced by his use of the feminine singular pronoun as 'she further described' what happened. Yet because no woman was there, it follows that his claim of one woman implicating all three of them in the fatal beating was also false.

There was more. 'Mr. Powlett deposed that one of the jins [sic] had without either threats or solicitation [on] his part described to him the circumstances attendant on the murder of the two unfortunate whalers . . . and had in corroboration of her statement produced the bloody bludgeons with which the inhuman wretches had completed their butchery.'[8] Since the bludgeons or waddies had been left close to the victims' burial site, that was the only place and time they could have been produced for Powlett to see, so he was reinforcing his lie that at least one of the women had gone with him to the whalers' grave. This invented confession by a woman who was never at the grave was the basis of his evidence and of the prosecution case against the rebels.

Because confessions made under duress were not admissible as evidence, Powlett was challenged by Redmond Barry, the young Irish barrister defending the accused. 'Was this a voluntary confession?' he asked, to which Powlett replied 'Most decidedly, there was no threat held out to her whatever'.[9] Since there was no woman there at the grave, no such confession was made, voluntary or otherwise. The only confession was the one made immediately after the five rebels were captured — the one reported by Constable Johnson. But as the three women told a clergyman, that was made only after Powlett's men had threatened 'to kill them if they did not tell all about it — who they had killed'.[10] Because they were unbaptised, however, they could not testify in court to that potentially mitigating fact. But it has been observed that Barry's challenge was valid.

> There is a very clear argument that anything said by the Tasmanians at that time or subsequent to the dispersal,* given its conduct generally and the salvoes of shots and the threats made with guns to the women's heads, should have been completely discounted by the court as unfair and inadmissible, even in 1841.
>
> This would have been reasonably well understood by Powlett . . . [11]

Corporal Johnson's testimony included confirmation of the killers' motive. He swore that 'Mr. Powlett asked them what made them shoot the whalers; one of them, I cannot say which, said he thought it was Mr. Watson . . .'[12] Timme himself confirmed that motive when he spoke up during the hearings.

> The prisoner Bob . . . said he met the two whalers and asked if they had shot [at him] the night before. They said not. Bob said he thought it was them and said the ball passed through his jacket. Next time he saw them he thought it was Watson, that was the reason why he shot them.[13]

Timme well knew what Watson looked like after four days camped with the miner and his family, and since he had accosted the whalers only an hour or two before the killings, he should also have recognised them. But Cook and Yankee were ambushed from behind a sandhill. The shooters would have risen quickly from concealment and taken hasty aim without verifying their victims' identities. It was enough that they 'thought it was Watson'. The motivation, so often repeated, has never been in doubt. As a newspaper observed, Pevay too 'confessed that revenge had led him to commit the murders'.[14]

When the whaler Samuel Evans took the stand he gave a detailed statement about events at the time of the killings (quoted at pp. 180–181 above). So much evidence had to be heard that the *Port Phillip Gazette* commented on 'the protracted character of the examination, large benches of Magistrates having sat since Tuesday, to adjudicate on the case; the investigation commenced on Friday, continued Saturday,

---

*   The attack on the rebels' camp and its immediate aftermath.

was resumed on Monday, and proceeded with on Tuesday . . .' Every hearing drew a capacity crowd, one of whom, 'In a peculiar but hardly surprising breach of protocol', was John Walpole Willis, the judge who was to try the prisoners.[15] Not present, however, and surprisingly never called to testify were two of the three men who led the manhunt and took part in the capture: Samuel Rawson and William Thomas.

On the final day, 30 November, Barry was absent when St John 'committed Bob and Jack to take their trials for the wilful [sic] murder of William Cook and the man known as Yankee, and the three lubras Matilda, Truganini and Martha for being accessories before and after the fact'.[16] By then the evidence given had already convinced the public of the prisoners' guilt, to which opinion the *Port Phillip Gazette* gave voice. 'The crimes alleged against them have been too clearly made out to leave any chance of acquittal, and their employment under Mr. Robinson for such a number of years, precludes any hope of mercy on the plea of ignorance.'[17]

§

When Robinson visited the prisoners on 2 December, taking with him Rev. Joseph Orton, founder of the Wesleyan Missionary Society's mission to the Australian Aborigines, he noted that Timme was again unambiguous about the rebels' motive for killing Cook and Yankee: 'Bob said Mr Horsefold [sic] told them Watson shot Isaac and he meant to have shot Watson'.[18]

The trial was scheduled to begin on 4 December, two days after that visit, with the prosecution case being led by another Irish lawyer, the crown prosecutor James Croke, but it was adjourned until 15 December. Although no explanation for the postponement has been found, it is perhaps germane that Ensign Rawson, who ought to have been a material witness, was slated to leave Port Phillip, which he did on 7 December, never to return.[19] That seems to have suited the prosecution, which made no attempt to delay his departure or even to obtain a deposition from him before he sailed. Yet on 29 November, only eight days before Rawson left, Judge Willis had told Crown Prosecutor Croke that 'steps should be taken to prevent witnesses leaving the Colony', after Croke informed him that witnesses in a larceny case he was prosecuting had left Port Phillip.[20] In the light of subsequent events it is plausible that the trial was adjourned explicitly to ensure Rawson was out of the way before it resumed and consequently could not be called to testify.

Supporting that hypothesis are several problematic events that occurred between the trial's adjournment and its resumption. On 9 December Assistant Protector Thomas visited Robinson and then went on to see Powlett. Thomas's note of the meeting with Powlett is brief but significant: 'See Crown Commissioner, hear Waler [sic] Evans Examined'.[21] Why 'Examined'? Evans had already given sworn evidence to the committal. Powlett plainly had some other reason for summoning the whaler to his office six days before the trial resumed. Seen through the lens of what subsequently happened in court, it is deducible and near-certain that Powlett was persuading Evans not to testify. Hearing that would naturally have disturbed Thomas. He left Powlett's and went to see Croke. Two days later Croke informed Robinson of Thomas's visit to him, after which Robinson recorded an enigmatic précis of what Croke told him about that meeting.

> Called on Croke[,] gave him names of VDL natives.* Thomas came to Croke about the VDL natives. Croke said the shooting with slugs at Watson would hang them.[22]

Much might reasonably be inferred from that cryptic note. The third sentence suggests that Thomas told Croke about what he had heard at Powlett's and that Croke, who considered Evans 'a most important witness', responded by telling Thomas it didn't matter because he could drop the murder charge if necessary and prosecute the rebels for the attempted murder of Watson and Ginman, which would not need Evans's testimony. Later, when Croke was retailing this to Robinson,

---

*   For the presentments to be prepared.

perhaps he remarked – wistfully, jokily, or purposefully – that things would be easier if Thomas were too busy to attend the trial.

Robinson's visit to Croke has been criticised as legally inappropriate and the discussions he had with him and Barry as highly improper.[23] Always eager to ingratiate himself with his superiors, Robinson, the chief defence witness, had also been getting inappropriately chummy with the judge before the trial. The two exchanged books.

In this hiatus between committal and trial, a salient fact deserves repetition. Because both Thomas and Rawson had participated in the rebels' capture, they should have been important witnesses at the hearings. Thomas had also accompanied Powlett to the whalers' grave, knew who else had gone, and had heard whatever was said and who said it, so his evidence should have been vital. And Rawson, although within days of leaving the colony, was still at Port Phillip throughout the committal hearings and could have given evidence. So it is disconcerting that neither he nor Thomas was called to testify before Major St John. Other than Powlett, the only witness who was present at the grave who did testify at the committal was Corporal Johnson, and at the trial he compliantly changed his story to agree with the lies of his superior officer, Commissioner Powlett.

Further, and even more pernicious, neither Rawson nor Thomas would be heard at the trial. One man's attendance was prevented by convenient happenstance, the other's by sinister decree.

§

Thomas undoubtedly expected to be called to testify at the committal hearings; that he was not seems to have strengthened his determination to attend the trial. The day before it was due to begin he was at Turruck with some of his Aboriginal charges, who wanted him to go to Merri Creek. 'I cannot till VDL[d] Blks tried' was his response.[24] The following day, Wednesday 15 December, four days after Robinson's meeting with Croke, the trial resumed. Thomas went into the Supreme Court at the south-eastern corner of King and Bourke streets, sat in the public gallery, and watched as the five prisoners were led in and Judge John Walpole Willis entered and took his seat on the bench. He was a contentious British jurist whom Governor Gipps once declared to be unfit for 'the calm and dispassionate administration of justice'.[25] After controversially serving in Canada and British Guiana, Willis was sent to Sydney in 1837 and feuded there with the chief justice. In 1841 he was packed off to Melbourne, where he clashed with the legal profession and some prominent citizens. Gipps also called him 'an apologist for the cruellest practices by some of the least respectable of the settlers on the Aborigines', although Willis had also passed judgments recognising Aborigines' right to rule their own affairs.[26] Conflicting opinions about him abound. While he was 'an able lawyer, honest and fearless, and alert to prevent fraud and oppression', he nevertheless 'lacked the judicial temperament'.[27] He was also seen as 'a man so irascible, disruptive and uncompromising that he was dismissed from two of his judicial posts and was unwanted in the third', although it should be pointed out that Willis's Canadian and Guinanan sackings were due mainly to his arrogance and naivete when he ran afoul of entrenched politico-mercantile cliques. He was the author of several well-regarded legal textbooks that reveal him 'as a thorough and highly skilled legal technician. His judgement, however, could be appallingly fallible . . .'[28] It is quite remarkable that during this trial he failed to see – or chose to ignore – many errors and inconsistencies in the prosecution's case and made aberrant rulings. He also demonstrated clear bias against the accused.

Willis began proceedings by acknowledging the persistent spectre of racial prejudice. He urged the empanelled jurors to be impartial because the trial involved Aborigines.[29] But there was an immediate setback. Powlett, the chief prosecution witness, failed to appear; no reason was noted. Willis therefore announced a five-day adjournment, saying:

> I cannot but now feel happy that fate of those sable prisoners which excited so much interest . . . is now about to be speedily determined. From what I have been enabled to learn, Mr. Powlett, the Crown Commissioner, a necessary witness, will be here on Monday next.[30]

Thomas left the court and went to visit the five accused in their cell. Then he called to see Robinson to warn him of strife he feared was brewing among bickering Aborigines in his protectorate. Robinson had also gone to court that morning and, inappropriately, had chatted with the judge 'about the blacks'. Having seen Thomas there, he now gave him a disturbing instruction. He ordered him to stay away from the trial when it resumed – in Thomas's words, Robinson told him 'that I must stop [with the quarrelsome Aborigines] until the trial is over'.[31] Thomas initially obeyed the order. He followed the squabbling tribesmen southward on Mornington Peninsula, which was ablaze with bushfires, until he reached Arthurs Seat on Saturday 18 December, then turned back. 'Could not proceed further on Acc^t of pending Trial', he wrote.[32] The following day he called on Robinson, who must have been surprised to see him, counter to instructions, back in Melbourne, although he noted in his journal only that 'Thomas called and reported the death of an Adelaide black by a Goulburn black'. The assistant protector was clearly resolved to attend court. A more drastic measure was needed.

The trial was to resume next day, Monday 20 December. Thomas rose early and dealt with some protectorate business before going to the courthouse. But when he tried to enter he was shocked to be refused admittance.

> Attended Court, thrust out by Judges Officer[.] Get you gone says he[,] only Magistrates here. I said I am a Magistrate[;] he looked foolish[.] I disgusted with his usage did not enter.[33]

His exclusion was outrageous. The courtroom was packed with spectators who were not magistrates and he had been freely admitted on the day the trial was adjourned. Evidently the court officer had since been ordered by higher authority to keep Thomas out so the prosecution could proceed unchallenged. Thomas, probably guessing who was responsible for the interdiction, did not press the matter and demand admission – a pity, for he was known to be a pious and decent man and he might have been able to change the outcome. It can hardly be doubted that Robinson was behind the embargo, and since he was to be the only witness for the defence, his acting to undermine it was irrational and repugnant. Yet in all probability he did it not from malice toward Thomas or the rebels but in a reflexive bid for collegiality with Croke and Powlett, educated men of higher status with whom he hoped to ingratiate himself.

With Thomas safely excluded, the trial proceeded. 'Small Boy, otherwise Robert Teminey Jemmy, Tunninerpareway otherwise Jack or Napoleon, Lallah Rook [sic] alias Truganini, Fanny alias Waterforden, and Maria Matilda alias Nantapolina, all aborigines, were indicted for the wilful [sic] murder of William Cook, and a man called Yankee, by shooting with a gun loaded with bullets, at Western Port', a newspaper reported. 'The first count charged Small Boy as principal, and the other prisoners as aiding and abetting; the second count charged all the prisoners as principals in the murder by striking, kicking, and beating.'[34] Judge Willis's notes repeat those addled details and who was charged with what, including the curious fact that Timme was charged with shooting both whalers, rather than just one, while Pevay was indicted only for bludgeoning Cook.[35] By the prisoners' reported confessions Pevay had fired the first shot, the one that killed Yankee, so its omission from the indictment is odd.

Barry entered pleas of not guilty to all charges and the trial continued. The accused, although undoubtedly reassured by the presence in court of the chief protector of Aborigines, must have found the prolix proceedings incomprehensible, the wigged and gowned pomposity bewildering, and the formal language of legal process far beyond their understanding of English. None of the accused had been baptised; none, therefore, could give sworn testimony.

The prosecution stumbled early when the whaler Samuel Evans failed to appear and could not be found. Despite Thomas's warning to Croke, it was a serious setback for the prosecutor. Evans would have testified that when he and the other whalers were nearing Watson's hut on the day Cook and Yankee were slain, they had encountered the five rebels, meaning that he could attest to the prisoners' armed presence in the vicinity just before the killings. He had also seen people with guns running to the beach immediately after the shooting, and he had seen people watching Cook and Yankee's burial from a distance, after which he had helped pursue the watchers through the sandhills. That was all crucial and Croke was confounded by his witness's failure to appear. Evans, probably having been suborned during his meeting with Powlett six days earlier, had apparently fled Melbourne. Perhaps Powlett had recognised potential weak points in Evans's deposition: that he never identified the Palawa he had encountered that day as the people he had seen running to the beach, whom he had thought were the absent miners. And his having been fired on without warning by Watson and his two-man posse might also be problematic. Were the court to hear that armed and trigger-happy whites had been nearby at the time of the killings, Redmond Barry could have planted doubt in the jurors' minds about who really fired the fatal shots. Best that Evans be persuaded to be unavailable.

His nonappearance was such a serious blow to the prosecution that Croke believed his case was now unprovable. His only recourse was to do what he had informed Thomas he would do if that happened: he told the judge he would abandon the murder charge altogether and instead prosecute the prisoners for the attempted murder of Watson and Ginman. But Willis refused to allow it. He did not think it was right to proceed on a minor charge, he said, when a more important one was against them – a ruling that experts have described as aberrant. 'Cases invariably proceed on lesser charges if problems of proof are apparent. It is the prosecutor's role to make the call on these matters. Judges do not make or intervene in these decisions.'³⁶ Flummoxed by Evans's absence and wrong-footed by Willis's rebuff, Croke was at a complete loss. He turned for guidance to Powlett, the cause of his problem, and they conferred.

> Mr. Croke after a little hesitation said, in consequence of a conversation he had [at] that moment with Mr. Powlett . . . he would not abandon the charge of murder as he thought he would be enabled to prove it.³⁷

Mr Powlett's self-confidence is damning. Here was the crown prosecutor admitting to the judge that without Evans he would have insufficient evidence to prosecute, yet Powlett was able to provide assurances that his testimony alone would be enough to prove the Crown's case. He was obviously confident of his own credibility and the unassailability of his evidence, which would be supported, as he must have known, by perjurious testimony from Watson and Johnson. Consequently Croke, with his case now resurrected by Powlett's intended perjury, proceeded as planned.

Barry, however, tried to dissent. He argued that the prosecution's evidence was mainly circumstantial. The reported confessions were unreliable, he said, because they were made by people in a state of terror and there had been no European witnesses to the killings. Powlett was undeterred. He testified to the trial, as he had to the hearings, that the confession had been made only after some of the prisoners were marched to the gravesite, which he said was six miles from where they were apprehended. (Rawson said it was three.) Six miles – 10 kilometres – implied two to three hours' march, sufficient time after their capture for the prisoners' fear and excitement to have abated and Trukanini's confession to have been calmly made. Powlett then repeated his most damning lie. He swore that at the gravesite, without threats or prompting, Trukanini had incriminated Pevay and Timme as the killers of Cook and Yankee.

One witness with no reason to lie was the whaler Thomas Robins, whose account resembled Evans's at the committal. He told the court what he had seen when he left Watson's hut to investigate after hearing the fatal shots fired.

> I saw four people on the hill near the hut, *I could not distinguish their colour* . . . [O]ne minute after the shots were fired *three of the four* went down to the beach and one stopped on the hill [emphases added]. I did not see a gun in the hands of the person who stopped on the hill. I saw two guns in the hands of some of the party before they came down.[38]

Robins's statement that *three* people went down to the beach – as Corporal Johnson had told the *Port Phillip Herald* – confirmed Trukanini's active part in the killings. She was the third person; the others were Pevay and Timme. But if Robins's inability to identify the gun-carrying people as blacks registered with Barry, he failed to capitalise on it.

When William Watson took the stand he, like Powlett, swore to tell the truth, then laced his evidence with lies. He testified that Trukanini told him, when she guided him and Powlett to where the bodies were buried, that the three women had stayed on the hill after the men shot the whalers. Pevay and Timme alone had gone down to the beach to the victims.

> [Trukanini] said she had stood on the high bank when the men were killed. She hid herself behind a bush with the other women as she was scared when she saw a man wounded and struggling on the sand.[39]

Watson's inventions are obvious. He had no need to be guided to the burial site because he already knew where it was, having himself helped to bury the bodies only 300 metres from his own hut – an obvious lie Barry should have seized on. Trukanini was not their guide to the gravesite: she was at Massie and Anderson's having her wound dressed. And Watson himself was not at the grave to listen to this supposed confession; only Powlett and Thomas, the police, and the male prisoners were there. Confirmation was in Rawson's journal, which showed that Powlett and Thomas took with them to the burial site only 'two of the prisoners and the police', which is corroborated by Thomas's diary.[40] The two prisoners were Pevay and Timme. Trukanini was never at the whalers' grave to blame the men while claiming self-exculpation, nor was Watson there to hear her. His evidence was wholly invented. His collusion with Powlett is clear.

Powlett himself was a careless perjurer whose lies contradicted one another. The evidence he gave at the trial differed from his testimony at the committal. At the trial he told blatant lies: that 'Truganini . . . when I asked her where the whalers were buried . . . conducted me to the place[.] Prisoners Bob and Jack accompanied us about six miles from where they were taken . . . Truganini pointed out the grave . . .'[41] Yet at the committal Powlett had testified that 'I was shown the place where the men was murdered . . . *the women* pointed it out to me [emphasis added]'. Two lies, each contradicting the other.[42] If Judge Willis, who had attended the committal, noticed the anomaly, he made no comment.

When Corporal Johnson was sworn in he reiterated the confessions he said he had heard Pevay and Timme make, as reported in the *Port Phillip Herald*. But in compliance with his superior officer's perjury he now added to his story Trukanini's fictitious presence at the gravesite, and he falsely placed the men's confession there too. 'The two men and Truganini took us to the place [where the victims were buried]', he swore. 'The two black men Bob and Jack said they had shot the whalers . . .'[43]

The facts bear recapitulation. The prosecution case depended on Powlett's, Watson's, and Johnson's testimonies that Trukanini had gone with Powlett to the gravesite and there incriminated Pevay and Timme as the killers. But Trukanini did *not* go to the grave – a fact attested by both Rawson and Thomas; both men's journals recorded that all three women were escorted to Massie and Anderson's. Rawson wrote that 'Powlett took *two of the prisoners and the police* about 3 miles further to examine the place where the two men had been murdered, while

I with the soldiers *and the other prisoners* returned . . . [to] Anderson's station [emphases added]'. Thomas's journal entry confirmed those facts and verified that he too was at the grave with Powlett and consequently knew who else was present and what was said. Crucially, he noted that '*men Blks* took *us* to the spot were [*sic*] killed 2 men' and that 'Rawson and party took *the women* towards the station [emphases added]'.[44] Thus two witnesses with no reason to lie recorded the truth about who went to examine the grave.

Surprisingly, Rawson subsequently amended his journal. No doubt to oblige Powlett, a senior official and a gentleman like himself, he doctored his original entry to concur with the lie Powlett and Johnson told in court. After modification, his journal read that *three* blacks, not two, had accompanied Powlett to the grave. The revision has not gone unnoticed.

> Rawson, rather remarkably, amended his journal entry at some indeterminate time. In doing so he crossed out the word 'two' and he replaced it with the number '3'. A third person, presumably Truganini, is now included in the party which went to the graves where Powlett has her making statements and admissions.[45]

Who really guided Powlett to the grave should have been irrelevant except that he knew the prosecution's case was weak, which prompted him to falsify a scenario whereby Trukanini went with him to the gravesite and there, without duress and by now calm and collected after a supposed 10-kilometre walk, denounced Pevay and Timme as the whalers' killers while exculpating herself and the other women. Yet Powlett himself had testified at the committal hearings that 'the women beat out [the whalers'] brains with the sticks'.[46] Nevertheless, his rank and class guaranteed that his integrity was unquestionable and his evidence unlikely to be challenged. Corporal Johnson would testify as ordered and the unbaptised Trukanini would never be able to swear that she had not been there.

Rawson never had to explain the revision to his journal because he took no part in the trial. On 7 December 1841, seven days after the committal hearings ended but eight days before the adjourned trial was due to begin, he and the rest of his detachment left Port Phillip in the steamer *Seahorse* to join their regiment in Sydney before sailing to India, and he never returned.[47] From that a plausible picture of chicanery can be conjectured. There would have been no reason for Rawson to amend his journal *after* leaving Port Phillip, knowing his ultimate destination was India. So the revision must have been made earlier, probably because, like Thomas, he expected to be called to testify at the hearings. His only reason for changing fact to falsehood at that time would have been to oblige another gentleman, probably one senior to him. Knowing that he was about to leave Port Phillip (although possibly expecting to be recalled to testify), there would be no harm in doing a senior chap a favour. The accused were only blacks, after all, and hadn't they confessed when apprehended? No bother at all, then, to shore up the prosecution, just in case. Merely a quick alteration to the diary . . .

With Rawson gone, only one potential impediment to a successful prosecution remained – William Thomas. But he could simply be kept out of court and was: he was never called to testify. Nor was Rawson recalled from Sydney to give evidence. So because 'Those whose job it was to protect the interests of the [accused] – the Chief Protector, their barrister and also, even, the judge – made no effort to ensure that all relevant evidence was led', the judicial process was hopelessly corrupted and justice was not served.[48] Moreover, the chief protector of Aborigines had conspired to make certain that the truth could never be told at the trial of those he was supposedly protecting. Add his callowness and other parties' perjury, collusion, and incompetence to the prevailing racist attitudes and it can be seen that the trial was not merely corrupt but vindictive. The ghosts of the Benalla killings and the Myall Creek executions haunted Judge Willis's courtroom that December as they had Major St John's committal hearings. Blacks had killed whites. They must be punished.

§

As this judicial farce stumbled toward its tainted end, the limitations of the 'brilliant young barrister' Redmond Barry became obvious. He seems to have had little experience as a Supreme Court advocate – his training was mostly in mortgages and conveyancing – and his value to the accused was negligible.[49] He failed to notice or challenge the prosecution's lies and inconsistencies and provided only a weak defence. His eloquent oration to the jury took entirely the wrong approach: he told them that because of the dispossession of Aboriginal people and the injustices inflicted on them, 'the feelings of the wild and untutored savage must predominate, and only slumber to burst forth with redoubled fury on the first opportunity'.[50] He did little more by way of defence than encourage the jurymen to exercise great caution when considering the circumstantial evidence, urging them to give the accused the benefit of any doubt they were entertaining. Adding to his uselessness, he was terrified of the 'vituperative and eccentric' Judge Willis. '[Barry's] diaries show that the gross provocation of Willis from the bench often reduced the young barrister to a state of almost unendurable tension.'[51]

While Barry's failings helped to doom the accused, the unassailable pillar of the prosecution's case was the implicit integrity of Frederick Powlett. He was an Englishman of impeccable social rank: a descendant of the last duke of Bolton and the son of a chaplain to the Prince Regent. He had come to Australia with Sir John Franklin and was of unimpeachable probity because of his rank and heredity. As a senior colonial official at Port Phillip he was 'a well known and much respected figure. He was a confidant of Lieutenant-Governor Charles La Trobe and was agent for his property, as well as for Lady Jane Franklin's . . . He had a high sense of honour . . . was fair and impartial, both as a lands commissioner . . . and as a magistrate.'[52]

Fair and impartial? Not always.

§

In his diary, former assistant protector James Dredge, a Methodist preacher, blamed Robinson's ineptitude for the rebels' predicament, yet the chief protector of Aborigines was the only witness called in their defence. He could do little more than praise the prisoners' character and their services to him over the years, but his opening words helped condemn them: 'They have a knowledge of the principles of religion and the existence of a supreme Being, and know right from wrong'. No equivocation now. If they weren't quite Christians, they were near enough.

He was loquacious in his evaluation of Timme.

> I know of Bob having undertaken a journey, with my concurrence, in the service of Messrs. Langhorne and Bacchus, to Adelaide; the character [reference] given of him to me was extremely good. Mr. Langhorne owed his life and those of his party to him; from the Murray blacks when they attacked his party . . . Bob has been in my service thirteen years; he was a lad when I got him, and he accompanied me in my first journey to Port Davy [sic]; I afterwards sent him back on account of his youth; on my subsequent journeys, he was with me, and conducted himself satisfactorily; he was respectful; I never knew him dishonest, and he was always industrious . . .[53]

Then he fossicked through mind and memory for similar redemptive words about Pevay, but those he found were few and feeble. '[H]e was with me up to my last expedition up to September last – and his conduct also has been most satisfactory', he said.[54] And that was all. Yet only a few months later he was to report to La Trobe (perhaps with belated remorse) that during their expedition to the Western District Pevay had 'rendered most valuable service. His conduct during the whole course of the journey deserved the highest praise.'[55]

Continuing in defence of the women, Robinson testified as effusively as he had in support of Timme, especially praising Trukanini and her having saved his life during Wyne's Arthur River attack in 1832. In mitigation he told the court that 'The women are not allowed by the men to act according to their own will – they are in entire subjection to the men, in absolute thraldom [sic]'.⁵⁶ His testimony served the women well. The harsh spotlight of guilt swung onto the men alone.

But Barry, recognising the hopelessness of exonerating Pevay, now chose to encumber him with all blame. 'Even if there was anything to criminate one man', he said in closing, 'there was not against the other, for he was clearly coerced by his companion; as for the women, there was nothing whatsoever to criminate them'.⁵⁷ Timme's allegation to Corporal Johnson that Trukanini had helped to beat Cook to death was ignored by all, although the *Port Phillip Herald* told its readers she had admitted her part in the clubbing.⁵⁸ Pevay and Timme themselves were to point out that she was, at very least, an aider and abettor.

> Both prisoners had all along admitted their guilt, but it was not until the night preceding their execution that they disclosed full particulars. Jack, who was all along the ring-leader in the outrages at Western Port, was, it seems, the actual murderer of the unfortunate whites, for Bob refused to have any share in the matter until threatened by Jack, and urged by Truganina . . . to remember the massacre of their relatives . . . by the Van Diemen's Land whites.⁵⁹

Barry's defence of the men proved useless. Even though Willis's notes summarised the prosecution's case as 'Circumstantial Evid'ce – Circum'l confession', it was enough to convince him.⁶⁰ Having declared that murderers should not be permitted to escape justice, he made an 'extraordinarily prejudicial' three-hour address to the jury that quoted from a report Robinson had made to the Legislative Council in 1838. It described Palawa during the Black War as 'extremely insidious in their attacks both on persons and property'.⁶¹ As one legal expert has observed, that 'encouraged the jury to regard all Aboriginals from Van Diemen's Land as inherently savage and violent, as if this somehow made up for the circumstantial nature of the evidence in the case'.⁶² Willis left the jury little doubt about the verdict he expected from them.

> There is a duty that you owe to yourselves and to your fellow subjects, to protect not only their property, but more especially their lives, and by your verdict to prevent if possible (should you deem the prisoners or any of them to have been actors in them), the recurrence of similar acts of aggression.⁶³

The trial lasted all day. At 7.30 pm, with Willis's verbose summing-up echoing in their ears, the jury retired to consider their verdict. Little deliberation was needed. After 30 minutes they returned to the courtroom, where John Roach, the foreman, declared that Pevay and Timme were guilty but the women were not. The jury also recommended mercy for the men because of their previous good character 'and the peculiar circumstances of the case'. Willis reserved sentencing until the following morning.

Back in the dock next day, 21 December, Pevay and Timme watched the grim-faced judge don the black cap, although it is unlikely that they understood the significance of the petty ritual. Willis's grandiloquent formal sentencing was equally incomprehensible.

> Painful as it is at all times to pronounce the Sentence of the law upon a fellow creature, yet this pain is greatly increased when the delinquent has not the consoling hope of his crime being pardoned hereafter, by means of true repentance and the mercy and forgiveness of Almighty God. The light of Christianity, the only rational piety, if ever distinguishable in your minds, can but have glimmered for a moment, instead of continuing to illuminate by its calm splendour, your journey through a world of misery, and directing you to the Haven of Eternal Rest. All men, even in an uncivilised state, are said to entertain, however imperfectly and however clouded with vain imagination, some expectation of a future state. May the latest [*sic*] spark, if it exist in your minds, kindle, by God's blessing, that holy

> flame of piety and repentance, that world must close upon you, for I can hold out no hope of pardon.
>
> Your punishment that awaits you is not that of vengeance, but of terror, that others by the example you will afford, may be deterred from similar transgression. The civilisation and instruction imparted to you, under the kind protection of Mr. Robinson, who has behaved like a father to you, and who has brought you to these shores, has not, I lament to say, been attended with the salutary consequences that might reasonably have been expected. You are not like the wild Aborigines who inhabit the native forests of this district. You are not . . . ignorant savages about to be made amenable to a code of law of which you are absolutely ignorant, and the spirit and principles whereof are foreign to your mode of thought and action. You, for years, have associated with and become familiar with the manners, customs, and ordinary laws of the British people, sufficiently so to know at least that the circumstances of which you have been convicted, could not have been committed by you with impunity. What I have said to you will be better explained to you by those under whose care you will be until the period of your execution.[64]

Having told them there was little hope of salvation for their souls because they were not Christians, Willis then contradicted himself by telling them Robinson's success in Christianising them had helped determine their fate.

> You have been long enough with Mr. Robinson to have become acquainted with the scriptures, and that holy volume enjoins life for life, and that when this world closed on you, your souls live in another world. The sentence which the law awards, and justice now compels me to pronounce, [is] that you be taken hence to the place from whence you came, and that on such day as his Excellency may appoint, you be conveyed to a place of execution – of public execution – and there you be severally hanged by the neck till you be dead, and may

God in his infinite goodness have mercy on your souls and pardon your sins.[65]

Willis recommended against clemency. 'The case strikes me as one of great atrocity', he wrote to La Trobe. 'There were also charges of arson and robbery against the Prisoners, which their conviction for murder rendered it unnecessary to try. It now therefore rests with His Excellency the Governor to decide whether these wretched men, or either of them, shall be speedily executed; or reprieved until their case be submitted to Her Majesty.'[66] He wanted the prisoners executed by an Aboriginal hangman as a deterrent to other Aborigines, but La Trobe left the decision to Robinson.[67]

The *Port Phillip Herald* was also in no doubt that Pevay and Timme should hang.

> The oft-repeated and, in certain circles, the so-popular argument of pseudo-philanthropists that the soul is the property of the blacks, and therefore the laws of nature force them to resist invasion on the part of the whites, cannot be advanced as ... an excuse ... [A] most dangerous precedent has been introduced ... and if the blacks, now convicted of one of the most aggravated murders on record, do not suffer that punishment which such atrocious crime deserves, it will be impossible for the authorities ever again ... in any case of a capital offence, to assert ... the amenability of blacks to British law.[68]

Another journal, the *Port Phillip Gazette*, opined that the trial had confirmed all Aborigines' 'ineradicable love of destruction and, as a consequence, the imperative necessity of coercion in their management'. However, it recommended mercy for Pevay and Timme, suggesting that they be incarcerated for life in the prisons of Cockatoo Island.[69] It was the only voice to call for their reprieve, but it soon fell silent.

One man, however, did not give up hope. Perturbed by the whole nefarious business, Assistant Protector Thomas sent a report to La Trobe after the trial. It never reached the superintendent and subsequently disappeared, so its precise wording is unknown. But its subject is clear and indisputable because 19 months later, on 23 July 1843, long past any need for lenity, Thomas was still troubled enough to write to La Trobe about the vanished report, asserting that it might have saved Pevay and Timme had it been delivered.

> But the recollection that had one of my former reports gone faithfully up to the Government (which was sent back to me with severe reproof) those two unfortunate Aborigines who suffered at Melbourne might still have been in existence.[70]

The report would have gone via Robinson, Thomas's immediate superior (and a man never averse to reproving his underlings), for forwarding to La Trobe. But Robinson refused to accept it and sent it back to Thomas with a rebuke, after which it was never seen again. Robinson's journal entry for 30 December 1841 suggests that the document was disturbing. It reads: 'Mr Bertram, overseer at Narre Narre Warreen [sic] called a.m., was, he says, sent by Thomas. He brought an extraordinary and slovenly report, I could not sanction . . . Expect it is all an absurdity.' Since Thomas's report must have been intended to directly or indirectly apprise La Trobe of the skullduggery that defiled the rebels' trial, it would undoubtedly have seemed extraordinary to Robinson, who appears to have been unaware that witnesses had lied. But it is not known who was responsible for its disappearance and Thomas's own journal sheds no light on the matter.

Regardless, he alone emerges from the whole sorry saga of apprehension and punishment with his integrity intact, his humanity untainted.

§

Initially Pevay, who was aged about 30, and Timme, two or three years younger, seemed unconcerned by their sentence, convinced that the jury's recommendation for clemency would save them. 'At first they showed a feeling with regard to their position, which could be construed either into solid apathy or savage indifference, but which, from their silence, it was impossible exactly to define', one newspaper commented.[71]

> When informed, after their trial, that their sentence was sent to Sydney, they lost none of their buoyancy of spirits, they thought that they would be reprieved, and continued laughing and talking with their usual merriment, frequently playing at ball with a bundle of rags rolled up as a substitute.[72]

But, as the *Port Phillip Herald* observed, it was an unpropitious time for black men to be seeking clemency. It cited the Myall Creek murderers' execution.

> When ... colonists call to their recollection that in Sydney white men suffered the extreme penalty of the law, and we justly admit, for taking summary vengeance against the natives, and that they if guilty of a similar offence are liable to a similar punishment, the public will instantly perceive that whilst the laws protect the blacks, the white man's blood must go unavenged.[73]

In the prevailing circumstances Governor Gipps and the Executive Council were not inclined to pardon blacks convicted of killing whites, especially after La Trobe, in submitting Willis's notes and comments to Gipps, said he could offer him no words in either Pevay's or Timme's favour. On 3 January 1842 the Executive Council confirmed the sentence and set 20 January as the execution date. The news shocked the condemned men.

> Since they have been aware of their fate ... they have seldom spoken, and frequently stand motionless for hours ... but their expressed belief since their sentence that they will again visit Van Diemen's Land, and hunt through that country, cannot give us any reason for being at all cognisant of their situation as it demands.[74]

'Shooting at Watson would hang them'

Their fate was final now, fixed and immutable. The buoyant spirits of one of the condemned sank into a dark slough of despond. When Robinson visited them on 17 January he noted that Pevay was sullen but Timme was in tears.

17

'He hung beautiful'

EXECUTION OF THE BLACKS. Tomorrow the last vengeance of the law is to be carried into effect against the guilty natives of Van Diemen's Land whose outrages and trial before the Supreme Court, have occupied ... so much public attention.

The two men who were brought as guilty will be hung at the site of the new gaol building on the hill which runs parallel with the north line of La Trobe Street. Their sentence will be carried out at seven o'clock in the morning and thus will close the last scene of their tragic and exciting history.[1]

When all hope of reprieve was dashed, Timme's demeanour had changed. He became frightened and demoralised, lost his appetite, could not sleep, and wept constantly. Pevay, however, remained in 'a state of perfect unconcern'.[2]

After their discharge from court, Trukanini, Planobeena, and Mathabelianna remained for the moment at Port Phillip, camped in the grounds of Robinson's South Yarra home. When Robinson told Planobeena on the eve of execution what was about to happen to the two men, she 'wept exceedingly, first said she would go [to visit Pevay], at last her feelings overcome, said no my like to see his face'.[3]

The night before the execution Pevay ate and drank heartily – half a loaf of bread and three pannikins of tea – but Timme refused food and tobacco and was distraught when Robinson visited them. They were attended by Rev. Adam Compton Thomson, who stayed with them until 2 am and reported that both men were attentive to his prayers.

At 4.30 am, after only two hours' sleep, the condemned men were awakened and given breakfast. Pevay ate a solid meal of bread and tea, then lit his pipe and smoked contentedly, also offering it to Timme, who declined it and all offers of food, consuming only a little tea. At once stage Pevay laughed and snapped his fingers and loudly declared he did not care a fig for anything.

On a small hill not far away, in early morning sunshine, spectators were already crowding around the execution site, chattering excitedly as they jostled for prime viewing places around the drop.

After breakfast Robinson went to the jail to farewell the condemned men, taking Wurati's son Droyyerloinne. Pevay and Timme were shaved and told to dress in all-white clothing – coarse shirt, trousers, cap, stockings, and cape – but Timme had to be coerced into complying. One of the four attending clergyman, Rev. Joseph Orton, wept at this, and Robinson, who disapproved of dressing up the victims, reported that he too was much affected. Disconcertingly, the white garments were provided by Judge Willis himself; he had personally delivered them to the prisoners that morning. His reason for sending them to their death so bizarrely clad is unknown, although he possibly intended to highlight the ethnic as well as the moral blackness of the condemned.

Both men were in a state of mental suffering, according to Robinson, but a newspaper disagreed.

> [Pevay] seemed perfectly unconcerned and even gay; he laughed heartily when his attendant was assisting him to put on the stockings, and expressed his unconcern at his approaching fate, saying, that after his death he would join his father in Van Diemen's Land and hunt kangaroo; he also said that he had three heads, one for the scaffold, one for the grave, and one for V.D. Land; his companion remained totally silent during these arrangements.[4]

The likely truth of the matter was recorded by Orton.

> At 6 o'clock I attended the gaol and had some conversation with them, the one named Bob appeared to be sensible of the dreadful event that awaited him ... but seemed to be truly penitent and sincerely to cry for mercy. Jack was less concerned and exhibited an air of indifference to the last – though not without emotions of fear as to his approaching [end].[5]

With four clergymen and the evangelistic Robinson present and prayerful, the cell was rife with religiosity. Robinson asked Thomson to baptise Timme, having jotted 'Baptize Robert' in his journal the previous day. Although the prisoners' supposed embrace of Christianity had made possible their conviction, its superficiality was obvious to the attending priests, and Thomson refused.

> [Rev.] Thomson said he should not baptize Bob because he had no knowledge of the notion of the instructions, although he said he knew the fundamental principle Jesus Christ came into the word to save sinners; Jesus Christ was the Son of God; he died for our sins. He, Bob, repeated for his sins, knew he was a sinner, that God made him, was in heaven, everywhere.[6]

No such sacrament was requested for Pevay.

At 7 am Rev. Thomson returned, accompanied by several magistrates and the sheriff. Following Divine Service in the yard attended by all the prisoners, Pevay and Timme were ushered to Robinson's cart, waiting with two grey horses in its shafts. Screened sides had thoughtfully been attached to the vehicle – 'a painted cloth stretched around on poles fastened to the corners of the frame' – in order to hide the condemned men from morbid public gaze – a bizarre clemency, it might be thought, for prisoners who were about to be put to death before thousands of gawking men, women, and children. The two beshackled Palawa climbed with Thomson into the vehicle for their journey to the scaffold. When they were settled the driver geed the horses into a walk and the cart with its escort of police and mounted police moved off, accompanied by a crowd of several hundred onlookers.[7] With Timme weeping bitterly all the way, the procession trundled 'up Collins, round by William, down Lonsdale and via Swanston street, where it passed slantwise ... to the gallows hill' opposite the new public library.[8] A temporary gibbet had been erected there on a partly cleared site at the back of a new jail under construction – now the Old Melbourne Gaol – whose incomplete walls were crowded with spectators.[9] Almost the entire populace, 'all apparently anxious to gratify that morbid feeling of curiosity which renders an execution a treat to the lower orders of the British', were assembled there to enjoy the free entertainment.[10]

> An immense crowd ... between four and five thousand people [attended], the greater part of whom were *women and children*. From the laughing and merry faces which were assembled ... the scene resembled more the appearance of a race-course than a scene of death. The walls and body of the new gaol were literally packed with spectators as anxiously awaiting the awful scene as if it were a bull-bait or a prize-ring.[11]

So numerous and tightly packed were the onlookers that the police escort had to force a path through them to allow the cart to reach the scaffold.[12] The structure was crude and flimsy, a 'killing contrivance of the roughest and most inhuman kind'.

> The gallows was formed of two upright posts about twenty feet [six metres] in height with a cross beam at the top to which the ropes were attached; the scaffold was formed of a plank two feet [60 centimetres] wide fastened to the gallows at one end by a hinge, and supported at the other by a prop which being pulled away let fall the drop.[13]

The notably makeshift trapdoor was propped up with bricks and sticks and the platform was so narrow that it could hardly accommodate John Davies, the novice executioner. A sheep thief transported for life, he was a short man of about 45 whose scarred face was garlanded with carrot-coloured beard. He had been victor in an 18-man contest for the job, for which he was promised £10 and his freedom.[14] Next to where he waited at the foot of the gallows were two plain coffins, which eager spectators were standing on to gain an elevated view. Also keen for a better perspective were a contentious number of Aborigines who had climbed trees around the site (and who behaved with notable decorum throughout).[15] Another onlooker with a superior viewpoint was himself a commanding spectacle: the publican Black Byng, son of a South Carolina slave. His sheer size astride his prancing white horse in the brilliant morning sunlight made him unmissable. Colour of another kind was added to the proceedings when Captain Beers marched in with a military guard in bright uniforms.

As Pevay and Timme began to climb down from the cart, their chains jangling with every movement, 'two constables stepped up to hand the prisoners out, and the start back which Bob gave showed the terror inflicted by the sight of the unexpected populace; he came out, however, immediately, after trembling violently, followed by Jack, calm and imperturbable to the end . . . Bob's agitation increased with every passing moment, and his moans were terrible to hear'.[16] An onlooker commented on the incongruity of white clothing on their black bodies, 'the contrast of which, with their nearly jet black hands and faces gave the criminals an appearance particularly revolting'.[17] At the foot of the scaffold they were subjected to 20 minutes of religious solemnity – 'a farce of prayer reading', one newspaper called it – which was frequently interrupted by shouts of 'Cut it short!' from the impatient crowd eddying around the prisoners and uttering 'explosions of uproarious merriment'.[18] Pevay remained calm as the two men knelt with the clergyman, but Timme was visibly terror-stricken. Prayers completed, the condemned men stood. As their arms were being pinioned behind them Timme 'broke out in the most heart-rending groans; the terrified and piteous looks he threw around him . . . was terrible to witness; he trembled violently'.[19]

Although the chief protector of Aborigines had absented himself from the proceedings, former assistant protector James Dredge attended and recorded the scene in his diary.

> The executioner tied their hands before they went up the ladder and chains hung from their ankles, making it nearly impossible for them [to ascend].
>
> The poor wretches, in getting up the ladder, deprived of the use of their hands, were obliged to cling to the bars with their knees and chins and be partly dragged and partly pushed up to slaughter . . .
>
> Jack was the first to ascend the ladder which he did with tolerable firmness. Poor Bob had to be literally dragged to the fatal platform.[20]

Even as Pevay reached the platform, Timme was still beseeching people in the crowd to save him, 'pressing against everyone that spoke to him as if to catch at some chance of salvation'.[21] Pevay, however, was relaxed and patient as he waited to be put to death. He had once told Robinson that Palawa believed in an afterlife; dying meant they simply 'walked about from one tribe to another', so he was unafraid. He asked the hangman not to cover his eyes until he could see his friend when he came up. But Timme, near collapse at the foot of the ladder, was helpless to climb it, so Davies clambered down and dragged him up.

> It was gratifying to see the universal kindness with which they were treated, soothed by every one round, and tenderly handled by the executioner.[22]

A hush settled on the spectators as Timme was hauled into view atop the platform. He was shivering violently and his terror was contagious. Pevay too began to tremble. The executioner became anxious, fearing personal injury if their quaking tipped him off the platform's narrow fragility. He hurriedly fixed a noose around each man's neck and jerked caps down over their eyes before scrambling down the ladder to safety. As Rev. Thomson intoned the words 'in the midst of life there is death', Davies and his assistant tugged on the rope that released the trapdoor. The two rebels dropped – but only about 30 centimetres, not far enough to break their necks. 'There was a dead pause, and a cry of shame from the crowd', a witness remembered. 'The two twisted and writhed convulsively ... in a manner that horrified even the most hardened'.[23] The assistant executioner John Styleman hastily kicked away the prop that supported the trapdoor and this time the two Palawa plummeted all the way. '[A] sharp cry was heard from Bob as he fell, but from Jack only a heavy sound, as if the wilfully pent breath had been forced out of the body by the violence of the jerk'.[24] Pevay appears to have died instantly, his bulk a final blessing. ('He hung beautiful', Davies said.[25]) The lighter and slimmer Timme did not. His badly adjusted noose had slipped and he continued to thrash in agony, 'his chest labouring and heaving violently, his fine athletic frame ... dreadfully convulsed' as life was torturously strangled out of him.[26] 'The bodies swung to and fro for a few moments, but presently settled downwards; there were one or two violent muscular movements, and both were dead.'[27]

Sickened, the crowd began to boo and jeer, yelling insults at the executioner, who 'grinned horribly a ghastly smile'. The journalist Edmund Finn noted that many of the women spectators 'who were as loquacious as chattering monkeys before, now changed their tune and got up a cry, which, for loudness ... would do full credit to a full chorus of demented banshees'.[28]

Gradually the tumult died and the spectators drifted away, leaving the white-clad black bodies suspended in the midsummer sunshine for the hour stipulated by law. Then they were taken down and laid in the waiting coffins, the lids were affixed, the cart loaded. Tumbril became hearse. It slowly bore them the short distance to an unconsecrated tract, hastily set aside for an Aboriginal cemetery only three days earlier, which adjoined the hallowed ground of the Christian graveyard. Waiting at the graveside to receive them were the chief protector of Aborigines and Droyyerloinne, the only Palawa mourner. With a hymn and prayers from Rev. Orton the two tortured bodies were lowered into the earth. Robinson wrote that he was distressed by the tragic scene.

William and Mary Watson, who had been in the crowd watching the execution, followed the cart to the burial ground. As the first shovelfuls of earth thudded onto coffin lids they approached Robinson to ask if they might be compensated for the possessions they had lost when their hut was stripped and burnt. They had petitioned Governor Gipps, they said, but had had no response.[29] Robinson's reply is not known, but it has been observed that 'the stolen items used as evidence would have been returned at the conclusion of the trial, and the court testimony states that the whalers helped to transport goods from Watson's hut on October 7, the day after the killings. Not only was Watson crass, he was on the make, and quite prepared to lie.'[30]

While Watson and Robinson were conferring, Orton went to Robinson's home to console the three women. 'I saw the wives of the two blacks who had suffered', he wrote. 'They were sitting pensively in their native mia-mias apparently deeply affected . . . they wept bitterly . . .'[31] The women confirmed again the motive for the killings – they had thought it was Watson, they said – and told Orton that Cook had not begged for his life, as reported, but had pleaded to be put out of his misery. He had also made an anguished confession.

> One of the whalers who was still alive when the blacks came up beg'd them to kill him, as he could not survive, and that it served him right for he had killed many blacks.[32]

James Dredge had been profoundly impressed by Pevay's courage on the scaffold. He 'seemed indifferent to everything' and 'seemed to leave the world without a struggle, as if as if the bitterness of death had long passed', he wrote.[33] But the execution had been a nauseating spectacle and Dredge had been nauseated. That night, still sickened, he committed to his journal the depth of his repugnance, calling the hanging 'an affecting, appalling, disgusting, execrable scene' whose like he hoped never to see again.[34] He was spared a reprise. There were no more Palawa rebels. Not in Port Phillip. Not anywhere.

Epilogue

Tasmania was uninterested in the tragic demise of two of its few surviving Indigenous sons, especially so far away. Only once, on 18 February 1842, was their execution noted in a Tasmanian newspaper, when the *Hobart Town Advertiser* reprinted a report of the hangings from the *Geelong Advertiser* of 24 January. Having been extirpated from their homeland, Palawa were no longer newsworthy in it. The handful of living remnants were immured, and helpfully dying, on a remote Bass Strait island. Out of sight, out of mind.

Yet the newspaper did sense the tragedy that underlay the execution.

> There is no excuse to offer, nothing to justify or excuse the outrages of which they were guilty, we cannot therefore murmur, though we deeply regret, that such should have been their fate.

In its musings about Pevay's and Timme's demise the *Geelong Advertiser* briefly mentioned two heroic acts, otherwise unrecorded and now unverifiable, supposedly performed by Timme during the Friendly Mission. 'Twice during that momentous period Mr. Robinson owed the salvation of his life to the intrepidity and self-devotion of Bob . . .' It seems unlikely. Probably the writer was mistakenly crediting Timme with Trukanini's twice having saved Robinson's life on Arthur River.

To the men's execution-eve assertion that cheating by settlers had ignited their breakout, the *Geelong Advertiser* contributed a supportive codicil.

Epilogue

> For their services [to the Friendly Mission] ... Colonel Arthur ... gave the blacks who assisted Mr. Robinson ... 600 sheep, which with their produce, amounting to four or five times that number, are now at Flinder's [sic] Island, but leave was denied them to bring their property with them, when they followed Mr. Robinson to [Port Phillip], and *to their dissatisfaction on this score may be attributed, in a great measure, their entering upon the commission of the outrages which have placed them in their present situation* [emphasis added].

§

For the few surviving Palawa exiles at Port Phillip, and the whites who had been drawn into the breakout and its aftermath, life after the executions went its random way.

George Augustus Robinson wrote nothing in his post-execution journals of his feelings about the breakout, the hangings, or his two executed companions, a silence that might charitably be construed as remorseful. He remained chief protector of Aborigines until pensioned off when the Port Phillip Protectorate was abolished at the end of 1849, the year after his wife Maria died. In 1852 he returned to England and the following year married Rose Pyne, who bore him five children. For the next five years he and she lived in Europe before finally settling in Bath. Robinson's well-rewarded services in Tasmania and Victoria had made him wealthy but, despite that, he was never accepted by the higher strata of English society he aspired to. He died at Bath in 1866, aged 75.

Frederick Armand Powlett, aged 54, died the year before Robinson, ending a career in public office that included a brief stint as acting colonial treasurer. As well as perjuriously ensuring the conviction of Pevay and Timme, his distinctions included being a founder of Melbourne Cricket Club.

Samuel Rawson sailed from Sydney in the *Kelso* in June 1842 for service with his regiment in India and never returned to Australia. He had a long military career, retiring in 1866 with the rank of major, and died at Chiswick in 1882, outliving all other major players in the breakout and its repercussions.

William Thomas remained an assistant protector until the Protectorate's abolition, after which his services were retained as chief government adviser on Aboriginal affairs. He served in several important roles in which 'His bravery and moral conviction were undoubted, but his advocacy of Aboriginal causes made him unpopular in colonial society'.[1] Thomas died at his Brunswick home in 1867.

John Walpole Willis, after being sacked in 1843 for incompetence, was never given another judicial post. He returned to England and lived as a country squire, eventually being appointed lord lieutenant of Worcestershire. His death was in 1877 at the age of 84.

James Croke rose to become solicitor-general of Victoria and later a member of the Victorian Legislative Assembly. He died in England in 1857.

Redmond Barry became a judge of the Victorian Supreme Court, in which role he is best remembered for sentencing Ned Kelly to death. He died in 1880, 12 days after Kelly's execution.

William Watson, who disappeared from history's pages after the executions, is believed to have died in 1875 in Geelong.

John Davies was penalised for bungling the execution. To show their displeasure, authorities paid him only half of the promised £10 fee and delayed for nearly two years the other portion of his emolument, his ticket of leave. Five months after executing Pevay and Timme he officiated at the hanging of three bushrangers, but it was his final execution. In 1847, when last heard of, he was a self-employed shoemaker in Brighton.

Walter George Arthur became an activist after being returned to Flinders Island in August 1842 with most of Port Phillip's few Palawa survivors. In 1846 he composed a petition to Queen Victoria requesting removal of the unpopular Flinders Island administrator Henry Jeanneret. In October the following year he, his wife Mary Ann, and the 12 other surviving internees at Wybalenna were

Epilogue

transferred to Putalina (Oyster Cove), south of Hobart, where Walter worked a nearby farm and battled alcoholism before joining the crew of a whaling ship in 1859. He drowned in May 1861.

Wurati did not make it back to Wybalenna with the others. He died during the return voyage in 1842 and was buried on Green Island.

Droyyerloinne, his son, remained in Port Phillip. A veteran of several abscondences, he died the year after his father.

Myyungge, Wurati's other son, was another frequent absconder. He too was returned to Flinders Island, although later than the others, and was eventually transferred to Putalina, where he partnered with Mathabelianna before dying in 1848.[2]

Thomas Thompson's fate is uncertain, but he stayed at Port Phillip, where he was last heard of in 1851.[3]

Planobeena's life after the executions was scantily documented. She was returned to Flinders Island with the others in 1842 and married a man named Parloorer. They were both transferred in 1847 to Putalina, although Planobeena did not stay there, after which the records are silent. She is thought to have died between 1851 and 1855.

Mathabelianna was another whose life was sparsely recorded after the return to Flinders Island, although, with Trukanini, she continued to abscond. She was subsequently removed to Putalina but left there and disappeared from history. Her death was likely between 1851 and 1854.

Trukanini too was returned to Flinders Island, where she married a man named Mannapackername (died 1847) and continually absconded. In 1847 she was sent to Oyster Cove with the pitiable remnant of surviving Palawa. When Robinson visited them there in 1851 she refused to acknowledge his presence. At Oyster Cove she partnered with William Lanne, sometimes referred to as the last male Palawa, who died in 1869.[4] After the death in 1873 of the last of the other women, Trukanini was taken to live among the alien race that had dispossessed and devastated her people. Wrongly dubbed 'the last of the Tasmanians', she died in Hobart on 8 May 1876. Although she has been painted as a tragic heroine, it must be remembered that, in extremis, she willingly incriminated her partner Timme to exculpate herself. Perhaps, however, she suffered the most prolonged and torturous punishment of all.

§

Like all the other Aboriginal tombs that would soon seed their unconsecrated half-acre of Melbourne, Pevay's and Timme's graves were never marked, so time and the relentless metastasis of urban sprawl soon hid all trace of them from sight and sorrow. As settlement grew to city, the land was thought too valuable to be merely the necropolis of two rebel Palawa and the unknown number of unmonumented Kulin who followed them into its grasp. It could be put to more remunerative use. So the boneyard became a livestock market, then a wholesale fruit and vegetable market, and finally a much larger and more colourful bazaar. Today whatever substantial might remain of Pevay and Timme is thought to lie beneath the noisy churn of trade and tourism that is the Queen Victoria Market, between sheds E and F.

Their spirits, however, refused effacement.

More than 180 years after they died some essence of them and their futile grab for freedom lingers in Melburnians' ken, niggling and unignorable. Like Ned Kelly, hanged 38 years after they were, Pevay and Timme continue to fascinate people. In 1875, 33 years after their deaths, an artist named Wilbraham Liardet painted a watercolour titled *The First Execution*, which depicted, symbolically rather than accurately, the two condemned men in Robinson's cart on their way to the gallows. In ensuing years the rebels also became the subject of numerous articles, papers, and books, many of them rife with inaccuracy and specious reasoning. Such persistent interest led in 2008 to formation of a community group called the Tunnerminnerwait and Maulboyheenner Commemoration Committee, which aimed to observe each anniversary of their execution – a curious honour, perhaps, for two convicted murderers. Six years later the City of

Epilogue

Melbourne commissioned and published a 40-page monograph titled *Tunnerminnerwait and Maulboyheenner: The involvement of Aboriginal people from Tasmania in key events of early Melbourne*.[5] Its title goes some way toward explaining the most recent awareness of the two hanged men: Melburnians curious about their city's infancy were wondering how Tasmanian Aborigines came to be there and what two of them did to earn such a melancholy place in its history. The city followed the booklet's publication by commissioning both a painting of the execution scene and a commemorative marker to the two men. The Wadawarrung artist Aunty Marlene Gilson completed the painting *Tunnerminnerwait and Maulboyheenner* in 2016, which was also the year that the public marker, *Standing by Tunnerminnerwait and Maulboyheenner*, was erected on the corner of Franklin and Victoria streets near where the temporary scaffold had stood in 1842. Designed by artists Trent Walter and Brook Andrew, a Wiradjuri man, the marker is constructed of bluestone, aluminium, and steel. It bears the following inscriptions:

> **Front**: Tunnerminnerwait Maulboyheenner
> **Left side**: Standing by Tunnerminnerwait and Maulboyheenner / 2016 / Brook Andrew and Trent Walter
> **Right side**: This artwork was initiated by Tunnerminnerwait and Maulboyheenner Commemoration Committee, which holds a gathering here annually to honour the two men who were executed by public hanging on this location at midday [*sic*], 20 January 1842. Commissioned by the City of Melbourne

It is undoubtedly the only structure erected anywhere in Australia, if not the world, to *honour* – a surprising choice of verb – two killers executed according to law. The word may best be seen as an expression of belated recognition of, and, by inference, regret and guilt for, the hangings, and perhaps too for the injustice and mistreatment and lies that sent them to their deaths.

Victoria remembers them elsewhere too. At the Wonthaggi Wishart

Reserve, near the scene of their capture, the Bass Coast Reconciliation Network holds an annual commemoration event that includes a welcome to Country and a smoking ceremony.[6] Nearly two centuries after their death, Pevay and Timme clearly remain troubling reminders of the great and unforgivable crimes committed against Australia's Aboriginal people, specifically the racist acts spawned by the fascist-policies-with-a-Christian-mask that enabled Lutruwita to be violently wrested from its traditional owners and ultimately propelled Pevay and Timme to an agonising death on a shaky Melbourne scaffold.

§

Did Pevay and Timme premeditatedly kill Cook and Yankee in cold blood?

Undoubtedly.

Did they get a fair trial?

Undoubtedly not.

The two of them were hanged after a fault-riddled travesty of a trial, which has moved some critics – those who have never noticed the contradictions in the evidence or the aberrations in the legal process – to argue that the two men were merely criminals who got what they deserved. But the issue is not so simple. Perspective offers many angles of approach, many shades of opinion.

Consider the cause. While festering resentment, anger, and a desire to live free sparked the breakout, the rebellion was at first peaceable. What transformed it into a lethal rampage was James Horsfall's unfounded and inexplicable story that William Watson had murdered their comrade Prupilathina. A grab for freedom consequently became an angry drive for retaliation and revenge, not merely on Watson but on whites generally – they would smite those who smote them. So they attacked the posse that had tried to ambush them at Westaway's campfire. Instead of fleeing its superior numbers, they lingered to inflict ferocious payback on their pursuers. Even their thefts from settlers were, in part, small acts of revenge – reprisals and reciprocations for being cheated and mistreated.

Seen from a Port Phillip settler's viewpoint, however, the Palawa rebels were nothing but criminals. They raided settlers and stole food, clothing, weapons, and livestock. They shot at, wounded, and killed colonists. They evaded authorities. By any yardstick they were bandits, brigands, murderers. Worse, they were imports from Van Diemen's Land, unwanted and unwelcome. They had no right even to be at Port Phillip. That they were blacks deepened the dye of their crimes because their victims were white. Worst of all, they were blacks who had enjoyed the many advantages of civilising and religious instruction and paid employment, making their breakout treacherous as well as criminal – an unforgivable breach of faith. They could ride, shoot, and understand English. They fought with whites' weapons and black bushcraft and they knew whites' habits and customs and weaknesses, all of which colonisers dreaded in subject peoples. It made them doubly dangerous, doubly feared, doubly hated. Pevay and Timme's brutal end was no more than they deserved, and if it took perjury and collusion to deliver it, so what?

Other observers see things differently. They insist Pevay and Timme were freedom fighters rather than criminals, while still others have repudiated that claim because a freedom fighter, as *The Macquarie Dictionary* says, is 'one who joins in organised resistance, usually armed, against the established government, or the domination of his or her country by a foreign power'. Although Pevay and Timme's resistance was not organised and they were not trying to overthrow an established government, they were undeniably fighters for freedom – their own. As Redmond Barry pointed out during their trial, 'these men and their fellow countrymen once roamed over the green hills and wide plains of their native soil, the lords of all around, subject to no will but their own, no master but their own passions'.[7] And that was all they desired – to be their own masters. To be free.

Breakout!

So they broke out. Their aim was to liberate themselves from having to be white men's lackeys required to obey white men's laws. They wanted to live according to their own laws and customs. Sadly, that could never be, for they had to seek their freedom in what was irreversibly a British colony, and colonisation imposes subjection and disenfranchisement on the colonised. It also demands their compliance with the coloniser's laws, because imposition of those laws instantly annuls the subjugated people's own.

However you look at it, whatever you consider the rights and wrongs of the breakout, its causes and consequences, the die was cast for Pevay and Timme when they first stole from a settler, their fate sealed when they shot Watson and Ginman. But even had they killed no one, wounded no one, robbed no one, their end would still have been a tragedy. When an alien regime is forcibly imposed on a free people, the end is always tragic.

Acknowledgements

Although writing is perforce a solitary (and sometimes self-indulgent) occupation, I would have written little of consequence without the support and cooperation of my wise and wonderful wife Lou. My debts to her, literary and otherwise, are innumerable.

Every book about historic events is built on the bedrock of others' scholarship. The road for me, as for anyone today writing about Palawa history, was surveyed, paved, and signposted by several resolute historians, and I'm beholden to the foundation work of Ian D. Clark, Vivienne Rae Ellis, N.J.B. Plomley, Cassandra Pybus, Henry Reynolds, Jan Roberts, and Lyndall Ryan. Kate Auty and Lynette Russell's book *Hunt Them, Hang Them* was also a valuable resource.

It would be remiss of me not to additionally acknowledge Lyndall Ryan's personal kindness and encouragement over the two decades since she read *Steps to the Scaffold* in manuscript and wrote a generous encomium. She died while this book was in press, and I hope that in some small way it will help celebrate her life, her seminal work, and her warm collegiality.

Henry Reynolds's contributions also went beyond his foundation scholarship and friendly encouragement. With typical generosity he read the manuscript, made suggestions for its improvement, and wrote the insightful Foreword that places the story of Pevay and Timme in its wider historical context. I could not have asked for more.

I am indebted too to several experts who were forthcoming with assistance on specific matters: Ian Clark, Nicholas Clements, Julie Gough, Greg Lehman, Ian McFarlane, Kim Pearce, Annie Reynolds, Theresa Sainty, Gaye Sculthorpe, and Ian Terry. Brian Rollins once again generously shared with me his invaluable knowledge of the history of Emu Bay and the VDL Company. My learned and literate friends Michael Briggs and Ian Kennedy Williams willingly read draft chapters and offered frank and useful comments. My son Ben assisted with photographs of Flinders Island locations. And I acknowledge with gratitude the contributions of Tony Brown, Jacquie Ward, and Maria Macdermott at the Tasmanian Museum and Art Gallery, Alex Gionfriddo at the State Library of Victoria, and various staff members of Libraries Tasmania and the State Library of New South Wales.

I was delighted to be able to use Aunty Marlene Gilson's iconic painting *Tunnerminnerwait and Maulboyheener* as a cover illustration. For the necessary permissions and arrangements I thank the artist herself, Martin Browne of Martin Browne Contemporary, and Eddie Butler-Bowdon of Melbourne City Council. Eddie also kindly arranged for me to use a council photograph of the memorial *Standing by Tunnerminnerwait and Maulboyheenner*.

As always, my friends at Wakefield Press smoothed the process of turning manuscript into book. Thank you one and all: Michael Bollen, Maddy Sexton, Carney Sims, Polly Grant Butler, Julia Beaven and Jesse Pollard.

Bibliography

Books

Arkley, Lindsey (2000), *The Hated Protector: The story of Charles Wightman Sievwright, Protector of Aborigines 1839–42*, Orbit Press, Mentone, Vic.

Auty, Kate & Russell, Lynette (2016), *Hunt Them, Hang Them: The Tasmanians in Port Phillip 1841–1842*, Justice Press, Melbourne

Birnie, Joel Stephen (2022), *My People's Songs: How an Indigenous family survived colonial Tasmania*, Monash University Publishing, Clayton, Vic.

Bonnell, Max (2017), *I Like a Clamour: John Walpole Willis, colonial judge, reconsidered*, Federation Press, Alexandria, NSW

Bonwick, James (1884), *The Lost Tasmanian Race*, Sampson Low, Marston, Searle, and Rivington, London

Bonyhady, Tim & Lehman, Greg (2018), *The National Picture: The art of Tasmania's Black War*, National Gallery of Australia, Canberra

Bride, Thomas Francis (ed.) (1969), *Letters from Victorian Pioneers*, William Heinemann, Melbourne

Brodie, Nick (2017), *The Vandemonian War: The secret history of Britain's Tasmanian invasion*, Hardie Grant Books, Richmond, Vic.

Campbell, Alastair H. (1987), *John Batman and the Aborigines*, Kibble Books, Malmsbury, Vic.

Cameron, Patsy (2011), *Grease and Ochre: The blending of two cultures at the colonial sea frontier*, Fullers Bookshop/the Riawunna Centre, UTAS, Launceston, Tas.

Clark, Ian D. (ed.) (2000), *The Journal of George Augustus Robinson, Chief Protector, Port Phillip Aboriginal Protectorate, 1839–1852*, Heritage Matters, Melbourne

Clements, Nicholas (2014), *The Black War: Fear, sex and resistance in Tasmania*, University of Queensland Press, St Lucia, Qld

Clements, Nicholas & Reynolds, Henry (2021), *Tongerlongeter: First Nations leader & Tasmanian war hero*, NewSouth Publishing, Sydney

Cox, Robert (2021), *Broken Spear: The untold story of Black Tom Birch, the man who sparked Australia's bloodiest war*, Wakefield Press, Mile End, SA

Cox, Robert (2004), *Steps to the Scaffold: The untold story of Tasmania's black bushrangers*, Cornhill Publishing, Pawleens, Tas.

D'Arcy, Jacqueline (2019), *On His Majesty's Service: George Augustus Robinson's first forty years in England and Van Diemen's Land*, Matador Publishing, Kibworth Beauchamp, Eng.

Breakout!

Ellis, Vivienne Rae (1981), *Trucanini: Queen or traitor?*, Australian Institute of Aboriginal Studies, Canberra

Fels, Marie Hansen (2011), *'I Succeeded Once': The Aboriginal Protectorate on the Mornington Peninsula*, ANU Press, Canberra, accessed at https://press.anu.edu.au/publications/series/aboriginal-history/i-succeeded-once

Finlay, Grant (2019), *'Good people always crackenny in heaven': Mythic conversations in lutruwita/Tasmania*, Fullers Publishing Pty Ltd, Hobart,

Horton, Thomas & Morris, Kenneth (1983), *The Andersons of Western Port: The discovery and exploration of Western Port, Victoria, and the first settlers in eastern Victoria, Samuel Anderson, and his brothers, Hugh and Thomas, from 1797 to 1903*, Bass Valley Historical Society, Corinella, Vic.

Johnson, Murray and Ian McFarlane (2015), *Van Diemen's Land: An Aboriginal History*, UNSW Press, Sydney

Johnston, Anna & Rolls, Mitchell (eds) (2008), *Reading Robinson: Companion essays to Friendly Mission*, Quintus Publishing, Hobart

Land, Clare (2014), *Tunnerminnerwait and Maulboyheenner: The involvement of Aboriginal People from Tasmania in key events of early Melbourne*, City of Melbourne

Levy, M.C.L. (1953), *Governor George Arthur: A colonial benevolent despot*, Georgian House, Melbourne

McFarlane, Ian (2008), *Beyond Awakening: The Aboriginal tribes of North West Tasmania: a history*, Hobart, Fullers Bookshop, Riawunna, University of Tasmania

Plomley, Brian (1993), *The Tasmanian Aborigines*, Plomley Foundation, Launceston.

Plomley, N.J.B. (1976), *A Word-List of the Tasmanian Aboriginal Languages*, Plomley/Government of Tasmania, Launceston.

Plomley, N.J.B. (ed.) (1966), *Friendly Mission: The Tasmanian journals and papers of George Augustus Robinson 1829–1834*, 1st edn, Tasmanian Historical Research Association, Hobart

Plomley, N.J.B. (ed.) (2008), *Friendly Mission: The Tasmanian journals and papers of George Augustus Robinson 1829–1834*, 2nd edn, Queen Victoria Museum and Art Gallery/Quintus Publishing, Hobart

Plomley, N.J.B. (1991), *Jorgen Jorgenson and the Aborigines of Van Diemen's Land*, Blubber Head Press, Hobart

Plomley, N.J.B. (1992), *The Aboriginal/Settler Clash in Van Diemen's Land 1803–1831*, Queen Victoria Museum & Art Gallery, Launceston.

Plomley, N.J.B. (ed.) (1987), *Weep in Silence: A history of the Flinders Island Aboriginal settlement with the Flinders Island journal of George Augustus Robinson 1835–1839*, Blubber Head Press, Hobart

Bibliography

Purtscher, Joyce (1993), *Children in Queen's Orphanage Hobart Town 1828–1863*, I. Schaffer, New Town, Tas.

Pybus, Cassandra (1991), *Community of Thieves*, William Heinemann, Melbourne

Pybus, Cassandra (2020), *Truganini: Journey Through the Apocalypse*, Allen & Unwin, Crows Nest, NSW

Rae-Ellis, Vivienne (1996), *Black Robinson*, Melbourne University Press, Melbourne

Reynolds, Henry (1995), *Fate of a Free People: A radical re-examination of the Tasmanian wars*, Penguin, Ringwood, Vic.

Reynolds, Henry (1982), *The Other Side of the Frontier: Aboriginal resistance to the European invasion of Australia*, Penguin, Ringwood, Vic.

Roberts, Jan (1986), *Jack of Cape Grim: A Victorian adventure*, Greenhouse Publications, Richmond, Vic.

Rose, Michael (ed.) (1996), *For the Record: 160 Years of Aboriginal print journalism*, Allen & Unwin, St Leonards, NSW

Ryan, Lyndall (1996), *The Aboriginal Tasmanians*, 2nd edn, Allen & Unwin, St Leonards, NSW

Snowden, Dianne (2018), *Voices from the Orphan Schools: The children's stories*, NewPrint, Huntingfield, Tas.

Stevens, Leonie (2017), *Me Write Myself: The free Aboriginal inhabitants of Van Diemen's Land at Wybalenna*, Monash University Press, Clayton, Vic.

Toscano, Joseph (2008), *Lest We Forget: The Tunnerminnerwait and Maulboyheenner Saga*, Anarchist Media Institute, Parkville, Vic., accessed at https://stors.tas.gov.au/1527325

Weidenhofer, Margaret (ed.) (1967), *Garryowen's Melbourne: A selection from the chronicles of early Melbourne 1835 to 1852, by Garryowen* (Edmund Finn), Thomas Nelson, Melbourne

Windschuttle, Keith (2002), *The Fabrication of Aboriginal History: Volume One: Van Diemen's Land 1803–1847*, Macleay Press, Sydney

Other

Coutts, Peter & Wesson, 'Jane Bob and Jack', unpublished MS held at MS 2817 in the AIATSIS Library

Dean, Shirley (2000), 'Our Children, the orphans', BA (Hons) thesis, University of Tasmania, accessed at https://eprints.utas.edu.au/17911/1/Whole-dean-thesis.pdf

Fels, Marie Hansen et al. (2014), 'Mistaken identity, not Aboriginal heroes', *Quadrant Online*, 8 October

Fels, Marie Hansen (2023), 'Not a battle, not a war, but definitely defiance', *Quadrant Online*, 10 May

'The hanging of two Aboriginals', Excerpt from the diary of James Dredge, *The La Trobe Journal*, April 1971

Land, Clare (2018), 'The haunting story of Tunnerminnerwait and Maulboyheenner', *La Trobeana: Journal of the C.J. La Trobe Society Inc.*, vol. 17, no. 1, March, pp. 55–64

McFarlane, Ian (2002), 'Aboriginal society in North West Tasmania: dispossession and genocide', PhD thesis, University of Tasmania, accessed at https://eprints.utas.edu.au/220/2/02Whole.pdf

McFarlane, Ian (2001), 'Pevay: a casualty of war', *Tasmanian Historical Research Association Papers*, vol. 48, no. 4

Parry, Nancy (2003), 'Many deeds of terror: Windschuttle & Musquito', Evatt Foundation paper, 29 August

Rayner, Tony (1996), 'Mannalargenna: Plomley's incorrect identification of Mannalargenna as a chief of the Oyster Bay Tribe', unpublished paper Tasmanian Aboriginal Centre 1996: pp. 2–3. Copy in author's possession.

Rye Historical Society newsletter, April–June 2016, accessed at http://ryehistoricalsociety.weebly.com/uploads/5/5/4/3/5543545/white_cliffs.pdf

Stevens, Leonie (2010), 'The phenomenal coolness of Tunnerminnerwait', *Victorian Historical Journal*, vol. 8, no. 1, June, pp. 18–40

Willis, John Walpole, 'Judge Willis's note books', Book no. 12, Criminal Sessions 1841, Box 4, MS 000195, Royal Historical Society of Victoria Library, accessed online

The Western Port Times, vol. 1, no. 10, February 2019, pp. 10–15, in Horton, Thomas & Morris, Kenneth (1983), *The Andersons of Western Port: The discovery and exploration of Western Port, Victoria, the Life of the first settler in Eastern Victoria, Samuel Anderson, and his two Brothers Hugh and Thomas from 1797 to 1903*, Bass Valley Historical Society, Corinella, Vic.

Various newspapers as cited in the text.

Websites

Report of George Augustus Robinson's speech to the Australian Aborigines Protection Society, 19 October 1838, accessed at http://www.law.mq.edu.au/research/colonial_case_law/nsw/other_features/correspondence/robinson_speech_1838/

'Transcript of trial of Rob't Temmy Jemmy Small Boy, Jack Napoleon Tunninerpareway, Lallah Rookh Truganina, Fanny Waterpoordeyer and Maria Matilda Nallepolemmer (?Nattepolenniner) for Murder', Royal Historical Society of Victoria, 'William Walpole Willis, Note Book no. 12, Page 108, Dec'r 20th 1841', accessed at https://www.historyvictoria.org.au/the-judge-willis-casebooks/casebook-12-transcripts-and-commentary/

Transcript of 'Truganini, bushranger', accessed at the Koori History Website, http://www.kooriweb.org/foley/audio/trans_truganini.html

Notes

PROV is Public Records Office Victoria, TAHO is Tasmanian Archive and Heritage Office

Preface
1. Windschuttle, *The Fabrication of Aboriginal History: Volume one*, p. 70.
2. Cox, *Steps to the Scaffold*, p. 162.
3. Reynolds, *Fate of a Free People,* pp. 139–140 *et seq.*
4. *Australasian Chronicle* (Sydney), 15 February 1842.
5. Norman Mailer, 'Journalistic research', *The Spooky Art: Thoughts on Writing*, New York, Random House, 2004, p. 189.
6. *The Mercury*, 6 June 1876.
7. Nicholas Shakespeare, *In Tasmania*, Random House, Milsons Point, NSW, 2004, p. 112.

Prologue
1. *Geelong Advertiser*, 17 July 1841.
2. *The Chronicles of Early Melbourne*, excerpt in *The Herald* (Melbourne), 17 November 1882.
3. *ibid.*
4. In Weidenhofer, *Garryowen's Melbourne*, p. 109.
5. *Port Phillip Herald*, 21 January 1842.

Chapter 1 ~ 'The African slave trade in miniature'
1. *The Tasmanian almanack for the year of our Lord 1825*, Andrew Bent, Govt. Printer, Hobart.
2. Colonial Secretary to GAR 1.12.29, in Plomley, *Friendly Mission*, 1st edn, p. 89.
3. Greg Lehman, 'Regarding the savages', in Lehman & Bonyhady, *The National Picture*, quoting Shayne Breen, 'Extermination, extinction, genocide: British colonialism and Tasmanian Aborigines', in Rene Lemarchand (ed.), *Forgotten Genocides: Oblivion, denial, and memory*, University of Pennsylvania Press, Philadelphia, 2011.
4. Clements, *Black War*, p. 4.
5. Plomley, *Friendly Mission*, 11 July 1829.
6. G.A. Robinson to Maria Robinson, 24 May 1831, A7055, vol. 34.
7. Plomley, *Friendly Mission*, 1st edn, p. 82.
8. *ibid.*
9. *ibid.*
10. *ibid.*, pp. 62–3.
11. Cassandra Pybus ('Journey through the apocalypse: Ria Warrah, Wooredy and Truganini', *Griffith Review* 58, October 2017) has suggested that Robert 'probably belonged to the Mouheneenner [Muwinina], who had once lived around the Derwent River', which is plausible – although his having been raised by Clarence Plains settlers suggests his people were more likely to have been Mumirimina from the opposite side of the Derwent. But her contention that Trepanner 'had been captured with Eumarrah' is wrong. Lyndall Ryan (*The Aboriginal Tasmanians*, p. 135) stated that Trepanner was from the Stoney Creek band – Umarrah's band – and his early abscondence from the Friendly Mission with Umarrah and another man from the same

band suggests the accuracy of Ryan's contention, but he was verifiably not one of the four Palawa Robertson captured with Umarrah. According to Robinson, Trepanner was from 'the northern coast' (Plomley, *Friendly Mission*, 15 December 1829).
12   Trukanini's statement, as paraphrased in a letter dated 20 January 1873 from an unidentified writer to J.W. Graves, quoted in a letter of Graves's published in *The Mercury*, Hobart, on 4 June 1876.
13   Plomley, *Friendly Mission*, 9 July 1834.
14   Plomley, *Weep in Silence*, p. 849.
15   Denison King, in Plomley, *Friendly Mission*, 1st edn, pp. 227–228.
16   Plomley, *Friendly Mission*, 6 February 1830.

Chapter 2 ~ 'The cry of welcome was evinced'

1   *ibid.*, 1st edn, pp. 228–229, n. 60; https://www.orphanschool.org.au/showorphan.php?orphan _ID=2835. However, neither boy is listed in the school register.
2   https://archivesandheritageblog.libraries.tas.gov.au/the-orphan-schools/; https://www. orphanschool.org.au/suffer.php.
3   Pybus, *Truganini*, p. 77.
4   Plomley, *Friendly Mission*, 26 November 1830.
5   http://palawa-places.org.au/tarkariliya-tunnerminnerwait-and-maulboyhenner
6   Plomley, *Weep in Silence*, pp. 843, 851, 857. For a discussion of Timme's putative family connections, see Pybus, *Truganini*, pp. 296–298.
7   Plomley, *Friendly Mission*, 2nd edn, p. 497, n. 185; *ibid.*, 22 June 1831; https://www. utas. edu.au/telling-places-in-country/historical-context/historical-biographies/ timme.
8   *Hobart Town Courier*, 22 November 1828.
9   *ibid*; Cox, *Broken Spear*, pp. 134–135, 143. Robertson claimed Jemmy was a chief which, given his age – Robinson reported his still having been 'a lad' in 1830 – contradicts the notion.
10   His having an English nickname implies some interaction with settlers but nothing definite is known.
11   *Hobart Town Courier*, 7 March 1829; Cox, *Broken Spear*, p. 143.
12   Quoted in Campbell, *John Batman and the Aborigines*, p. 33.
13   *Hobart Town Courier*, 3 October 1829.
14   Two of the five captives, Cowertenninner and Umarrah, were then in the field as unwilling guides for roving parties, and the fifth was the Jemmy who had escaped from Constable Prior in February. Umarrah's wife Laoinneloonner, 'a fierce woman', was later freed by the government and killed 'by the tribes' at Great Lake before 1831 (Plomley, *Friendly Mission*, 9 January 1831.) Umarrah subsequently partnered with Wulaytupinya on an unknown date.
15   Cox, *Broken Spear*, p. 150.
16   It was reported in the *Port Phillip Gazette* on 22 January 1842 that Timme had once been part of Robinson's Bruny Island establishment, but the claim is wrong. Robinson himself was on Bruny only from March 1829 until the Friendly Mission left Hobart in January the following year, during which period Timme was either at large or in Richmond jail.
17   Plomley, *Friendly Mission*, 1st edn, p. 95.
18   *ibid.*, 17 January 1830.
19   *ibid.*, 1st edn, p. 105, n. 50. Umarrah had already been released from jail and had been groomed for some time to act as a British guide before he joined the Friendly Mission.

Notes

Chapter 3 ~ 'Plenty much blood, plenty cry'

1. *ibid.*, 23 May 1830.
2. *ibid.*, 19 June 1830.
3. *ibid.*, 20 June 1830.
4. *ibid.*, 1st edn, p. 232, n. 109.
5. Plomley, *Friendly Mission*, 21 August 1830.
6. *ibid.*, 20 February 1834.
7. Reynolds, *The Other Side of the Frontier*, pp. 133–134.
8. Curr to Directors, 13 August 1829, TAHO VDL 5/1, Inward Despatch no. 86.
9. *ibid.*, 16 November 1829, TAHO VDL 5/1, pp. 209–210, Inward Despatch no. 100.
10. *ibid.*, 8 January 1830, TAHO VDL 5/1, Inward Despatch no. 111.
11. Plomley, *Friendly Mission*, 22 September 1830.
12. However, the identification is not absolutely watertight. Three weeks after Pevay joined Robinson, the mission called at Circular Head, where Robinson socialised with Curr. On the following Sunday, still at Circular Head, Robinson conducted a church service. 'All the gentlemen was there', he wrote. 'Addressed the aborigines on the occasion in their own dialect, with which the gentlemen was highly pleased.' Although Curr and Pevay were presumably both present at the service, Robinson made no note of any interaction between them, whereas a greeting or some gesture of recognition might have been expected. Perhaps it was simply not worthy of mention in Robinson's journal. Plomley, *Friendly Mission*, 18 July 1830.
13. Curr to Colonial Secretary, 5 February 1830, TAHO.
14. Plomley, *Friendly Mission*, 21 June 1830.
15. *ibid.*, 11 July 1830.
16. Robinson to Colonial Secretary, 30 June/1 July 1830, in Plomley, *Friendly Mission* (1st edn), p. 233.
17. Plomley, *Friendly Mission*, 1 July 1830.
18. *ibid.*, 14 July 1830.
19. *ibid.*, 1st edn, p. 234, n. 123.
20. *ibid.*, 26 July 1830.
21. *ibid.*, 1st edn, p. 234, n. 131.
22. *ibid.*, 4 August 1830.
23. *ibid.*, 23 August 1830.
24. *ibid.*, 20 September 1830.
25. *ibid.*
26. *ibid.*
27. *ibid.*, 21 September 1830.
28. *ibid.*, 22 September 1830.
29. McFarlane, 'Pevay: a casualty of war', p. 288.
30. Plomley, *Friendly Mission,* 2 October 1830.
31. Cox, *Baptised in Blood*, p. 273.
32. Plomley, *Friendly Mission*, 12 October 1830.
33. *ibid.*
34. *ibid.*, 1st edn, p. 242.
35. *ibid.*
36. The fate of Lettelowhe and Merappe is uncertain. Robinson was given permission to free them from Launceston jail with Pevay and presumably did, but they do not seem to have joined the mission with Pevay after being liberated, and they subsequently disappeared from the records.
37. In *Broken Spear* (first printing, p. 185), I stated that the Palawa conciliated that day, 1 November 1830, included Manalakina and Woreterlettelarnnenne, but Robinson's journal for that date makes no mention of either man by name. In fact,

259

Woreterlettelarnnenne joined him on 15 November 1830 (Plomley, *Friendly Mission*, 1st edn, p. 277). Robinson first mentions Manalakina's being with the mission – and already on Swan Island – in the entry for 15 November 1830, but he is not named as one of the Palawa who joined him that day, so it is possible to say only that Manalakina joined him on an uncertain date between 1 and 15 November 1830. The error has been corrected in subsequent printings of *Broken Spear*.

38 Plomley, *Friendly Mission*, 1 November 1830.
39 *ibid.*, 17 December 1830.
40 *ibid.*, 19 December 1830.
41 *ibid.*, 15 October 1830.
42 *ibid.*, 28 May 1831.
43 *ibid.*, 14 April 1831; E. Stephens, 'The Tasmanian half-castes of the Furneaux Islands', *Journal of the Manchester Geographical Society*, vol. 14, 1898, pp. 355–366.
44 Plomley, *Weep in Silence*, pp. 821, 834.
45 Plomley, *Friendly Mission*, 1st edn, p. 1019; Anna Haebich, *Broken Circles: Fragmenting Indigenous families 1800–2000*, Fremantle, Fremantle Press, 2000, p. 639, n. 243.
46 Plomley, *Friendly Mission*, 21 May 1837; Plomley, *Weep in Silence*, p. 709; https://pressfiles.anu.edu.au/downloads/press/p110711/html/Text/ch11.html?referer=&page=18#footnote-13594-18-backlink.
47 Plomley, *Friendly Mission*, 1st edn, p. 83.
48 *ibid.*, p. 82.
49 *ibid.*, 30 December 1830.
50 *ibid.*, 20 April 1831.
51 *ibid.*, 29 April 1831.
52 *ibid.*, 4 May 1831.
53 *ibid.*, 29 April 1831.
54 *ibid.*, 4 May 1831.
55 It is curious, however, that Robinson did not name him in his journal when he noted his boarding the cutter. He could be expected too to have recognised Timme, whom he had last seen only 12 months earlier, and made some appropriate note.

Chapter 4 ~ 'Make haste, black fellow run away'

1 Plomley, *Friendly Mission*, 15 May 1831.
2 *ibid.*, 7 June 1831.
3 Teengerreenneener or Richard, whom Robinson called 'a domesticated Aborigine', had been working for a settler named Brumby at Longford and was taken to Robinson in Launceston on 20 April 1831.
4 Plomley, *Friendly Mission*, 7 July 1831.
5 *ibid.*, 17 July 1831.
6 Rayner, 'Mannalagenna'; Plomley, *Tasmanian Aboriginal Place Names*, p. 11.
7 Plomley, *Weep in Silence*, p. 846.
8 Plomley, *Friendly Mission*, 18 August 1831.
9 *ibid.*, 20 August 1831.
10 *ibid.*, 21 August 1831.
11 *ibid.*, 28 August 1831.
12 Woreternattelargener, also spelt Wawtootitteyerlargenner, had the alternative names Tootetitteyerlargenner and Koleteherlargenner. Ningernooputener's alternative name was Lonederpunyer.
13 Plomley, *Friendly Mission*, 30 August 1831.
14 *ibid.*, 3 September 1831.
15 *ibid.*, 11 September 1831.
16 *ibid.*, 1 September 1831.

17 *ibid.*, 10 September 1831.
18 *ibid.*, 11 September 1831.
19 Executive Council minutes of 14 March 1831, in Levy, *Governor George Arthur*, p. 117.
20 Executive Council Minutes of 23 February 1831, *ibid.*, p. 120.
21 Executive Council Minutes of 14 March 1831, *ibid.*, p. 121.
22 The *Independent* (Launceston), 8 October 1831.

Chapter 5 ~ 'Greatly at a loss how to proceed'

1 *ibid.*
2 Plomley, *Friendly Mission*, 15 October 1831. In *Broken Spear* (first printing, p. 213) I wrongly stated that Robinson had 14 Palawa with him, but I had neglected to include Tanalipunya, who had joined the mission on 31 August 1831. The error was corrected in subsequent printings.
3 Plomley, *Friendly Mission*, 22 October 1831.
4 *ibid.*, 27 October 1831.
5 *ibid.*, 28 October 1831.
6 Cox, *Broken Spear*, pp. 64–66.
7 Plomley, *Friendly Mission*, 16 November 1831.
8 *ibid.*, 17 November 1831.
9 *ibid.*, 4 December 1831; Cameron, *Grease and Ochre*, p. 37.
10 *ibid.*, 28 December 1831.
11 *ibid.*, 19 July 1833.
12 *ibid.*, 14 December 1831.
13 *ibid.*, 27 December 1831.
14 Robinson, Speech to the Aborigines Protection Society, 1838. A fuller account of Robinson's momentous conciliation of the remnant Oyster Bay and Big River peoples is in Cox, *Broken Spear*, pp. 228–230.
15 However, the Tasmanian Museum and Art Gallery dates these portraits to 1837, which is after Pevay and Timme were incarcerated on Flinders Island. They were back on mainland Tasmania between March 1836 and July 1837 with Robinson's sons as they searched for a family of Palawa holdouts, during which time they had at least two sojourns in Launceston but did not go to Hobart. As there is no record of Bock's visiting Launceston during that period, the 1837 date for the portraits seems improbable and 1832 more likely.
16 Plomley, *Friendly Mission*, 4 April 1832.

Chapter 6 ~ 'We will kill them all by and by'

1 *ibid.*, 28 May 1832.
2 *ibid.*, 4 June 1832.
3 Plomley, *Weep in Silence*, pp. 813, 861; Plomley, *Friendly Mission*, 16 June 1832, 15 July 1832.
4 Plomley, *Friendly Mission*, 28 December 1830.
5 *ibid.*, 19 June 1832.
6 *ibid.*
7 *ibid.*, 20 June 1832.
8 *ibid.*, 22 June 1832.
9 *ibid.*, 23 June 1832.
10 *ibid.*
11 *ibid.*, 14 July 1832.
12 *ibid.*
13 *ibid.*

14   *ibid.*
15   *ibid.*
16   *ibid.*, 15 July 1832.
17   *ibid.*
18   *ibid.*
19   *ibid.*, 17 July 1832.
20   *ibid.*, 22 July 1832.
21   *ibid.*, 2 September 1832.
22   *ibid.*
23   *ibid.*, 30 August 1832.
24   *ibid.*, 2 September 1832.
25   *ibid.*, 3 September 1832. The Palawa Robinson described as 'TRUGERNANNA'S relative' was probably the Port Davey woman Tymedeen or Timemedeneme, whose husband Cordeve, a childhood friend of Wurati and Trukanini, was also present at Arthur River that day. Their relationship was possibly one of amity rather than family.
26   *ibid.*
27   *ibid.*
28   *ibid.*, 4 September 1832.
29   *ibid.*
30   *ibid.*
31   *ibid.*, 20 February 1834.
32   *ibid.*, 3 September 1832.
33   *ibid.*, 31 October 1832.

Chapter 7 ~ 'They are not at liberty to do as they choose'

1   When Planobeena joined the mission is unknown. It is inferable that she was left on Flinders Island in February 1832 when Robinson and the mission left for Launceston, yet Cottrell mentioned her being one of his guides as he trekked down the west coast toward his Macquarie Harbour rendezvous with Robinson, although, in that case, how and when she might have rejoined the mission are unknown. Very likely she had been with them, unobtrusive and unmentioned, after the mission had left Launceston on 4 April the previous year. Cottrell to GAR, 19 January 1833, in Plomley, *Friendly Mission*, 1st edn, pp. 804.
2   Plomley, *Friendly Mission*, 4 September 1832.
3   Cottrell to GAR, 7 December 1832, in Plomley, *Friendly Mission*, 1st edn, pp. 802–803.
4   Cottrell to GAR, 19 January 1833, in *ibid.*, 1st edn, p. 804.
5   *ibid.*
6   Plomley, *Friendly Mission*, 1st edn, p. 805.
7   *ibid.*, 28 April 1833.
8   *ibid.*, 8 May 1833.
9   *ibid.*, 11 May 1833.
10   *ibid.*, 21 May 1833.
11   *ibid.*
12   *ibid.*, 23 May 1833.
13   *ibid.*, 14 June 1833.
14   *ibid.*, 18 June 1833.
15   *ibid.*, 20 June 1833.
16   *ibid.*, 12 July 1833.
17   *ibid.*, 13 July 1833.
18   *ibid.*, 21 July 1833.
19   *ibid.*, 23 July 1833.

20 *ibid.*, 24 July 1833.
21 *ibid.*, 25 July–6 August 1833.
22 *ibid.*, 1st edn, p. 822.
23 *ibid.*, 19 August 1833.
24 *ibid.*, 21 August 1833.
25 *ibid.*, 4 September 1833.
26 *ibid.*, 5, 6 September 1833.
27 *ibid.*, 10 September 1833; *ibid.*, 1st edn, p. 818, n. 178.
28 *Hobart Town Courier*, 18 October 1833.
29 *ibid.*, 21 October 1833; *ibid.*, 18 October 1833.
30 Plomley, *Friendly Mission*, 1st edn, p. 823.
31 *ibid.*, p. 822.
32 *Hobart Town Courier*, 20 December 1833.

Chapter 8 ~ 'The entire Aboriginal population are now removed'

1 Colonial Secretary to GAR, 24 October 1833, in *Friendly Mission*, 1st edn, pp. 823–824.
2 Plomley, *Friendly Mission*, 7 December 1833.
3 *ibid.*
4 *ibid.*, 24 December 1833.
5 *ibid.*, 25 December 1833. Although no record exists of Robinson's previously having referred to Pevay as Black Jack, he was known as Jack and the adjectival 'Black' was often appended randomly to Palawa men's British-bestowed nicknames, including by Robinson. For instance the guide Teengerreenneener or Richard, usually called Dick, sometimes appears as Black Dick in Robinson's journal. Likewise Kikatapula or Tom Birch was also known as Black Tom. At the end of 1833 Robinson had no companion known specifically as Black Jack and no other guide than Pevay who was nicknamed Jack, so the reference was undoubtedly to Pevay.
6 *ibid.*, 29 December 1833.
7 *ibid.*, 14 January 1834.
8 *ibid.*, 25 December 1833.
9 *ibid.*, 31 December 1833.
10 *ibid.*
11 *ibid.*, 19 January 1834.
12 *ibid.*, 25 January 1834.
13 *ibid.*, 17 February 1834.
14 *ibid.*, 18 February 1834.
15 *ibid.*
16 *ibid.*, 27 February 1834.
17 *ibid.*, 28 February 1834.
18 *ibid.*, 4 March 1834.
19 *ibid.*, 13 March 1834.
20 *ibid.*, 14 March 1834.
21 *ibid.*, 6 April 1834.
22 *ibid.*, 7 April 1834.
23 See *ibid.*, 2 July 1834. According to Plomley (*ibid.*, 1st edn, p. 921), Planobeena was possibly also sent there at this time, but Robinson recorded that she was still with the mission on 16 July 1834. It should be noted however that, in a note on a report dated 9 September 1836, Robinson included Karnebutcher in a list of 'early deaths' with such people as Kikatapula, Eumarrah and Penderoin, all of whom died before the October 1835 shipment of captives to Flinders Island; see Plomley, *Weep in Silence*, p. 649.
24 *Trumpeter General*, 16 May 1834.

25 Plomley, *Friendly Mission*, 1st edn, p. 880.
26 *ibid.*, 18 June 1834.
27 *ibid.*, 14 July 1834.
28 *ibid.*, 9 April 1834.
29 *ibid.*, 16 July 1834.
30 *ibid.*, 1st edn, p. 926.
31 *Hobart Town Courier*, 10 October 1834.
32 *True Colonist*, 17 January 1835.
33 *Launceston Advertiser*, 15 January 1835. One of the men who died was presumably James Fuller, who drowned on 14 August 1834; see Plomley, *Friendly Mission*, 1st edn, p. 920.
34 Plomley, *Friendly Mission*, 1st edn, p. 926, apparently quoting George Robinson junior.
35 George Robinson junior to GAR, 2 February 1835, TAHO CO/280/56.
36 *Launceston Advertiser*, 15 January 1835.
37 *ibid.*, 22 January 1835.
38 GAR to Colonial Secretary 3 February 1835, TAHO CSO/280/56.
39 Ryan, *Aboriginal Tasmanians*, p. 172.

Chapter 9 ~ 'We don't want to live here'

1 GAR to Colonial Secretary, 25 February 1835, TAHO CO/280/60.
2 Pybus, *Truganini*, p. 162.
3 Plomley, *Weep in Silence*, pp. 300, 309. In *Friendly Mission* (1st edn, p. 921), Plomley suggested that Nollahallaker and Karnebutcher were transferred to Flinders Island on 24 April 1834, which is likely. Robinson's journal of 2 July 1834 notes Nollahallaker being on the island and wanting to leave it, as was Pagerly, who must have been shipped there with the other two. In the January 1836 census of Wybalenna internees Nollahallaker is tentatively identified (by Plomley) as Sabina, in which case she is recorded as having died of influenza on 3 March 1839. Plomley, *Weep in Silence*, pp. 867–868, 878–881.
4 Plomley, *Weep in Silence*, p. 868; Bonyhady & Lehman, *The National Picture*, p. 86. Ellis (*Trucanini*, p. 87) stated that Tanilpunya died on Flinders Island on 11 October 1836 but that is a misidentification for Meemelunneener ('Hannah'), Manalakina's final wife, with whom he partnered after Tanlipunya's death. In *Broken Spear* (p. 246) I wrongly stated that Tanlipunya had died on Flinders Island.
5 *Hobart Town Courier*, 2 October 1835; *Bent's News and Tasmanian Three-Penny Register*, 30 April 1836.
6 *True Colonist*, 5 August 1836.
7 *Colonial Times*, 19 February 1839.
8 Plomley, *Weep in Silence*, 1 October 1835.
9 *ibid.*, 5 October 1835.
10 *ibid.*, 14 October 1835.
11 *ibid.*, 17 October 1835.
12 Allen to GAR, 30 October 1835, A7062, vol. 41.
13 Plomley, *Weep in Silence*, p.623.
14 *ibid.*, 21 December 1835.
15 *ibid*.
16 Plomley, *Friendly Mission*, 1st edn, p. 276, 15 November 1830.
17 Reynolds, *Fate of a Free People*, p. 167; Rae-Ellis, *Black Robinson*, pp. 113–114; Plomley, *Weep in Silence*, p. 644; see also Lyndall Ryan, 'Historians, *Friendly Mission*, and the contest for Robinson and Trukanini', in *Reading Robinson*, pp. 147–159.
18 Plomley, *Weep in Silence*, 25 December 1835.

19 *ibid.*, p. 314.
20 Lloyd Robson, *A History of Tasmania, Volume I*, Oxford University Press, Melbourne, 1983, p. 220.
21 Plomley, *Friendly Mission*, 1st edn, p. 685.

Chapter 10 ~ 'Too much dead man'

1 Wymurrick had survived his removal from country for only three months, dying on Flinders Island on 28 January 1833 not long after being taken on a visit to Hobart, after which 'he appeared to be labouring under a depression of spirits . . . I much fear that his visit to Hobart Town was the main cause of his death . . .' (Darling to Colonial Secretary, 20 February 1833, TAHO CSO1/1/319/7578, p. 169).
2 Plomley, *Weep in Silence*, 7 November 1835.
3 *ibid.*, 18 November 1835.
4 *ibid.*, 6 August 1831.
5 Plomley, *Weep in Silence*, p. 747.
6 *ibid.*
7 H.J. Emmett, 'Reminiscences of the Black War in Tasmania', 1870, NLA MS3311, p. 8.
8 Plomley, *Weep in Silence*, 27 November 1835.
9 *ibid.*, 5 December 1835, in Plomley, *Weep in Silence*, p. 313; *ibid.*, p. 927.
10 Pagerly's death is assumed to have been in 1834–35 because she is not identifiable in the census of internees taken in January 1836 and her name is among those in a November 1837 list of Palawa buried at Wybalenna, although her date of death is unknown. Plomley, *Weep in Silence*, pp. 878–881, p. 909.
11 Robinson to Colonial Secretary, 31 July 1835, TAHO CSO 1/807/17237.
12 Clements & Reynolds, *Tongerlongeter*, p. 198.
13 Plomley, *Weep in Silence*, 17 January 1836.
14 Nickolls to Colonial Secretary, 21 January 1835, CSO1/1/326.
15 *ibid.*
16 TAHO CSO 5/180/4240.
17 Plomley, *Weep in Silence*, 28 December 1835.
18 *Launceston Advertiser*, 29 September 1836.
19 Plomley, *Weep in Silence*, 4 August 1837.
20 Report of Major Thomas Ryan upon the Aboriginal Establishment, March 1836, RP vol. 24.
21 Plomley, *Weep in Silence*, p. 715.
22 Ryan, *Aboriginal Tasmanians*, p. 189.
23 Plomley, *Weep in Silence*, p. 97.
24 Nickolls to Montagu, 18 April 1835, in Plomley, *Weep in Silence*, p. 86.
25 Plomley, *Weep in Silence*, p. 633.
26 *ibid.*, p. 628.
27 Bonwick, *Lost Tasmanian Race*, p. 175.
28 Stevens, *Me Write Myself*, p. 91.
29 Plomley, *Weep in Silence*, 3 December 1837.
30 Ryan, *Aboriginal Tasmanians*, p. 185.
31 Cox, *Broken Spear*, p. 158.
32 Prospectus, *Flinders Island Weekly Chronicle*, 10 September 1836, in Stevens, *Me Write Myself*, p. 64.
33 In Rose, *For the Record*, pp. 3–19.
34 Plomley, *Weep in Silence*, 20 December 1835, 29 July 1837.
35 *ibid.*, 2 December 1835.
36 *ibid.*, 15 December 1835.

37 *ibid.*, 21 December 1835.
38 *ibid.*
39 *ibid.*, 3 January 1836.
40 *ibid.*, 18 February 1836.
41 *ibid.*, 21 January 1836.
42 Ellis, *Trucanini*, p. 88.
43 Plomley, *Weep in Silence*, 22 February 1836; *ibid.*, p. 631.
44 *ibid.*, 22 February 1836.
45 *ibid.*, p. 633.
46 *Hobart Town Courier*, 15 April 1836.
47 Plomley, *Weep in Silence*, p. 661.
48 *ibid.*, p. 679.
49 *ibid.*, p. 707.
50 *ibid.*, p. 665.
51 *ibid.*, p. 669.
52 *ibid.*, 21 July 1837; *ibid.*, p. 819.
53 *ibid.*, 21 July 1837.
54 Plomley, *Friendly Mission*, 1st edn, pp. 926–927.
55 Plomley, *Weep in Silence*, 24 July 1837.
56 *ibid.*, 29 December 1837.
57 For a discussion of the scanty evidence for so early a liaison, see Ellis, *Trucanini*, pp. 38–39.
58 Plomley, *Weep in Silence*, 29 July 1837.
59 Plomley, *Word-List*, p. 290.
60 Plomley, *Weep in Silence*, pp. 639, 709.
61 https://press-files.anu.edu.au/downloads/p110711/html/Text/ch11.html?referer=&page=18#footmote-13594-18-backlink.
62 Plomley, *Weep in Silence*, p. 666.
63 *ibid.*, 27 December 1836.
64 GAR to Colonial Secretary 12 January 1837, TAHO CSO 5/19/364, pp. 171–196.
65 Plomley, *Weep in Silence*, 26 December 1836.
66 *ibid.*, 3 August 1837.
67 *ibid.*, 8 August 1837.
68 *ibid.*, p. 98.
69 *ibid.*, 4 September 1837.
70 *Flinders Island Weekly Chronicle*, 6 [?] October 1837, in Rose, *For the Record*, pp. 3–19.
71 Plomley, *Weep in Silence*, 10 October 1837.
72 *Flinders Island Weekly Chronicle*, 11 October 1837, in Rose, *For the Record*, pp. 3–19.
73 *ibid.*, 18 October 1837.
74 Plomley, *Friendly Mission*, 29 June 1834.
75 Rae-Ellis, in *Black Robinson*, p. 128, translated *crackenny* as *die*, but Robinson recorded that *crackene* meant *stop*; see Plomley, *Weep in Silence*, p. 509.
76 Plomley, *Weep in Silence*, 15 October 1837.
77 *ibid.*
78 *ibid.*, 5 November 1837.
79 *Port Phillip Gazette*, 22 January 1842.
80 *Flinders Island Weekly Chronicle*, 6 November 1837, in Rose, *For the Record*, pp. 3–19.
81 Plomley, *Weep in Silence*, 17 November 1837.
82 *Flinders Island Weekly Chronicle*, 17 November 1837, in Rose, *For the Record*, pp. 3–19.
83 *ibid.*
84 The journal's demise might also have been influenced by Walter's general fall from grace that month. One of Robinson's daughters discovered Walter in bed with an

internee named Mary Ann (whom he later married), after which Robinson sentenced him to a week in the cells 'for misconduct'.
85 Plomley, *Weep in Silence*, 2 December 1837.
86 *Flinders Island Weekly Chronicle*, 21 December 1837, in Rose, *For the Record*, pp. 3–19.
87 The others were Maccamee ('Washington') and his wife Warrameenaloo ('Juliet'); Wowee ('Albert') and his wife Pieyenkomeyenner ('Wild Mary'); 'Edward' (Leepunner?) and his wife Teddehebuerer ('Clara'); 'Alexander' (Moomereriner?) and his wife Drunameliyer ('Caroline'); Teengerreenneener ('Pompy' or 'Richard' or 'Cranky Dick'); Pruplathina; and Walter George Arthur.
88 Plomley, *Weep in Silence*, 12 December 1837.
89 *ibid*.
90 *ibid*., 14 December 1837.
91 *ibid*.
92 *Flinders Island Weekly Chronicle*, 21 December 1837, in Rose, *For the Record*, pp. 3–19.
93 Plomley, *Weep in Silence*, 15 December 1837.
94 *ibid*., 14 December 1837.
95 *ibid*., 16 December 1837.
96 *ibid*., 19 December 1837.
97 In Stevens, *Me Write Myself*, p. 146.
98 Plomley, *Weep in Silence*, pp. 941–942.
99 Clements & Reynolds, *Tongerlongeter*, p. 180.
100 Plomley, *Weep in Silence*, 7 December 1835.
101 *ibid*., 25 January 1838.
102 *ibid*., 26 January 1838.
103 Plomley, *Tasmanian Aborigines*, p. xii.
104 GAR official report of 17 May 1837, quoted in Bonwick, *Lost Tasmanian Race*, p. 169.
105 Robinson Letterbook QVMAG CY548, in Stevens, *Me Write Myself*, p. 188; Finlay, *Good People*, pp. 224–225.
106 *ibid*., p. 190.
107 Stevens, *Me Write Myself*, p. 167.
108 Plomley, *Weep in Silence*, p. 749.
109 *ibid*., p. 771.
110 Report of Board of Enquiry, 25 March 1839, A7071, vol. 50.
111 Plomley, *Weep in Silence*, 20 January 1841.
112 *ibid*., 20 January 1837.
113 Judge Willis Note Book.
114 Plomley, *Weep in Silence*, 20 January 1842.
115 *Australasian Chronicle* (Sydney), 15 February 1842.
116 *Cornwall Chronicle*, 7 April 1838.
117 *ibid*., 9 June 1838.
118 Plomley, *Weep in Silence*, pp. 910–913.
119 *ibid., p. 779*.
120 *ibid*., 30 June 1838.
121 Neither Rolepa nor Nikaminik went to Port Phillip. Rolepa died at Wybalenna on 1 June 1840, Nikaminik at Oyster Cove on 27–28 May 1849 after being transferred from Flinders Island.
122 Plomley, *Weep in Silence*, p. 942.
123 Journal of George Robinson jun., RP vol. 50, 28 March 1839.

Chapter 11 ~ 'Get plenty of guns ready'
1 Clark, GAR Journal, 5 March 1839.
2 GAR to Maria Robinson, 16 March 1839, A7075.

3   GAR to La Trobe, 12 December 1839, PROV.
4   Minute attached by James Stephen, Secretary, Colonial Office, 9 May 1839, to letter from Sir George Gipps to Lord Glenelg, 10 November 1838, Public Records Office, London, Colonial Office, 280/105.
5   *ibid.*
6   Governor George Gipps, speech to the NSW Legislative Council, reported in the *Port Phillip Patriot and Melbourne Advertiser*, 20 August 1840.
7   William Thomas Journal, 6 May 1839.
8   GAR to La Trobe, 12 December 1839, PROV.
9   Clark, GAR Journal, 14, 15, 29 March, 7 April 1839.
10 According to Plomley (*Weep in Silence*, p. 839), Ben Lomond's natal name was Rolepana and he was a son of Rolepa and therefore a sibling of Timme.
11 Clark, GAR Journal, 3, 11 May, 29 July 1839.
12 Pybus, *Truganini*, p. 193.
13 Clark, GAR Journal, 7 August 1839.
14 Chief Protector's Office, Receipt, 31 December 1839, PROV.
15 Clark, GAR Journal, 10 August 1839.
16 Robinson to La Trobe, 20 December 1838, accessed at http://access.prov.vic.gov.au/public/component/daPublicBaseContainer?component=daViewItem&entityId=1164259547.
17 *South Australian Register* (Adelaide), 16 November 1839.
18 Arkley, *The Hated Protector*, p. 247; Coutts & Wesson, *Bob and Jack*; Port Phillip Herald, 24 December 1841.
19 Pybus, *Truganini*, p. 190.
20 Clark, GAR Journal, 17, 31 August, 4 September 1839.
21 William Thomas, 8 November 1860, Appendix No. 3, to the 'First Report of the Central Board appointed to watch over the interests of the Aborigines in the Colony of Victoria', *Victoria Legislative Council Votes & Proceedings*, 1861, in Fels, 'I Succeeded Once', pp. 80–81.
22 Clark, GAR *Journal*, 28 October 1839.
23 William Thomas (junior), *Reminiscences*, uncat. mss., set 214, item 27, Mitchell Library, Sydney, pp. 77–79.
24 Quoted in Fels, 'Not a battle', np.
25 Clark, GAR Journal, 29 August 1840.
26 *ibid.*, 16 March 1840.
27 Clark, GAR Journal, 30 March 1840.
28 *ibid.*, 7 June 1840.
29 Pybus, *Truganini*, pp. 197–198.
30 Fels, 'I Succeeded Once', p. 91, n. 184.
31 William Thomas Journal, 25 June 1840, in Fels, 'I Succeeded Once', p. 102.
32 GAR Journal, 13 June 1840.
33 William Thomas, Report for May 1840, series 11, unit 7, doc. 308, PROV.
34 Ellis, *Trucanini*, p. 100.
35 William Thomas, undated note, series 11, unit 7, doc.291, PROV.
36 Prupilathina is sometimes said to have drowned that month in Western Port while a crewman on a cutter belonging to Christopher Berry, but Cassandra Pybus has proposed a plausible account of Prupilathina's survival after his disappearance from Western Port; see her *Truganini*, pp. 203–204.
37 William Thomas Journal, CY2604, item 3, ML.
38 Clark, GAR Journal, 19 June 1840
39 *Port Phillip Gazette*, 5 August 1840.
40 *Port Phillip Patriot*, 20 August 1840.
41 Clark, GAR Journal, 24 August 1840.

42 *ibid.*, 12 November 1840. The entry for 25 October 1840 might suggest that Pevay was working for a colonist named Walter Coates, who took up land that year on the south bank of the Yarra: 'Mr Coats [*sic*] called to report that he had a mare killed on Thursday night last and suspected Jack a VDL native now in his service had killed it, no proof and the presumption is rather weak.' Next day he sent Assistant Protector Thomas to investigate but failed to note any outcome, although Jack's contract with Coates was renewed the following month and he was still working with Coates in December, so he was *not* Pevay, who was away droving in the first days of November (GAR Journal, 12 November 1840), but Batman's Jack, GAR Journal, 25, 26 October 1840, 9 November 1840, 4, 18 December 1840. Depending on the type of country traversed and the availability of feed and water, a cattle drive could travel from 25 to 40 kilometres a day, so the 150-kilometre journey from Goulburn River had probably taken from four to six days. Adding the time it took the drovers to get to Goulburn River before starting back suggests Jack and Wurati and the others had been away for at least 7–10 days – say from about the beginning of November – so 'Jack a VDL native' was at Coates's at that time and was unlikely to have been Pevay.
43 *ibid.*, 15 November 1840.
44 *ibid.*, 21 November 1840.
45 *ibid.*, 4 December 1840. Marie Hansen Fels, in 'Mistaken identity', np, seems to imply that Pevay was the culprit, but Robinson's journal for 20 December named Batman's Jack. That the other absconder was Thomas Brune is implied by GAR Journal entry for 20 December 1840. He was the only Palawa with his English surname spelt that way – the other two had their names spelt Bruny – but it is impossible to be sure because of Robinson's inconsistent spelling.
46 *ibid.*, 20 December 1840.
47 *ibid.*
48 Pybus, *Truganini*, p. 197.
49 Clark, GAR Journal, 24 February 1841.
50 Pybus, *Truganini*, p. 200.
51 Clark, GAR Journal, 24 February 1841.
52 William Thomas (junior), 'Reminiscences', uncat. mss., set 214, item 27, Mitchell Library, Sydney, pp. 77–79.

Chapter 12 ~ 'It was a big big country'

1 Niel Black diary, 9 December 1839, in Lowe, 'Forgotten rebels', p. 22.
2 In noting the climb, Robinson referred to Pevay as Jack VDL. Soon he began to record him as VDL Jack or simply VDL, although never consistently; Pevay and Napoleon were sometimes used interchangeably.
3 Clark, GAR Journal, 1 April 1841.
4 Pybus, *Truganini*, p. 201.
5 *ibid.*, p. 202.
6 Clark, GAR Journal, 21 April 1841.
7 *ibid.*, 10 May 1841.
8 *Port Phillip Patriot*, 29 November 1841.
9 Clark, GAR Journal, 24 April 1841.
10 *ibid.*, 30 April 1841.
11 Quoted in Stevens, 'The phenomenal coolness of Tunnerminnerwait'.
12 *The Argus* (Melbourne), 27 May 1890.
13 Clark, GAR Journal, 28 April 1841.
14 *ibid.*, 26 April 1841.

15 Robinson variously called this man Myatt or Myers and described him as a convict. Ian Clark, in a footnote to GAR Journal for 3 September 1841, identified him as Joseph Myatt.
16 GAR Journal, 30 April 1841.
17 *ibid.*, 28 April 1841.
18 *ibid.*, 14 January 1842.
19 *ibid.*, 7 May 1841.
20 *ibid.*
21 *ibid.*, 10 May 1841.
22 *ibid.*
23 *ibid.*
24 *ibid.*, 16 May 1841.
25 *ibid.*, 19 May 1841.
26 *ibid.*
27 *ibid.*, 29–30 May 1841.
28 Pybus, *Truganini*, p. 203.
29 Clark, GAR Journal, 8 June 1841.
30 *ibid.*, 29 April 1841.
31 *ibid.*, 13 June 1841.
32 *ibid.*, 25 April 1841.
33 *ibid.*, 31 July 1841.
34 *ibid.*, 1–2 July 1841.
35 *ibid.*, 4 July 1841.
36 *ibid.*, 9 July 1841.
37 *ibid.*
38 *ibid.*
39 *ibid.*, 10–11 July 1841.
40 *ibid.*, 15 July 1841.
41 *ibid.*
42 *ibid.*
43 *ibid.*, 1 August 1841.
44 *ibid.*, 4 June 1832.
45 Plomley, *Weep in Silence*, p. 831; *Australasian Chronicle* (Sydney), 15 February 1842.
46 *Port Phillip Patriot*, 29 November 1841.
47 Clark, GAR Journal, 29, 30 August 1841, 5, 19 September 1841.
48 *ibid.*, 14 October 1841.

Chapter 13 ~ 'Now was the time for revenge'

1 William Thomas (junior), 'Reminiscences', uncat. mss., set 214, item 27, Mitchell Library, Sydney, pp. 77–79.
2 Plomley, *Friendly Mission*, 30 December 1830.
3 Clark, GAR Journal, 14 January 1842. Timme is known to have worked for Michael Solomon of Moodie Yallo station and John Highett at Pallarangun, as well as for Alfred Langhorne, James Horsfall at Ballymarang and Robinson and his sons (Pybus, *Truganini*, p. 215).
4 Pybus, *Truganini*, p. 190; Samuel Johnson, *A Dictionary of the English Language*, 1755, accessed online.
5 Thomas Papers, reel CY2605, frame 294, ML; Pybus, *Truganini*, pp. 200–203.
6 Clark, GAR Journal, 2 December 1841.
7 Fels, 'Mistaken identity', np.
8 William Thomas Journal, 6 September 1841.
9 Pybus, *Truganini*, p. 203.

Notes

10 Although it has been claimed more than once that the raid on Jamieson's was by the Palawa rebels, contemporary Victorians believed local Aborigines were responsible, as suggested by Jamieson's note informing La Trobe of the raid, which he said was by 'a large party of Aborigines', not by two men and three women.
11 Massie to La Trobe, 7 October 1841, VPRS 19, Box 20, File 41/1568 PROV.
12 Finn, *'Garryowen': The chronicles of early Melbourne 1835 to 1852*, vol. 1, pp. 350–351.
13 *Port Phillip Herald*, 24 December 1841.
14 Quoted in *Port Phillip Gazette*, 1 December 1841.
15 *ibid*.
16 *Port Phillip Patriot*, 14 October 1841.
17 Fels, 'Mistaken identity', np; Horton & Morris, *The Andersons of Western Port* excerpt, p. 10; Roberts, *Jack of Cape Grim*, pp. 61–62.
18 Massie to La Trobe, 7 October 1841, VPRS 19, Box 20, File 41/1568, PROV.
19 The Palawa rebels, hardly a large party, were probably not responsible for this raid. The attackers 'were supposed to be Gippsland natives', according to Charles Wale Sherard (who lived at Jamieson's 1841–43) in a letter to La Trobe dated 10 August 1853, quoted in *Letters from Victorian Pioneers* (1898 edition), pp. 36–37.
20 Jamieson to La Trobe, 4 October 1841.
21 *Burke's Family Records*, p. 500, accessed online.
22 Pybus, *Truganini*, pp. 210–211.
23 *Port Phillip Gazette*, 1 December 1841.
24 Deposition of Samuel Evans, VPRS24. Box 1 Whaler's case, no. 43 1841, in Auty & Russell, *Hunt Them*, p. 60.
25 *ibid*.
26 *Port Phillip Gazette*, 1 December 1841.
27 *Port Phillip Herald*, 26 November 1841, quoting Corporal William Johnson of the Border Police.
28 Thomas Robins's testimony in Judge Willis Note Book no. 12 page 108; *Geelong Advertiser*, 27 December 1840; Fels, 'Mistaken identity'; Roberts, *Jack of Cape Grim*, pp. 61–63; Massie to La Trobe, 7 October 1841, in Horton & Morris, *The Andersons of Western Port* excerpt.
29 *Port Phillip Gazette*, 1 December 1841.
30 Samuel Rawson, *Journal of An Expedition After Some Van Diemen's Land Blacks Who Were Committing Depredations at Western Port on the Southern Coast of New Holland*, October–November 1841, National Library of Australia, MS 204/1, 10 October 1841.
31 *Port Phillip Patriot*, 14 October 1841.
32 Clark, GAR Journal, 14 October 1841.
33 *Port Phillip Patriot*, 14 October 1841.
34 Clark, GAR Journal, 31 October 1841.
35 *Port Phillip Gazette*, 1 December 1841.
36 *ibid*.
37 Roberts, *Jack of Cape Grim*, p. 64.
38 Rawson Journal, p. 3.
39 *Port Phillip Gazette*, 1 December 1841.
40 *ibid*.
41 Despite the severity of their wounds, both men survived. However, Westaway took two years to recover and never returned to Settlement Point, and Bates was said to have remained a cripple for the rest of his life (*Western Port Times* excerpt).
42 *Port Phillip Gazette*, 1 December 1841.
43 *ibid*.; *Port Phillip Herald*, 26 November 1841.
44 *ibid*.

Chapter 14 ~ 'They would fight to the last'

1. William Thomas Journal, 26 October 1841.
2. *ibid.*, 28 October 1841.
3. Pybus, *Truganini*, p. 216.
4. *Port Phillip Patriot*, 28 October 1841.
5. *ibid.*, 29 October 1841.
6. He is called Ayse in Clark's transcription of one entry in Robinson's journal, but that is a misreading of Airey. The Airey referred to was one of the two retired naval officers of that name who were officials in the colony at the time. Clark, in a footnote to GAR Journal for 3 November 1841, identified him as George Sherbrooke Airey, Commissioner of Crown Lands for the Geelong District.
7. In Roberts, *Jack of Cape Grim*, p. 66.
8. *Port Phillip Gazette*, 6 November 1841; *Sydney Herald*, 24 November 1841; Pybus, *Truganini*, p. 216.
9. Roberts, *Jack of Cape Grim*, p. 68.
10. Rawson Journal, in Roberts, *Jack of Cape Grim*, p. 68.
11. *ibid.*, p. 69.
12. *ibid.*
13. *Port Phillip Herald*, 9 November 1841.
14. Rawson Journal, in Roberts, *Jack of Cape Grim*, p. 70.
15. *Port Phillip Herald*, 9 November 1841.
16. Clark, GAR Journal, 1–4 November 1841.
17. La Trobe to GAR, 31 October 1841, VPRS 16, vol. 2, p. 342, PROV, in Roberts, *Jack of Cape Grim*, 66.
18. Clark, GAR Journal, 1 November 1841.
19. *ibid.*, 3 November 1841.

Chapter 15 ~ 'By ¼ past 6 it was all over'

1. H.H. Meyrick letter dated 25 November 1841 in *Letters* to his family, 1840–1847, La Trobe Library, Manuscript 7957.
2. Thomas to Robinson, 5 November 1841, VPRS 11, Box 8, Item 411, PROV.
3. Thomas to Robinson, 11 November 1841, VPRS 11, Box 8, Item 412, PROV.
4. Powlett to La Trobe, 16 November 1841, VPRS, Box 22, File 41/1835, PROV.
5. Judge Willis Note Book.
6. *ibid.*
7. *Port Phillip Herald*, 26 November 1841.
8. *Port Phillip Gazette*, 1 December 1841.
9. *ibid.*
10. William Thomas Journal, 17 November 1841.
11. *ibid.*; Pybus, *Truganini*, p. 219.
12. William Thomas Journal, 18 November 1841, in Auty and Russell, *Hunt Them*, p. 47.
13. Rawson Journal, p. 33 *et seq.*
14. *ibid.*
15. *ibid.*
16. William Thomas Journal, 19 November 1841.
17. *ibid.*
18. *ibid.*
19. 'Truganini and the murders at Coal Creek' at http://wonthaggihistoricalsociety.org.au/files/plod/Truginini_at_Wonthaggi.
20. Rawson Journal, quoted in Roberts, *Jack of Cape Grim*, pp. 76–77.
21. Horton & Morris, *The Andersons*, p. 79, citing Rawson's Journal, 8 October–19 November 1841. All too many writers have claimed that the wounded woman was

Notes

either Planobeena or Mathabelianna, but 'Only one of the outlaws was injured. This was Trugeraninni . . .' (Horton & Morris, *The Andersons*, p. 80). See also Johnson and McFarlane, *Van Diemen's Land*, p. 270.
22 Rawson Journal, *ibid*.
23 *ibid*.
24 *Sydney Herald*, 14 December 1841.
25 William Thomas Journal, 20 November 1841.
26 Joseph Orton Papers: Journal 3:185 entry for 20 January 1842, in Auty & Russell, *Hunt Them*, p. 48.
27 Judge Willis Note Book.
28 Corporal William Johnson, Deposition, 30 November 1841; see also Johnson's trial testimony in Judge Willis Note Book.
29 Judge Willis Note Book.
30 *Port Phillip Patriot*, 29 November 1841.
31 Wiliam Thomas Journal, 20 November 1841.
32 Rawson Journal, *ibid*.
33 William Thomas Journal in Auty & Russell, *Hunt Them*, p. 55.
34 Frederick Powlett's testimony as reported in the *Port Phillip Patriot*, 23 December 1841; Corporal William Johnson testimony in Judge Willis Note Book no. 12 page 108.
35 *Australian Dictionary of Biography*, vol. 1, Samuel Anderson, p. 14, accessed online. Some writers, contemporary and otherwise, have claimed Trukanini showed Powlett where the victims were buried, but Pevay and Timme alone guided Powlett to the gravesite while Trukanini was being treated by Hugh Anderson for her bullet wound. See p. 207 of text. Others have claimed it was not Trukanini but one of the other women who was wounded. The misconception probably arose because of Powlett's false testimony that Trukanini had accompanied him and Thomas to the gravesite, so by implication it must have been one of the other women who was wounded. Thomas, in a much later manuscript, inexplicably claimed that nobody was wounded by all the gunfire and that he found Trukanini hiding under a blanket (Thomas Journal, note at p. 410).
36 William Thomas Journal, 20 November 1841, in Auty & Russell, *Hunt Then*, p. 55.
37 *Port Phillip Gazette*, 29 November 1841.
38 *Port Phillip Herald*, 26 November 1841.
39 Clark, GAR Journal, 26 November 1841.

Chapter 16 ~ 'Shooting at Watson would hang them'

1 William Thomas Journal, 1 April 1839, in Roberts, *Jack of Cape Grim*, p. 19.
2 Garryowen, *Chronicles*, pp. 448–451; GAR Journal 30 September 1841.
3 *Port Phillip Patriot*, 29 November 1841.
4 *Port Phillip Gazette*, 1 December 1841.
5 *ibid*.
6 *ibid*., 29 November 1841.
7 *ibid*., 1 December 1841.
8 *Port Phillip Patriot*, 29 November 1841.
9 *Port Phillip Gazette*, 1 December 1841.
10 Joseph Orton Papers: Journal 3:185 entry for 20 January 1842, in Auty & Russell, *Hunt Them*, p. 48.
11 Auty & Russell, *Hunt Them*, p. 52.
12 *Port Phillip Gazette*, 1 December 1841.
13 *ibid*.
14 *Australasian Chronicle* (Sydney), 15 February 1842.
15 Auty & Russell, *Hunt Them*, p. 57; *Port Phillip Gazette*, 1 December 1841.

16 *Port Phillip Gazette*, 1 December 1841.
17 *ibid.*
18 Clark, GAR Journal, 2 December 1841.
19 *Port Phillip Gazette*, 11 December 1841.
20 Paul R. Mullally QC in 'Cases not in note books', Royal Historical Society of Victoria, accessed online at https://historyvictoria.org.au.
21 William Thomas Journal, 9 December 1841.
22 Clark, GAR Journal, 11 December 1841.
23 Auty & Russell, *Hunt Them*, p. 64.
24 William Thomas Journal, 14 December 1841.
25 John V. Barry, 'Willis, John Walpole (1793–1877)', *Australian Dictionary of Biography*, accessed online.
26 Toscano, 'Lest we forget', p. 22.
27 John V. Barry, 'Willis, John Walpole (1793–1877)', *Australian Dictionary of Biography*, accessed online.
28 Bonnell, *I Like a Clamour*, p. 2; *ibid.*, pp. 28–29; *ibid.*, p. 16.
29 *Port Phillip Gazette*, 18 December 1841. According to the *Port Phillip Gazette* of 23 December 1841 the jurors were John Sutch, Thomas Wilkinson, Henry Worsley, Walter Veitch, Henry Townend, Edward Sawtell, William Witton, John Rankin, Robert Russell, Charles Scott, John T. Smith and John Roach (foreman).
30 *Port Phillip Patriot*, 16 December 1841.
31 William Thomas Journal, 15 December 1841.
32 *ibid.*, 18 December 1841.
33 *ibid.*, 20 December 1841.
34 *Port Phillip Patriot*, 23 December 1841. The name and spelling variations are verbatim.
35 Judge Willis Note Book no. 12 p. 108.
36 Auty & Russell, *Hunt Them*, p. 65.
37 *Launceston Advertiser*, 6 January 1842, report extracted from the *Port Phillip Herald*.
38 Robert [sic] Robins Deposition, in Roberts, *Jack of Cape Grim*, p. 85.
39 William Watson Deposition in Roberts, *Jack of Cape Grim*, p.85.
40 Samuel Rawson Journal; Testimony of Corporal William Johnson, in Judge Willis Note Book.
41 Judge Willis Note Book no. 12 p. 108.
42 *Port Phillip Gazette*, 1 December 1841.
43 Judge Willis Note Book; *Port Phillip Patriot*, 23 December 1841.
44 William Thomas Journal in Auty & Russell, *Hunt Them*, p. 55.
45 Auty & Russell, *Hunt Them*, p. 56.
46 *Port Phillip Gazette*, 1 December 1841.
47 *ibid.*, 11 December 1841; *Sydney Herald*, 13 December 1841.
48 Auty & Russell, *Hunt Them*, p. 62.
49 *ibid.*, p. 13.
50 Redmond Barry's speech, quoted in McFarlane, 'Aboriginal society in North West Tasmania', p. 240.
51 Peter Ryan, 'Barry, Sir Redmond (1813–1880)', *Australia Dictionary of Biography*, accessed online.
52 P.M. Sales, 'Powlett, Frederick Armand (1811–1865)', *Australian Dictionary of Biography*, accessed online.
53 *Port Phillip Herald*, 24 December 1841.
54 *ibid.*
55 Ian D. Clark, 'In quest of the tribes: G.A. Robinson's unabridged report of his 1841 expedition among Western Victorian Aboriginal tribes; Kenyon's "Condensation" Reconsidered', *Memoirs of the Museum of Victoria*, vol. 1, no. 1, 1990, p. 121.
56 Judge Willis Note Book.

Notes

57 *Port Phillip Herald*, 24 December 1841.
58 *ibid.*
59 *Port Phillip Patriot*, 24 January 1842.
60 Judge Willis Note Book.
61 Bonnell, *I Like a Clamour*, p. 182.
62 *ibid.*
63 *Port Phillip Advertiser*, c. 24 December 1841.
64 Arkley, *The Hated Protector*, pp. 249–250, quoting *Port Phillip Gazette*, 22 December 1841; *Port Phillip Patriot*, 23 December 1841.
65 *Port Phillip Herald*, 24 December 1841.
66 Willis to La Trobe, 23 December 1841, VPRS 19/22 No. 41/1835.
67 Clark, GAR Journal, 14 January 1842.
68 *Port Phillip Herald*, 24 December 1841.
69 *Port Phillip Gazette*, 22 December 1841.
70 Quoted in Ian MacFarlane, *1842: The Public Executions at Melbourne*, p. 17, in Roberts, *Jack of Cape Grim*, p. 89.
71 *Australasian Chronicle* (Sydney), 15 February 1842.
72 *ibid.*, 1 February 1842.
73 *Port Phillip Herald*, 24 December 1841.
74 *Australasian Chronicle* (Sydney), 1 February 1842.

Chapter 17 ~ 'He hung beautiful'

1 *Port Phillip Gazette*, 19 January 1842.
2 *Australasian Chronicle* (Sydney), 1 February 1842.
3 Clark, GAR Journal, 19 January 1842.
4 *Port Phillip Herald*, 21 January 1842.
5 Joseph Orton Journal, quoted in footnote in Thomas Journal, p. 424.
6 *Port Phillip Herald*, 21 January 1842..
7 *Australasian Chronicle* (Sydney), 15 February 1842.
8 Garryowen, *The Chronicles of Early* Melbourne, excerpt in *The Herald* (Melbourne), 17 November 1882.
9 In several editions of the *Herald* in November 1882 following the above, various correspondents disagreed about the location of the gallows. One wrote that 'the blackfellows were hanged on the ground occupied by the old Supreme Court, within a few yards of the gaol, the wall of which were then being built', while another, also a witness, claimed the execution place was 'at the top of Russell street, where McKenzie street terminates'.
10 *Port Phillip Patriot*, 24 January 1842.
11 *Port Phillip Herald*, 21 January 1842.
12 Weidenhofer, *Garryowen's Melbourne*, p. 108.
13 *Port Phillip Patriot*, 24 January 1842.
14 Michael Adams, *Hanging Ned Kelly: Elijah Upjohn, the hangmen and the underbelly of colonial Australia*, Affirm Press, South Melbourne, Vic., 2022, p. 59.
15 About 20 of them, according to Garryowen's *The Chronicles of Early Melbourne*, excerpt in *The Herald* (Melbourne), 17 November 1882. However, in subsequent issues of the *Herald* that month some correspondents disagreed. One who said he had witnessed the execution claimed that 'more than a hundred [Aborigines] were up trees and scattered about', while another, also claiming to have been a spectator, remembered seeing only a single Aboriginal youth watching from a tree.
16 *Australasian Chronicle* (Sydney), 15 February 1842.
17 *Port Phillip Patriot*, 24 January 1842.

18 Garryowen, *The Chronicles of Early Melbourne*, excerpt in *The Herald* (Melbourne), 17 November 1882.
19 *Port Phillip Gazette*, 22 January 1842.
20 James Dredge Journal, in Roberts, *Jack of Cape Grim*, p. 93.
21 *Port Phillip Gazette*, 22 January 1842.
22 *Australasian Chronicle* (Sydney), 15 February 1842.
23 Garryowen, *The Chronicles of Early Melbourne 1835–52*.
24 *Australasian Chronicle* (Sydney), 15 February 1842.
25 *Portland Guardian*, 2 February 1942.
26 James Dredge Journal, in Roberts, *Jack of Cape Grim*, p. 94.
27 *Australasian Chronicle* (Sydney), 15 February 1842.
28 In Weidenhofer, *Garryowen's Melbourne*, p. 109.
29 Clark, GAR Journal, 20 January 1842.
30 Fels, 'Mistaken identity', np.
31 Joseph Orton Journal, 20 January 1842, Mitchell Library, in Marguerita Stephens, *The Journal of William Thomas, Assistant Protector of Aborigines at Port Phillip and Guardian of the Aborigines of Victoria 1839–1867*, vol. 1, p. 424, Victorian Aboriginal Corporation for Languages, 2014.
32 *ibid*.
33 James Dredge Journal, p. 78.
34 *ibid*., in Roberts, *Jack of Cape Grim*, p. 93.

Epilogue

1 D.J. Mulvaney, 'Thomas, William (1793–1867)', *Australian Dictionary of Biography*, accessed online.
2 Pybus, *Truganini*, p. 285.
3 *ibid*., p. 290.
4 William Lanne was one of the family of holdouts who escaped from Robinson's sons' mission in 1836–1837. He, his parents, and his brothers surrendered – because they were lonely, they said – at Cape Grim in December 1842. By the end of 1847 all of them except William and his brother Barnaby Rudge were dead.
5 Available online at https://www.melbourne.vic.gov.au/sitecollectiondocuments/ tunnerminnerwait-and-maulboyheenner.pdf
6 Quoted in Arkley, *The Hated Protector*, pp. 247–248.

Index of Names

A

Airey/Airy, – 190, 194
Alexander (Moomereriner?) 126
Allan, Robert Innes 156, 176, 191
Allen, Jack (See Batman's Jack)
Allen, James 104, 109, 111, 113, 165, 173
Anderson, Hugh 199, 200, 207,
Anderson, Samuel 177, 199
Andrews, – 186
Armstrong, Thomas 184, 185
Arthur, George (Lt Gov.) 3, 4, 10–11, 15, 43, 44, 69, 83, 101, 113, 243
Arthur, Walter George (Palawa) 10, 107, 115, 123, 139, 146, 147 152, 244

B

Bacchus, Henry 194, 226
Bailey/Bayley, Jennett 199, 200
Baker, John 'Black' 33
Barry, Redmond 211–227, 244, 249
Bates, Thomas 186–187
Batman, John. 11–12, 146, 172
Batman's Jack (Palawa) 10, 146, 156
Beers, – (Capt.) 138
Ben Lomond (See Rolepana)
Bennett, Charles 186–187
Bertram, – 231
Black Jack (See Pevay)
Black, Niel 158
Black Tom (See Kikatapula)
Bob (See Timme)
Bock, Thomas 51, 172
Boomer Jack 7
Bourke, John 184
Broughton, – (Bishop) 154
Brune, Thomas 115, 124, 127, 146, 156, 162
Bruny, David (See Myunngge)
Bruny, Peter (See Droyyerloinne)
Buller Bullup (Aborigine) 197
Bunbury, Richard 169, 170
Buxton, John 186–187
Byng, John 'Black' xxiv, 238

C

Campbell, Alexander (Capt.) 161–163, 167
Cape Grim Jack (See Pevay)
Caroline (See Drunamellyer)

Charlotte/Sharlotte (Aborigine) 146, 147, 152, 153
Clark, – 113, 124
Clow, Thomas 194
Clucas, – 37, 41
Cook, William 180–181, 205, 212, 218–220, 227, 241
Cottrell, Anthony 68–69, 70–72, 81
Count Alpha (see Wurati)
Croke, James 213–220, 244
Curr, Edward 17–20, 23

D

Davies, John 237, 239, 240, 244
Davy/David Bruny (See Myyungge)
Deewooradedy 76, 77
Dick/Cranky Dick (See Teengerreenneener)
Dove, Thomas (Rev.) 114, 135, 154
Dowwunggi 121
Dray/Draymuric 6, 73, 74, 76, 77, 79, 102
Dredge, James 145, 226, 239, 241
Droyyerloinne 6, 146, 173, 235, 240, 245
Druemerterpunner 127
Drunamellyer 127
Duterrau, Benjamin 83, 100–101

E

Eliza Robinson (Palawa) 138
Evans, Samuel 180–181, 212, 214, 219–220
Everitt, – 42

F

Fanny (See Planobeena)
Fanny Hardwicke 33
Fletcher, – 148
Fossey, Joseph 15
Franklin, Jane (Lady) 138
Franklin, John (Sir) 132–133, 144, 146, 225
Friday (see Nikaminik)

G

Ginman, Elizabeth 177
Ginman, William 177, 178, 182, 219
Gipps, George (Gov.) 151, 154, 209, 216, 232, 241
Gisborne, Henry Fysshe 151
Gould, William Buelow 72

H

Hawdon, John 183–4, 196
Heaton, – (Mrs) 18
Heaton, John 18
Heedeek 63, 68, 70–72, 90
Helyer, Henry 18
Highett/Hyatt, John 152, 166
Horsfall/Horsefold, James 160, 176, 213, 248
Howard – 180

I

Ireland, John 186
Isaac (See Prupilathina)

J

Jack (See Pevay)
Jack Allen (See Batman's Jack)
Jaggy Jaggy 151
Jamieson, Robert 177, 179, 182, 183, 184, 193, 197
Jemmy (See Timme)
Jemmy/Little Jemmy (See Prupilathina)
Jinman (See Ginman)
Jock (See Planobeena)
Johnny Franklin (Aborigine) 146, 150, 173
Johnson, William (Cpl) 205, 207, 211, 212, 215, 222

K

Karnebutcher 53, 62, 87, 91
Keeghernewboyheenner 16
Kelly, Ned 244
Kickerterpoller (See Kikatapula)
Kikatapula xviii, xx, 5–6, 10, 12, 14, 21, 23, 33, 36, 38, 40–41, 42, 45, 47, 48, 51, 53, 110
Kirk, William 171–172
Kit (See Nollahallaker)
Koinerbareake (aka Ryenbaroke) 68
Kolebunner (See Kulipana)
Kulipana 42

L

Karnebutcher 53, 62, 87, 91
Keeghernewboyheenner 16
Kelly, Ned 244
Kickerterpoller (See Kikatapula)
Kikatapula xviii, xx, 5–6, 10, 12, 14, 21, 23, 33, 36, 38, 40–41, 42, 45, 47, 48, 51, 53, 110
Kirk, William 171–172
Kit (See Nollahallaker)
Koinerbareake (aka Ryenbaroke) 68

Kolebunner (See Kulipana)
Kulipana 42

L

Lacklay (See Prupilathina)
Lalla Rookh (See Trukanini)
Langham, John 183–184, 210
Langhorne, Alfred 147, 148, 175, 188, 226
Lanne, William 245
Laoinneloonner 12
Larmoderic 107, 137, 174
Larratong 63
La Trobe, Charles Joseph 147, 151, 154, 155, 157, 165, 179, 183, 194, 198, 225, 230, 231, 232
Lawerick 68
Leepunner (aka Edward) 118, 130
Lenergwin 90
Le Soeuf, William 145
Lettelowhe 27, 28, 29
Liardet, Wilbraham 246
Limont, William (Tpr) 205
Linermerrinnecer 23, 24
Lively (Aborigine) 197
Loathdidebope 66, 90
Loethebrah 35
London, Sarah 199–200
Lonini, Joseph 199–200
Lowe, Watkin 7
Luggenemeener (aka Big Tuery) 10, 11, 13, 107, 120
Lydgugee (See Trukanini)

M

Maccamee (aka Washington) 123
MacKay, George 154, 155
Mailer, Norman xx
Malapuwinarana (see Timme)
Manalakina 39, 40–42, 45, 46, 51–52, 56, 57, 62, 74, 76, 77, 78–79, 80, 83, 89, 100, 101, 107, 109
Mannalargenner (See Manalakina)
Mannapackername 245
Maria (See Mathabelianna)
Mary (Palawa) 4, 5
Mary Ann Arthur 244
Massie, Robert 177, 179, 181
Mathabelianna 121–123, 139, 146, 149, 156, 167, 173, 174, 175, 181, 191, 234, 245
Matilda (See Planobeena)
Maulboyheener (see Timme)

Index of Names

Mayterpueminner (See Mathabelianna)
McCray, Farquhar   194
McKay, Alexander   24, 60
McKenzie, Michael   33
Meemellunneener   110
Meeterlatteener (aka Rebecca)   146, 159, 172
Memerlannerlargener   42, 43, 46
Merappe   27, 28, 29
Meredith, George   121–122
Meyrick, Henry   146
Mitchell, Thomas (Maj)   167
Moorina   6
Moultehelargener   107, 124–125
Mundy, Fitzherbert   184, 185–6, 196
Mutteellee (See Wurati)
Myatt/Myer, Joseph   162, 168, 170–171
Myyunngge   6, 9, 136, 139, 173, 245

N

Napoleon (See Pevay)
Narrucker   22, 23–4, 60
Ned –   180
Neerhepeereminer   107, 114, 121
Newel, Paddy   7
Nicermenic (See Nikaminik)
Nickolls, Henry   108, 111
Nikaminik   23–24, 25, 107, 138
Ningernooputener   42
Nollahallaker   xxi, 54, 56, 58–61, 62, 68, 87, 88, 91, 99, 102
Nooerer   106
Noringbake   60
Numbloote (aka Sydney, Jenny)   111, 116, 118, 128, 130, 139

O

Old Joe (Aborigine)   207
Orton, Joseph (Rev)   213, 235–6, 240, 241

P

Paddedevenehenoke   60, 63, 64
Pagerly   6, 14, 21, 25, 33, 35, 38, 45, 51, 53, 62, 71, 79, 87, 91, 326
Pangum   107, 116
Pannabuke   56, 57, 63, 121
Paraweena   7
Parewareatar   7, 12, 13, 14, 16, 42
Parish, James   32, 33
Parker, Edward   145, 150
Parloorer   245
Pedder, John Lewes   44

Peevay/Pevay   xv, xvii–xxi, 16–22, 23–28, 29–30, 32, 33, 34–36, 38, 39–41, 43, 45, 48, 50, 51, 54–62, 64–67, 70, 71, 74, 75, 77, 78, 80, 81, 85, 86, 87–89, 92, 100, 102, 107, 111, 114, 118, 125–126, 130, 134–136, 137–138, 149–150, 155–157, 158–173, 174–179, 181, 183–184, 187, 191–193, 199–200, 204–208, 210, 212, 218, 220, 221, 222, 226–227, 228, 230, 231–233, 234–241, 246–248
Pordeboic   16, 60, 63, 89, 138
Penderoin   16, 57, 63, 65, 81, 87, 88, 99, 100, 107, 137, 174
Pendowterer (See Pintawtawa)
Pennemorenoke (aka Pennemorehenudic, Benjamin)   120
Pierrapplener (aka Diana)   33, 107
Pillah (aka Phillip)   125
Pintawtawa   16, 21, 23, 28, 60, 107, 137, 174
Plairnrooner   42
Planobeena   4–5, 32–33, 35, 36, 37, 41–43, 45, 46, 48, 52, 70, 71, 76, 78, 79, 80, 85, 87, 93, 101, 107, 117, 118, 128, 130, 138, 139, 146, 149, 162, 173, 174, 175, 177, 181, 191, 204, 234, 245
Plorenernoopperner (see Planobeena)
Poky Poky (Aborigine)   197
Pompy (See Teengerreenneener)
Powlett, Frederick Armand   182, 184–186, 188, 190–194, 198–199, 200–207, 210–212, 214–215, 216–217, 219, 220–221, 223–224, 225, 243
Prior, – (Const)   11, 12
Probelattener (See Prupilathina)
Prupilathina   39, 43, 45, 62, 68, 101, 111, 118, 122, 130, 138, 139, 146, 149, 152–153, 166, 173, 175, 176
Pulara (aka Jumbo)   35
Pung (See Woretermoteteyer)
Pyne, Rose   243

R

Rawson, Samuel (Ensign)   179, 182, 184–186, 188, 190, 191–195, 198–199, 200–207, 210, 213–214, 215, 220, 221, 222–224, 243
Reynolds, Henry   xix
Richard (See Teengerreenneener)
Roach, John   228
Robert (See Timme)
Robert (Palawa)   6, 8, 14, 21, 25, 31, 38, 43, 45, 52
Robertson, Gilbert   10–11, 12, 13
Robins, Thomas   180, 181, 205, 220
Robinson, Charles (son of GAR)   1, 8, 72, 73, 93–95, 101, 107, 118–120, 149, 156

Robinson, George (son of GAR) 72, 93–95, 118–120, 136, 139, 153

Robinson, George Augustus xxi–xxiii, 1–5, 7–8, 9–10, 13, 14–16, 20–28, 29–35, 37–70, 72–93, 95–96, 99–100, 101–103, 104–106, 107, 108–118, 119, 120–137, 138, 139, 143–148, 149, 150–152, 154–157, 158–173, 175, 183, 194, 197, 198, 210, 213, 214–215, 217, 218, 226–227, 229, 230, 231, 233, 234, 235, 236, 240, 241, 242, 243, 245

Robinson, Maria (daughter of GAR) 85

Robinson, Maria (wife of GAR) 139, 146, 243

Robinson, William (son of GAR) 101, 147, 166

Robson, – (Capt.) 86

Rolepa (aka King George) 10, 107, 111, 125, 138, 146

Rolepana (aka Ben Lomond) 10, 11, 146–147, 172, 173

Ross, – 165

Ruffy, – 156, 190

Rutherford, Thomas 176

Ryan, Lyndall 95

Ryan, Thomas (Major) 112–113

Rynuwidicer 88

Ryrie, William 151

S

Salter, George 94

Sawtell, Edwin 194

Semiramis (See Numbloote)

Sharpe, John 71

Sievwright, Charles 145

Smith, Malcolm Laing 28

Solomon, Michael 173, 188–189

Sparrow, – 186

Stansfield, William 46, 71

Stephen, James 143–144

St John, George Frederick (Major) 210, 213

Styleman, John 240

T

Tanalipunya 45, 52, 63, 83, 89, 99–100

Tanaminawayt (see Pevay)

Tanganuturra (aka Tibb) 35, 38, 45

Teengerreenneener 34–35, 38, 53, 62, 74, 76, 88, 92, 101, 118, 128–130

Tekartee (See Tikati)

Thom, John 200

Thomas, William 145, 147, 152, 153, 157, 160, 166, 173, 176, 188–189, 190, 194, 196–197, 198, 199–205, 206, 209, 210, 213, 214–216, 217–218, 221–223, 224, 230–231, 244

Thomas, William jnr 166, 173, 174

Thompson, Thomas 139, 173, 189, 191, 245

Thomson, Adam Compton (Rev.) 234, 236, 239

Thomson, James 33

Thursday (Palawa) 13–20

Tikati 33, 51

Tillarbunner (See Batman's Jack)

Tillenner 34, 35

Timemernidic 107, 138

Timme/Timme xvii–xx, 7, 8, 9–13, 33, 34–36, 38, 42, 45, 47–48, 49, 50, 51, 52, 62, 68, 70, 75, 78, 80, 83, 85, 89, 100, 101, 107, 111, 116, 117, 118, 120, 123, 125–126, 128, 130, 134–135, 136, 138, 139, 146, 147–148, 152, 153–154, 156, 159–160, 166, 172, 173, 174, 175–176, 178, 180, 181, 183, 187, 189, 191, 199, 201, 204–207, 210, 212, 213, 218, 220, 222, 223, 226, 227, 228, 231–233, 234–241, 242

Towterer 74, 75–76

Trepanner 6, 14

Trukanini xviii–xix, xx–xxi, 6–7, 14, 21, 24, 25–26, 33, 35–36, 38, 45, 51, 62, 53, 64–67, 68, 70, 71, 75, 79, 83, 85, 87, 92–93, 100, 101, 109, 111, 116, 117–118, 119, 121, 124, 128–130, 139, 147, 149, 152, 153–154, 155–156, 159, 166, 173, 174, 175–176, 177, 178, 179, 181, 189, 191, 204–207, 213, 218, 220, 221–222, 223, 226, 227, 234, 242, 245

Tuereringher (See Pagerly)

Tunnerminnerwait (See Pevay)

Turnbull, – 33

Tyrell, – 37, 41

U

Umarrah 6, 10, 14, 38, 39, 40, 42, 43, 45, 46, 47, 48, 51, 52

V

VDL (See Pevay)

VDL Jack (See Pevay)

W

Walyer 20, 23, 26, 28

Warrameenaloo (aka Juliet) 33

Watson, Mary 177–178, 241

Watson, William 176, 177–179, 180–182, 183, 206, 207, 210, 212, 213, 214, 219, 220, 221–222, 241, 244

Westaway, George 184, 185–187, 190, 197, 199

Whitcomb, George 95, 118

Willis, John Walpole (Judge) 213, 214, 216–230, 235, 244

Index of Names

Windschuttle, Keith   xiii–xiv
Wooraddy (See Wurati)
Woreternattelargener   33, 42, 48, 116
Woretermoteteyer (aka Pollerwotteltelterrun, Margaret)   32, 35, 37, 41, 107
Wottecowwidyer (aka Harriet)   134
Wowee   130
Wulaytupinya   46, 47, 51, 53
Wurati (aka Count Alpha)   6, 14, 21, 23, 25, 26, 30, 33, 38, 45, 51, 62, 64, 65, 68, 71, 74, 75, 83, 100, 101, 111, 117, 118, 125, 128, 130, 139, 147, 149, 159, 173, 205
Wymurrick   16, 57–58, 59, 60–61, 63, 107, 137, 174
Wyne   63, 64–67, 70–71, 72, 78–79, 80

Y

Yankee   180–181, 205, 212, 213, 218, 220

Wakefield Press is an independent publishing and
distribution company based in Adelaide, South Australia.
We love good stories and publish beautiful books.
To see our full range of books, please visit our website at
www.wakefieldpress.com.au
where all titles are available for purchase.
To keep up with our latest releases, news and events,
subscribe to our monthly newsletter.

Find us!

Facebook: www.facebook.com/wakefield.press
Twitter: www.twitter.com/wakefieldpress
Instagram: www.instagram.com/wakefieldpress

www.ingramcontent.com/pod-product-compliance
Lightning Source LLC
Chambersburg PA
CBHW040745020526
44114CB00048B/2913